Desert Victory 1943

What did I see in the desert today,
In the cold pale light of the dawn?
I saw the Honeys creaking out,
Their brave bright pennants torn;
And heads were high against the sky,
And faces were grim and drawn.

L. Challoner

Deser
Rats

Desert Rats

The Desert War 1940-3 in the Words of Those Who Fought There

JOHN SADLER

AMBERLEY

This one is for Trevor – fellow desert enthusiast and indefatigable researcher on the Tunisian campaign

First published 2012

Amberley Publishing
The Hill, Stroud
Gloucestershire, GL5 4EP

www.amberley-books.com

British Library Cataloguing in Publication Data.
A catalogue record for this book is available from the British Library.

ISBN 978 1 84868 337 2

Typesetting and origination by Amberley Publishing
Printed in Great Britain

Contents

Introduction

This volume is intended as a companion to the author's *An End to the Beginning*, itself a narrative account of the events leading up to and the course of the Second Battle of El Alamein in 1942, with a brief conclusion through Tunisia to the final Axis capitulation. In layout, therefore, it is very similar and no apologies are made for those elements which, being essential to both, are repeated. The intention is very different in that this seeks to amplify the oral history of the period and tell the story, as far as is possible, in the words of those who were there. The narrative comes from the mouths of survivors rather than the author and is not intended to be comprehensive in the same way.

For clarity I have retained the timeline and dramatis personae as both may be deemed useful to the reader. Nonetheless, I have deleted the appendices from the earlier volume as they are essentially technical in detail and do not of themselves add to the value or impact of oral testimony. Several of the experiences related here appear in the earlier work and the author must thus apologise to any reader who feels they are treading familiar ground but to omit these would significantly weaken the whole. For similar reasons I have omitted many of the detailed footnotes; this volume is a recollection, an attempt to visualise the campaign through the eyes of those who fought. Those seeking a detailed historical narrative should turn to my own previous work or any of the many other excellent accounts of the desert campaigns readily available in print.

Those quotations included within the narrative are gleaned from written documentary material and recorded interviews, some by the author – the majority from other secondary sources. These are reproduced verbatim wherever possible, some obvious errors have been corrected and I have abridged certain passages to suit the overall flow of the text. All original verse is by Samantha Kelly.

This book, like its predecessor, could not have been written without the generous assistance of a number of organisations and individuals, particularly Peter Hart and the staff of the Imperial War Museum Sound Archive, Richard Groocock at the National Archive and Tristran Langlois of National Army Museum, Steve Shannon from the DLI Museum, Liz Bregazzi and Gill Parkes of Durham County Record Office, David Fletcher of the Tank Museum, Bovington, Roberta Twinn of the Discovery Museum, Newcastle upon Tyne, Rod Mackenzie of the Argyll and Sutherland Highlanders Museum, Thomas B. Smyth of the Black Watch Museum, Paul Evans of the Royal Artillery Museum, Anna Tiaki of the Alexander Turnbull Library, New Zealand, Christopher Dorman O'Gowan for information concerning his late father Brigadier E. Dorman-Smith, John Stelling and Henry Ross of North War Museum Project, Dr Martin Farr of Newcastle University, Barry Matthews of Galina Battlefield Tours, Trevor Sheehan of BAE Systems Plc, John Rothwell, James Goulty, Sir Paul Nicholson, Major (Retd) Chris Lawton MBE, Colonel Arthur W. Charlton, Colonel Anthony George, John Fisher, John Shepherd, Mary Pinkney, Brian Ward, Jennifer Harrison, the Hon. Christopher Vane, Neville Jackson, the late Nigel Porter, Timothy Norton, Kit Pumphrey and Sir Lawrence Pumphrey, Graham Trueman, Adam Barr for help with photography, Rosie Serdiville, Sarah-Jayne Goodfellow and most particularly to Samantha Kelly for all of the original verse extracts. Special thanks are due to Jonathan Reeve, my editor at Amberley, for yet another successful collaboration.

As the author I remain, as ever, responsible for all errors and omissions.

John Sadler, Mid Northumberland, Autumn 2012.

Glossary

AA – Anti-aircraft
AFV – Armoured fighting vehicle
AP – Armour piercing
A&SH – Argyll and Sutherland Highlanders
AT – Anti-tank
ATS – Auxiliary Territorial Services
BAOR – British Army of the Rhine
Bde – Brigade
BEF – British Expeditionary Force
Bivvy – Bivouac
Bn – Battalion
CIGS – Chief of the Imperial General Staff
C in C – Commander in Chief
CLY – County of London Yeomanry
CO – Commanding officer
Coy – Company
CP – Command post
CRA – Commander, Royal Artillery
CSM – Company Sergeant-Major
CWGC – Commonwealth War Graves Commission
DAF – Desert Air Force (RAF)
DAK – Deutsches Afrika Korps
DCM – Distinguished Conduct Medal
De-lousing – Minefield clearance
Div – Division
DLI – Durham Light Infantry

DSO – Distinguished Service Order
ENSA – Entertainments, National Service Association
EP1 – Egyptian Pattern Mark 1 mine
FANY – First Aid Nursing Yeomanry
FAP – Forward Aid Post
FDL – Forward Defence Locations, i.e. the front line
FOO – Forward Observation Officer
FUP – Form-up position
GOC – General Officer Commanding
GSO1 – General Staff Officer 1st Class
GSO2 – General Staff Officer 2nd Class
HE – High explosive
HLI – Highland Light Infantry
IO – Intelligence Officer
I-Tank – Infantry Tank
KD – Khaki drill
KRRC – King's Royal Rifle Corps
LOB – Left out of battle
LRDG – Long Range Desert Group
MC – Military Cross
MG – Machine gun
MP – Military Police
NAAFI/EFI – Navy, Army and Air Force Institutes/Expeditionary Forces Institute
O Group – Orders Group
OH – Official History
OKH – *Oberkommand des Heeres*
OKW – *Oberkommand der Wehrmacht*
OP – Observation Post
PBI – Poor bloody infantry
POL – Petrol, oil and lubricants
QM – Quartermaster
RA – Royal Artillery
RAC – Royal Armoured Corps
RAF – Royal Air Force
RAP – Regimental Aid Post
RAC – Royal Armoured Corps
RAOC – Royal Army Ordnance Corps

RASC – Royal Army Service Corps
RE – Royal Engineers
Regt – Regiment
REME – Royal Engineers Mechanical Engineers
RHA – Royal Horse Artillery
RN – Royal Navy
RND – Royal Naval Division
RSM – Regimental Sergeant-Major
RTU'd – Returned to unit
RTR – Royal Tank Regiment
SAS – Special Air Service
Scarper – Disorganised and precipitate retreat, verging on rout
SIW – Self-inflicted wound
SOE – Special Operations Executive
SP – Self-propelled; refers to artillery
TA – Territorial Army
TAC HQ – Tactical headquarters
TAVR – Territorial Army Volunteer Reserve
WD – War Department
WO – Warrant Officer
W/T – Wireless telegraphy
USAAF – United States Army Air Force
USAMEAF – United States Army Middle East Air Force
VC – Victoria Cross

Hitler, he's only got one ball,
Goering's got two but very small,
Himmler's got something similar
Poor old Goebbels' got no balls at all

Army doggerel

Introductory: 'The Blue'

A few yards from where I was standing there was a depression in which there were several bodies hastily covered with sand, here and there a leg or arm protruding and part of a machine-gun barrel also sticking up. I was idly watching these as the last of the vehicles passed, and was waiting to be picked up. My opposite number was on the British side of the minefields some distance away, also waiting. It had been very hot, around 100 degrees I should think, but now the sun was beginning to set and it was getting colder. I put on my greatcoat, although I had been wearing shorts and khaki shirt all day, when I noticed the arm that was sticking out of the sand with its fingers outstretched. As I looked I saw the fingers slowly close to a clenched position. I felt my hair bristle as I was certain the poor fellow must be dead underneath the sand, for the hand was already turning black. I felt very relieved when I suddenly remembered the sharp difference in temperature that was causing this contraction. However, I was glad when our relief truck arrived and picked me up.[1]

Ground

The great swathe of the Sahara Desert covers a vast expanse. It has an enduring aura of romance and exoticism, experienced by very few of those who fought in the Desert War. Desert ('the Blue') threw up a whole catalogue of factors to hinder military activity and increase the misery of individual combatants. For these, British and Dominion, the Germans, Italians, French, Greeks and others, it seemed they had arrived in the very cauldron of a particular version of hell:

My three strongest recollections are: the heat, sweat pouring and oozing from me, until I ached and itched with it ... the strange lack of fear ... the seemingly endless hours of utter boredom, observing a low ridge about 2,000 yards away with nothing moving, nothing happening, except the sun beating mercilessly down and one's eyes straining (as I remember our gunner putting it) 'at miles and miles of f*** all'.[2]

The epic tapestry of the Desert War from 1940 to the end of 1942 unfolds primarily in the Libyan Desert, a natural amphitheatre wherein great armies wheeled and charged, stood at bay, gave and took ground. Men poured out their lifeblood over featureless, rock-strewn ridges barely showing above the scorched desert floor. Tanks, like dusty men o' war cruised and fought, largely untroubled by the human landscape that defined other battlefields.

A captain in 2 HLI recorded his first impressions of this alien terrain:

The first time one goes up into the desert one is completely amazed by the flat terrain. We used to motor around the desert finding our way by sun compass. It was a gadget which had been produced by British officers in the 1930s. It was a very accurate compass. Roughly, the sun marked the nomen [gnomon] – the same piece of equipment you have on a sundial clock – which threw a shadow, and if your compass was correctly set, that was the mark you kept your direction on.[3]

Along the Mediterranean coast, runs the fertile coastal strip, along which most of the main settlements are located. This agreeable plain is bounded inland by a line of limestone cliffs, steep and bare, dragged through with narrow defiles or wadis. Atop the cliffs and running southwards in a gentle decline, is a bare plateau, scorched by the hot sun and scoured by millennia of harsh winds. The surface is comprised of rock and layered grit, like the topping on a primeval cake, varying in density from metres to centimetres. Where the base rock is denser, low hills have been left, insignificant humps or irregular ridges, possession of which was to be vital to the armies and demand a vast sacrifice in blood and materiel.

For the British, the desert has always had the lure of romance. Britons, from Doughty to Ranulph Fiennes, have enacted a love affair with empty spaces and dusty Bedouin. None more famously than T. E. Lawrence who, in *Seven Pillars of Wisdom*, followed the tradition of Doughty and Burton in bringing the desert alive to generations of armchair travellers. In the Second World War Ralph Bagnold in creating the LRDG, first of the 'private armies' that turned the vast expanses into a Special Forces theme park, launched a new wave of romanticism and established the British as the army which was clearly at home in the desert, something neither the Italians nor Germans were able to emulate.

What did I see in the desert today,
Besides the sand and the rocks,
Where the distance fades into misty grey
And the shimmering mirage mocks?
I saw the lonely hare
Leap from the hidden form,
As the crashing notes of the One-o-fives
Foretold the coming storm.
I saw the startled plovers rise
From the wadi by the well,
And quick among the tortured scrub
Scampered the light gazelle,
When the clangour of our armour rose
Insistent in the west,
And, fluttering, the spent A.P.'s
Came bounding o'er the crest.

L. Challoner[4]

Few of those who were to fight, Allied or Axis, had much idea of what to expect. Hans Schilling who had volunteered for service in the Panzerarmee Afrika after being called up early in 1941 and drafted into the 71st Infantry Regiment put himself forward largely out of boredom:

The company commander had read out a notice calling for volunteers to go to North Africa and I had put myself forward. About twenty-five of us from my company decided 'why not'. We knew nothing about North Africa or the war there, but Africa sounded more interesting than anything else ... First we went to a barracks near Saarbrucken where we were issued with our tropical uniform. They measured us very carefully to see that everything fitted perfectly. Compared to the normal outfitting of uniform this was a different kettle of fish. Everything had to be just so; boots not too big or small, jacket and trousers fitting well – or you were given others to try on. There was no attempt made to brief us on what it was like in Africa – just something stuck on a notice board we were supposed to read about regulations for wearing the tropical uniform. We were told nothing about medical and hygiene problems, or about the climate.[5]

One of the even less endearing aspects of life in the desert was the ubiquitous khamseen or sandstorm. Bob Sykes, a British tanker, had his first taste while serving with Aussies at Tobruk:

> I was cleaning my rifle and .38 when one of the Aussies said, 'I should wrap them up well Bob, we're in for a Queenie of a dust storm.' I could not see anything, and I couldn't see how he could tell. But after about an hour I heard a very new noise, rather like a train coming, and way out a big black bank of cloud was rushing towards us. The Aussie said: 'Get your clobber inside, put your blanket over the entrance and get in quick.' … I thought I had seen it all up to now. The sandstorm came at us like an express train at about 40 mph with increasing gusts of wind. All the oxygen seemed to go out of the air, and the flies were maddening and swarming. The heat was terrific and I sweated so the sand caked on to me – in my eyes, nose and ears.[6]

Harsh Awakenings

East of the featureless expanse lay the lush lands of the Delta, teeming, cosmopolitan, redolent with Ottoman mystery and decadence. During the war years, Egypt was host to a collection of poets and writers, prominent among whom was Lawrence Durrell who in 'Near El Alamein' wrote:

> This rough field of sudden war –
> This sand going down to the sea, going down,
> Was made without the approval of love,
> By a general death in the desire for living.[7]

It was the noted swashbuckler and commando Patrick Leigh Fermor who penned Durrell's obituary in 1990. He had known the poet from his days in Special Operations:

> We met in 1942 … under a tree in Amy and Walter Smart's garden in Zamalek, and talked far into the night. He was at the heart of a group of gifted poets and writers – Robin Fedden, Bernard Spencer, Terence Tiller, Charles Johnston and several others – who were working between Cairo and Alexandria, at the embassy or in the various press sections, the British Council and Cairo University …[8]

Though unremittingly harsh the desert was not devoid of either flora, fauna or, for that matter, inhabitants: '… there was virtually no animal or insect life. Just the occasional jerboa – the desert rat (a nice friendly little fellow) – the scorpion and an occasional gazelle. The Arabs and their camels kept well out of the way.' Gazelles were game and a variant to the harsh ration diet; hunting itself was a useful diversion:

> We spied six of them in a line. The distance was only about five hundred yards. All of us fired at once hitting three. One went down on the spot, another kept limping on and the third kept falling and rising alternately. When we arrived we found the fallen gazelle still alive but unable to get up as his leg had been blown off. Nevertheless he made frantic, pathetic efforts to do so. As I watched him I was struck with pity for the little animal. But the fact was that we were in need of meat put salve on my conscience … I shall never forget the death of that animal. At first we decided to blow its brains out at close range but somebody said it would make too much of a mess that way, so Skinners elected to stand ten yards away and put a bullet through the brains. Skinner fired, the head was hit, thick blood spouted from the hole but the gazelle didn't die. It began to jerk and quiver spasmodically …[9]

Flies were another indigenous if less attractive feature:

> Flies were a terrible nuisance. More often than not you'd be drinking a cup of tea and you would have to put your hand over the top and sip it between the thumb and forefinger to stop the flies otherwise they would be lining up around the rum to dive in.[10]

James Patch, an RA gunner, in search of high adventure, joined the LRDG and saw a great deal of desert conditions:

> There were all kinds of different surfaces to travel on. There was the seria for instance mile after mile of perfectly smooth hard sand. I've seen a truck going along at 60 mph with nobody in the driving cab at all. The driver would set his hand throttle and the truck would just go on. And we knew we weren't going to hit any bumps or obstacles. All four members of the crew would get on the back of the truck and just let it go … At other times though, just getting through soft sand was another matter altogether. We often had to dig our way with sand trays all day long – and that was quite exhausting. At other times you'd have to zigzag all day through rocks and up and down wadis.[11]

Such places became natural foci for area defence or supply stations. Without wishing to push the naval analogy too far, fighting in the largely featureless desert placed a premium on navigation, demanding an exact use of the compass:

> So five miles beyond Sidi Barrani we branched off into the open desert and bumped along over boulders and scrub as far as 'Fred Karno's Circus'. This was the name given to the gap in the wire on the Libyan-Egyptian frontier, at the southern end of the Halfaya escarpment. By this time we were beginning to realise just what driving in the desert meant. The sun was merciless, even at this time of year and our loads were floating about the lorry, bursting open tin after tin of priceless petrol.[12]

In addition to the magnetic compass, often upset by the steel in vehicles, the sun compass was also relied upon.

> It was our first effort at movement, using only compass and sun compass. Fortunately, we had some guide in a row of telegraph poles that stretched away towards the forward area along the desert tracks.[13]

During the inter-war years much work had been done by that eclectic group including two who were both to serve in LRDG: Ralph Bagnold and Andrew Clayton. One of the even more colourful of this colourful bunch was the Hungarian Lazlo Almasy (fictionalised as the hero of Michael Ondaatje's *The English Patient*). Due to their combined efforts the empty canvas of the desert was marked by the network of ancient trails, with every feature in an otherwise bare landscape plotted and surveyed including the white bones of escarpments, sunken depressions, oases, salt marshes and dry wadis that could spring to brilliant life after rains.

For newcomers like Hans Schilling, the desert experience was a distinct novelty in a variety of ways:

> I had done my basic training in the infantry and so I expected we would all be sent to an infantry unit. But we were sent off to all sorts of units, and I ended up by going into Service Corps 4B, which is medical staff. I had no idea at all of what was going on, and I was surprised to find myself attached to Afrika Korps Headquarters as driver for Major-General Bayer, the Surgeon-General of the Afrika Korps. And this is where I found out what it was like to serve in Africa … It amazed me to see how people were walking around out of uniform and I thought they would not get away with that back in Germany. Everyone in Africa seemed to have a different uniform, and they got away with it. There

were a lot of fellows who had tried to make their uniforms look older and bleache
to make them white. White caps were the fashion and so I bleached mine until it was bone
white. I put lots of soap into it and let it dry out in the sun. It turned out though this was
a mistake because it got filthy very quickly and I had to clean it more often. The bleaching
took away what we called the factory 'bullet proofing' in the material, and when this was
lost there was no protection against dirt getting into the cloth.[14]

Schilling's first taste of action or near action involved a brush with
German military police:

All that we arrived in Africa with was our tropical uniform and personal kit. Everything else
was issued to us there. While I was the driver for Major-General Bayer I only had a rifle a
Kar 98K, but I did not see any action during this period. One day though, in the spring of
1942, there was a panic on somewhere, an attack was in progress and we had to go through
a place manned by Feldgendarmerie. A great long line of trucks had pulled up and the
General told me to drive on. So I pulled out of the line of traffic and took the Opel Admiral
up to the front. A Feldgendarmerie ran out to me waving his little round indicator, yelling at
me to stop, but I drove on and this man jumped up on the running board and held his pistol
at my head. Heaven knows what he called me, but it was bad. The general then stood up in
the back seat so the man could see his rank badges and he really dressed this man down. He
was only a Hauptfeldwebel and the general really let him have it: 'Look up front, can't you
see the sign on my car, look at me – if I tell my man to drive on, he drives on.'[15]

During the summer months, from May to October, the climate is
scorching hot, a blisteringly and relentless sun, furnace-bright and
searing dry. Only in the evenings before the dark cold of night, before
the sun sinks, is the broiling fire of day mellowed into evening cool.
Winters are drear and damp with frequent heavy downpours. Torrents
flow down the scree-riven wadis but water is soon soaked up by the
parched and greedy desert. There is great and ascetic beauty and the
desert can exert a powerful, almost obsessive pull. Dawn and sunset can
be infinitely memorable and the stars glow with a clear cold light that
conjures biblical images. Soldiers were thrown back on their recall of
heroic conflicts as depicted in the *Iliad*:

Wilfred Owen said that the poetry is in the pity; but that was in another war. This later
war was one of great distances and rapid movement and for me the poetry came when
least expected, in the interstices of a generally agitated existence, in the rush of sudden

contrasts, and the recognition that, whatever else changes, one's own mortality does not.[16]

Subsistence

Q 'Were they good days for you?

A 'Oh yes. Happy days with my men ... I have always longed to meet them again. Where are all the Geordie men I loved and commanded now?[17]

The desert offered little to sustain man. Rations, which inevitably come to prominence in the minds of fit young men, deprived of alluring sustenance, became a focal point for 'grousing', the litany of complaint which is the birthright of all soldiers:

You can stew it, you can fry it

But no matter how you try it

Fundamentally it remains the same,

You can hash it, you can slash it,

With potatoes you can mash it,

But when all is done you've only changed the name.

'A Cook's Thoughts on Bully'

For the infantryman food, the lack of it and the consistent unpalatability of what was offered were major practical considerations, as Hans Schilling recalls:

Food was always a problem in the desert, and it was the same for everyone. I spent a lot of time with the Afrika Korps HQ and the officers ate the same food as we did. The generals might get an odd orange or banana but that was it. After Tobruk was captured in 1942 we all had a lot of bully beef. It was a pleasant change from the terrible old Italian tinned meat, called 'AM', but we got sick of the bully beef too after a while. The other regular issue of Italian food we had was a type of big, thick, square biscuit. We called them 'cement plates', and I felt sorry for the fellows who did not have good teeth because you had to grind it. The only vegetables we ever saw were the dehydrated stuff, we would throw them into boiling water and see them grow. I was always grateful for the German black bread 'Dauerbrot' because it was good.[18]

It must at times have seemed almost unbelievable that such titanic efforts were exerted by both sides to win these arid, seemingly endless acres: 'In the desert, men asked "Why?" again and again. There had to be some good and justifiable reason for fighting in such inhospitable climes. No men fought merely for the sake of fighting.'[19]

For the most part, infantry inhabited trenches, much as their fathers had done on the Western Front, though these were less permanent affairs. To dig down into sand was not difficult but, where the surface had been whittled away by wind and the limestone exposed, powered tools were necessary to gouge out shallow trenches and fox-holes, supported by a rough parapet of stones, 'sangars'.

Battles were large and terrifying though relatively rare. Smaller actions at platoon or company level were far more common and there was a constant need for patrolling, either light reconnaissance or the beefier and bristling fighting patrol:

> Recce patrols were messy affairs if we had to go through the pockets of some poor devil who had been killed and had been left lying out in the sand for a couple of days. People talk about rigor mortis, but after a day or two the limbs were flexible again and indeed, after a week or so, a quick pull on an arm or leg would detach it from the torso. Two day old corpses were already fly blown and stinking. There was no dignity in death, only masses of flies and maggots, black swollen flesh and the body seeming to move, either because of the gases within it or else the thousands of maggots at work. We had to take documents, identity discs, shoulder straps, anything of intelligence value. Pushing or pulling these frightening dead men to reach their pockets was sickening. Of course, we couldn't wash our hands – one rubbed them in sand – sometimes we rubbed them practically raw if it had been a particularly disgusting day.[20]

'Desert Rose' sounds like an attractive form of flora. To the Allied army however it denoted an altogether more basic convenience – the field latrine. For temporary arrangements the hollow shell of a petrol container was buried with another laid on top at a suitable angle to form a urinal. Where more creature comforts were needed, a deep trench was sunk with a hessian sheet on timber frame arranged above. Chlorine was applied liberally. Cleanliness and hygiene were essential in the desert climate where dysentery and other horrors stalked. The tending of these facilities was not itself without hazard as Private Kenneth Lovell of D Company 16 DLI discovered:

CSM Baker had given me the job of trying to keep down the germs in our rather primitive latrines. To give some sort of privacy some big 80 gallon petrol drums had been laid longwise around their sides. He said, 'Get some cans of petrol, pour the petrol in and chuck a match on top. It won't do much but it might keep the germs down!' I did this with a couple of other chaps and we got to the last one. There wasn't much petrol left so I chucked it in, set light to it and sent one of the other chaps to get another can of petrol. When I returned I threw some earth into the pot to smother any remaining flames. Then, satisfied it was safe, I threw the contents of the can in. There was a hell of a 'WHOOSSHHH!' and a bloody great sheet of flame shot up towards me.

Lovell decided that a quick retreat was necessary but his hopeful leap to safety landed him on the crumbling slope of the pit and his boots afforded no purchase!

... Despite all my efforts, I fell back and with a splash landed in the shit! They say the more you stir the more it stinks – I can assure you that's very true![21]

Personal cleanliness and liberal application of AL63 (anti-louse powder) were equally emphasised. Opportunities for washing one's person or attire were often limited for the soldier coated in a caked carapace of stale, dried sweat and dust. Cuts and scrapes could swiftly become infected and morph into most unpleasant weeping ulcers:

Once ashore our first work was to build ourselves a camp. Within a few hours a tented camp had sprung up on the edge of the desert. We lived in this for three weeks and suffered the worst outbreak of 'spit and polish' that we had ever received ... But the value of this apparently excessive discipline was soon realised when we reached the battle area; we then found that the British troops were expected, by all other nationalities, to be the finest disciplined troops in the world.[22]

For the majority of the young men who served in these campaigns any form of overseas travel, indeed any travel at all was a novelty. To such innocents the Levant appeared a distant and exotic place:

Waiting for a taxi, he breathed the spicy, flaccid atmosphere of the city and felt the strangeness of things about him. The street lamps were painted blue. Figures in white robes, like night shirts, flickered through the blue gloom, slippers flapping from heels; the women, bundled in black, were scarcely visible.[23]

Few could deny that their apprehensions were overlaid by a sense of adventure:

> We sailed along the Red Sea for a century, it seemed. The heat was insufferable. Sleep was an impossibility; tempers were frayed and fights developed freely ... Curiosity replaced apathy. Stage by stage, and those men who had been to Egypt before found themselves in popular demand and frequent visitors to the canteen.[24]

At first their destination appeared almost delightful.

> As we clambered ashore we stamped and rubbed our feet delightedly ... We ran the sand slowly through our fingers; it was warm and real and comforting. I could never have believed then that I would hate this self-same sand so bitterly; the crumbled, remorseless rock that sucked at the lifeblood of us who tried to master her vastness in the following months.[25]

They would find that the epithet, 'Desert Rat' was not accorded to novices as of right; it had to be earned, the recognition of an apprenticeship in desert warfare and survival:

> ... The name given to themselves by the soldiers of the Eighth Army ... it became an expression of pride among the men. It soon became the entitlement only of experienced desert fighters and could not be claimed by any newcomer to the desert.[26]

Driver Robert Crawford and his comrades had cause to be grateful to two old sweats who rescued them from their own faulty navigation:

> These were two of the original Eighth Army who knew all the tricks of the Desert. They taught us in a few moments how to make a petrol fire from sand, water and petrol in a disused tin. They showed us how to make porridge from biscuits and an appetising meal from bully beef. Finally they taught us how to sleep comfortably on the floor of the desert; and, incidentally, made us feel the simpletons we really were.[27]

For every desert warrior the transition from raw newcomer to seasoned campaigner was a distinct learning curve, as Hans Schilling soon found out:

As for equipment – it amazes me now when I look at photos and I wonder how the dickens we carried all that stuff around. I remember the most important things we kept and the rest we left behind whenever we had to move. We just could not carry all the stuff we were issued with. The most important thing was always to keep your rifle and ammunition. It was a court martial offence to lose these. And the other pieces you tried to hang on to were your messkit, your cap and woollen overcoat (the nights were cold in the desert) and a bit of spare underwear. Everything else was excess. The first stuff we used to get rid of were things like the mosquito netting and the gas mask. Some men used to keep the gas mask canister, it was useful for filling up with ammunition or any spare food you had ...[28]

In such surroundings the comradeship of war was inevitably heightened. Men might express fine sentiments and extol the nobility of sacrifice but such poetic expressions soon wilted in the face of reality. Endless hours of tedium, dirty, sweaty, beset by a constant and ravenous horde of flies, troubled by looseness of the bowels and all the other complaints that add endless misery to a soldier's life, enlivened only by odd moments of sheer terror. The code of behaviour which evolved was dictated by pure pragmatism:

Your chief concern is not to endanger your comrade.
Because of the risk that you may bring him, you do not light fires after sunset.
You do not use his slit trench at any time.
Neither do you park your vehicle near the hole in the ground in which he lives.
You do not borrow from him, and particularly you do not borrow those precious fluids, water and petrol.
You do not give him compass bearings which you have not tested and of which you are not sure.
You do not leave any mess behind that will breed flies.
You do not ask him to convey your messages, your gear or yourself unless it is his job to do so.
You do not drink deeply of any man's bottles, for they may not be replenished. You make sure that he has many before you take his cigarettes.
You do not ask information beyond your job, for idle talk kills men.
You do not grouse unduly, except concerning the folly of your own commanders. This is allowable. You criticise no other man's commanders.
Of those things which you do, the first is to be hospitable and the second is to be courteous ... there is time to be helpful to those who share your adventure. A cup of tea,

therefore, is proffered to all comers …

This code is the sum of fellowship in the desert. It knows no rank or any exception.[29]

Before even food, water was the absolute essential and keeping those at the front adequately supplied remained a quartermaster's nightmare, be he British, German or Italian as Hans Schilling confirms:

Water was always the scarce commodity, and everyone guarded his water carefully to make sure there was no spillage. At the front we tried to carry two water canteens, and we always hoped that after that was gone there would be more. When we were in Egypt I can remember trucks going back as far as Derna – that's 500 kilometres – to pick up water. And once, while I was driver for the General, there was an uproar at some water filling station; people were running around yelling 'the British are here', but it turned out to be only one truck. We went over and saw two British soldiers being pulled out of the truck, which was a British truck with a 'Balkenkreuz' [German cross] painted on its side. This was common enough – we used more British trucks than German – but these were Tommies who had joined our line of trucks getting water rations. When they were asked what unit they belonged to they could not give a satisfactory answer and so we caught them. This was way behind the front line – these two Tommies just drove in out of the desert. It always used to amaze us how the British could do this, how they managed to live in the desert, but they had better training for this and they had supplies of food and water and petrol buried in the sand which we had no idea existed.[30]

Discipline was essential though the fire of combat tempered the parade ground bellowing of peacetime and the drill sergeant into a more businesslike focus:

Discipline such as we had formerly known disappeared. In its place came a companionship. Officers no longer issued orders in the old manner. They were more friendly and more with the men. They realised that this was a team. We, for our part, never took advantage of this new association. While orders were given, except in emergency, more in the nature of requests, they were obeyed even more punctiliously than under peacetime conditions. It was a case of every man pulling together, willingly. From what we had seen of the German Army, no such relationship existed, and it was not long before we discovered this was our strength.[31]

War Without Hate

Krieg ohne Hass ('War without Hate') – was a description attributed to

Rommel himself and insofar as war can ever truly be said to represent chivalry then it was here. The British had a high regard for the Desert Fox, both as a fighting soldier of the highest calibre and a man of impeccable honour. Some years after the war Lieutenant-General Johann von Ravenstein observed:

If the warriors of the Africa Campaign meet today anywhere in the world, be they Englishmen or Scots, Germans or Italians, Indians, New Zealanders or South Africans, they greet each other as staunch old comrades. It is an invisible but strong link which binds them all. The fight in Africa was fierce, but fair. They respected each other and still do so today. They were brave and chivalrous soldiers.[32]

Humour, as ever, was the soldier's balm: 'A typical example of the sort of thing that amused us was the story that Hitler had secretly contacted Churchill with the offer to remove Rommel from his command in return for Churchill retaining all his generals in theirs.'[33] Though the soldiers in the line observed a strict blackout procedure the sky to the east was lit up with the rich glow of the Delta cities. The brightness and gaiety of easy living these represented could not have contrasted more tellingly with the drab but dangerous austerity of the front. The contrast between the rigours of the line and the luxury of Cairo, 'Unreal City' could not have been greater:

To an outsider like Alan Moorehead (celebrated war correspondent and latterly author) coming upon Cairo early in the summer of 1940, a world of Edwardian privilege seemed to define the city's ambience. 'We had French wines, grapes, melons, steaks, cigarettes, beer, whisky and an abundance of all things that seemed to belong to rich, idle peace. Officers were taking modern flats in Gezira's big buildings looking out over the golf course and the Nile. Polo continued with the same extraordinary frenzy in the roasting afternoon heat. No one worked from one till five-thirty or six, and even then work trickled through the comfortable officers borne along in a tide of gossip and Turkish coffee and pungent cigarettes.'[34]

As water in the desert was the most scarce and precious of commodities at the same time as being the prime essential, troops at the front were given an extra cause to despise the 'desk wallahs' in Cairo, enjoying their very different war:

We imagined that every staff officer in Cairo lived in the lap of luxury, that was to say he had water. I remember on one of the circulars that came round, a wag who had written a long poem about these staff officers in Cairo who he called the 'Gaberdine Swine' – as their uniforms were made from gaberdine material. At the end of every stanza he had put in a chorus: 'And every time they pulled the chain/Went three days rations down the drain.'[35]

The charmed literary circle that was to produce those remarkable editions of *Personal Landscapes* included Robin Feddon whose pacifist stance had particularly irritated Ambassador Lampson:

We can't have Englishmen indulging in pacifist views, not only as a matter of general principle to which we must adhere and rigidly enforce but also because it makes us look extremely silly just at a time when I am belabouring the Egyptian Prime Minister into issuing stringent instructions to all provincial Mudirs that they must punish any defeatist or treasonable views on the part of any of their inhabitants of their Mudirieths.[36]

Though Cairo might be a cushy billet some, at least, were very much aware of what awaited men preparing to deploy 'up the Blue' or on leave. Hermione, Countess of Ranfurly was one:

It is always the same. These young men come on leave or courses to Cairo or Palestine, or for a while they are on the staff. They take you out to dinner and talk of their families and what they are going to do after the war; they laugh and wisecrack and spend all their money in the short time they can be sure they are alive. Then they go down to the desert leaving their letters, photographs and presents to be posted home. So often they never come back.[37]

If the beauties of the desert could move this generation of war poets then even the simple army convenience could raise an ode:

Of all the Desert flowers known.

For you no seed is ever sown

Yet you are the one that has most fame,

O Desert Rose – for that's your name.

There's thousands of you scattered around,

O' Desert Rose, some square, some round,

Though different in variety,
At night you're all damned hard to see.

Although you're watered very well
You have a most unfragrant smell;
And just in case you do not know,
O' Desert Rose, you'll never grow.

For you are not a Desert Flower,
Growing wilder every hour;
You're just a bloomin' petrol tin,
Used for doing most things in.

'To a Desert Flower'[38]

Resonances

As the desert campaign ground on, undistinguished places in that barren landscape, barely heard of would become household names:

We got out of our trucks and turned off to the left at a crossroads. Presently, we drew up at the empty sidings. There was a sort of goods yard and a compound surrounded by barbed wire on a line of crazy poles. Behind the station buildings stood a row of shattered shacks with their doors hanging open. The whole place was littered with empty barrels and broken crates, and everywhere the brickwork was chipped and pockmarked by machine gun bullets. Where the road crosses the metals stood a signal, its arm inappropriately set at 'safety'. The entire neighbourhood seemed to be completely deserted and, as I mounted the platform, I read on the front of the building the name of the place, 'ALAMEIN'.[39]

Prior to the Desert War, few people had heard of this insignificant halt some fifty miles west of Alexandria. Indeed, there was little to see. This rather shabby halt had the advantage of being close to the sea and it was possible to access the beach. This provided a welcome and refreshing experience for weary and dusty soldiery undertaking the train journey eastwards to Mersa Matruh:

To sun one's bones beside the
Explosive, crushed-blue, nostril-opening sea

(The weaving sea, splintered with sails and foam,

Familiar of famous and deserted harbours,

Of coins with dolphins on and fallen pillars.)

Bernard Spencer[40]

At about the time General Sir Claude Auchinleck (the 'Auk') assumed the mantle of Middle East Command in July 1941, replacing General Wavell, General Sir James Marshall-Cornwall, commanding garrison forces in the Nile Delta, was instructed to begin digging a series of defences anchored in the north on El Alamein. From that point the place was rapidly to become the seat of legend.

Certain preparatory moves had been undertaken as far back as 1940 when the threat from Graziani's army appeared most potent. These preliminaries were curtailed after the rout but further works were undertaken in the spring of 1941 before matters really got going that autumn after the Gazala fighting. Three large 'boxes' were now prepared. The first, most northerly, being around Alamein and intended to house a full division. The two additional positions, Deir el Quattara and the Jebel Kerag were each intended to hold a brigade. These positions were systematically strengthened by the construction of concrete pillboxes to hold AT guns and trench lines, secured with extensive wiring, the laying of mines and, in some instances, anti-tank ditches.

What did I see in the desert today?

Relics of what had died.

The pale, enamelled shells of snails

Wherein the spiders hide,

And the dark, fast-rusting shells of hate

Lie shattered side by side.

L. Challoner[41]

El Alamein was to assume prime importance to the Axis, though it was to be a place finally of despair and defeat. Hans Schilling remembers:

When things became really drastic at the front, after we had reached El Alamein, I decided I had done enough sitting around at HQ, or driving around. I wanted to make myself useful so one day when we were driving up to Tobruk I asked my General if he could get anyone else to be his driver. He was a Bavarian and came from Munich and he said to me in his Bavarian dialect: 'What – do you want to go to the front to do some shooting?' But he understood and I got my papers which posted me to a front line unit. I had to make my own way as best I could, asking directions and getting lifts as I went along. I was sent to join 90th Light Division. I went into Infantry Regiment 200, commanded by Major Briel ... When I arrived at my new unit, 1st Company in Infantry Regiment 200, the men took me under their wing and looked after me. When I heard the first artillery shells come over I dived for the nearest hole and covered myself but the other fellows just went on eating and smiled a bit; later we had quite a laugh.[42]

Field hospitals, command centres, stores and communications were housed underground, each served by water piped from reservoirs in the north fed via a pipeline from the Nile. With such large forces dispersed over a wide area the single coast road was both inadequate and exposed as a single line of supply. Consequently, a series of 'Sommerfield' tracks were constructed to remedy the defect. A total of eleven new airstrips were laid out. Mines, which had not featured significantly in the earlier battles, were becoming increasingly important. Both sides now relied heavily on minefields and, as the armies surged back and forth the fields changed hands so that new were laid on top of old. The area west of El Alamein thus became a dense and interlocking web of deadly mines, a major hazard for whoever sought to advance and one which had to be overcome before there could be any prospect of success.

Vital and often unsung work was carried out by the medical services of both sides, often working in the most difficult of conditions – Edgar Randolph joined the Australians as a field nurse and first saw active service in January 1941 during the Allied attack on Tobruk:

The casualties poured in. My mate, Bob Smith, and I were on the go for three days and two nights with no more rest than a ten-minute sit down. The place was like a butcher's shop. An Aussie DOA (Dead on Arrival) was passed to me to prepare for burial and lack of experience showed in the lad's death. He had a wound in his chest which had been covered with a field dressing. He was then whipped on to a stretcher and carried several miles. I had to get Smithy to help separate him from the stretcher as he had an exit wound in his back that you could put a fist into – not looked for and not treated. The poor devil had bled to death while he was being carried in.[43]

1

Desert War

20 June 1942 – Wounded are pouring into Palestine because the hospitals in Egypt are overflowing. Each day between nine and five I go down to a hospital in Jerusalem to help in the wards. I have no training so I do all the odd jobs such as washing soldiers, making beds and emptying things. Today I washed four heads which were full of sand. I am learning a lot about pain and courage and getting used to smells and sights. The soldiers make fun of everything and, even in the long ward where the serious cases are, no one ever grumbles. I cannot describe the courage of these men. Only when they ask me to help them to write home do I glimpse their real misery, some of them are so afraid their families will not want them back now they are changed. They call me 'Sugar'.[1]

In Armour

I was merely a trooper, a member of a tank crew in the Alamein campaign and certainly in no position to have any overall appreciation of the strategy and tactics of the battle. A good start is sometimes said to be half the battle, and certainly two things raised the spirits of the British forces before the Alamein battle was joined. The first was the appearance of the American Sherman tank on the scene …[2]

The Western Desert appeared to open up a vast canvas over which tanks, leviathans of the battlefield, could race, sleek as frigates or potent as ships of the line. Pure warfare where the featureless desert formed an inland sea, unencumbered by towns, rivers, forest or marsh and with a tiny, nomadic and largely unconsidered civilian population:

While the Western Desert of Egypt comprised a good deal of areas of soft sand – the Munassib Depression in particular – the Libyan Plateau was a fairly hard gravel desert and it was possible for light vehicles, scout cars, staff cars etc to reach speeds of 50mph if need be; tanks too could go at speeds limited only by their design.[3]

Reality inevitably proved to be somewhat different. Being in tanks was no sinecure; the risk of a ghastly death was omnipresent as trooper Powell recalled:

> Eventually the tank I was in was knocked out. I clearly recall the driver, a phlegmatic little Yorkshireman calling to us in the turret, 'My visor's gone. Next one we've had it' His tone was conversational almost casual. In a matter of minutes the tank was engulfed in flames. What surprises me is that I was not conscious of any explosion or sound just realising I was in the middle of a fire and myself on fire. The gunner was killed, the rest of us escaped.[4]

Relationships between infantry, armour and artillery were frequently based on ignorance, disdain and suspicion. Infantry in the desert felt exposed without armoured support and resented the ability of their mechanized comrades to withdraw from the front of an evening and their ability to stock up on luxuries. They did not understand the need for tanks to re-fuel and replenish and the intricacies of maintenance in trying desert conditions, dust and harsh surfaces taking a fearful toll on moving parts. The life took a toll of the men as well:

> War is an obscenity. No one knows this better than the soldier, sailor and airman, who see it in the raw. The hero is not shot in the shoulder for the heroine to bandage; he has his jaw blown off, or he is disembowelled. It matters not whether he is friend or foe – we were all in this bloody desert and this bloody war together. In the infantry it was worse; in tanks you did not always see the bodies – they were inside, burnt to a cinder.[5]

The inter-war years had seen a rivalry between the 'tank' school, led by Fuller and Liddell Hart and the 'cavalry' school, who chose to ignore telling lessons from the Great War. General Sir Percy 'Hobo' Hobart was a passionate advocate of the former and advocated to the full the Fuller/Liddell Hart concept of armoured warfare. This envisaged tanks as an independent, striking arm not dependent on a tail of infantry and guns but playing a cavalry role in firstly pinning enemy forces by a frontal feint then executing a series of flanking movements, not unlike the mounted caracole of previous centuries, to strike the foes from side and rear.

When I first arrived at Abbasia Barracks in Cairo straight from a convoy from England, my 'draft' of RAC officers had been told by an immaculately dressed cavalry colonel (with only one arm and a DSO): 'Two things. Forget everything you have ever learned in England. And learn to do as you are told.' No Sam Brownes, no polished buttons, no 'bull'. Bush jackets, suede boots (later to be called desert boots), perfumed hair shampoo, silk scarves (to keep out the sand), little or no saluting ... No kit just a change of pants and vest, socks, two blankets and a ground sheet. We lived in our tanks, armoured cars, whatever; rank could count only to the extent that you could earn respect. All took their turn in cooking, rearming, refuelling, checking of guns etc, etc, all slept together under the same tarpaulin.[6]

British doctrine was based essentially on a cavalry charge 'Balaklavering' – where tank fought tank; what was not fully considered was the crucial role to be played by anti-tank guns. Occasionally this paid dividends, in the halcyon early days when the enemy was solely the under-prepared Italians. Alf Davies of 1 RTR:

We arrived at a certain point at about five o'clock in the morning just before it got light, and we were expecting to see Italian tanks or infantry. But instead we saw about three hundred men, they all had candles – they were attending mass. Well you know there is no law and we just opened up with machine-guns – and candles, everything went flying elsewhere.[7]

As Italian armies disintegrated during the brilliant days of 'Compass' in 1940, British tanks, poorly armed as they were proved a match for the equally inferior Italian model: 'Topper' Brown of 2 RTR:

I managed to get into my gunner's seat and the next thing I saw as I looked through my sights was an M13 about thirty yards away, coming straight towards us ... Without thinking I pulled the trigger of the two-pounder, but as I didn't see any tracer I thought, 'Oh my God, I've missed.' I gave it another one, but just then one of the crew climbed out of the top, so I shot him. Daylight shone through the hole made by my first shot – was I relieved! We were so close that the tracer hadn't time to light up.[8]

If the odds on survival were better for the tanker than the footslogger, the nightmare vision of being trapped inside a burning hull haunted many. Even when those who burned were the enemy it was impossible to avoid horror:

We were horrified to see a figure with face blackened and clothes alight stumbling through the smoke. He staggered for some yards, then fell and in a frenzy of agony rolled frantically on the hard sand in a desperate effort to put out the flames. But to no avail. Gradually his flailing arms and legs moved more slowly, until at last, with a convulsive heave of his body, he lay still.[9]

Contrary to the imaginings of cynical infantry a tanker's life was not an easy one. True they retired to 'leaguer' at night but they themselves felt the Air Force enjoyed the 'cushiest number':

They fought went home, ate a prepared hot meal, slept in clean sheets while somebody else serviced and repaired their machines. In comparison, a tank crew drove and fought all day, then in the evening or often long into the night, they serviced and repaired the vehicle, then refuelled it before thinking about a meal and sleep.[10]

Protection, mobility and firepower are the three principal concerns of the tank designer and every variant thus embodies elements of compromise. A tank which moves fast cannot carry a greater weight of armour; a heavier tank is likely to be slower. Attempts were made to improve the armament on the Crusader Mark II and Valentine Mark II by replacing the obsolete 2-pounder with a 6-pounder which conferred limited benefits. The Crusader III suffered from the same lack of adequate armour and mechanical reliability. Valentine IX, while gaining a 6-pounder, lost its 7.92mm machine gun, a significant omission. It was not until the introduction of Sherman Marks II and III (fitted with twin diesel motors) that the Allies acquired a tank that could match its Axis opponents.

Shermans boasted strong tracks, heavier and deflective, sloping armour. The 75mm M3 main armament was a distinct improvement on its predecessors, including the 75mm M2 mounted in the sponson of the Grant tank. A further crucial disadvantage of Lee/Grants was the severe restriction imposed on the tanks seeking a hull-down position. Mounting its main gun in the sponson inevitably meant the turret remained fully exposed. Better M48 HE shells gave the Sherman more effective killing power against German armour. British Churchill tanks were other welcome newcomers to the Desert War. The Mark I was still lumbered with the 2-pounder, though the Mark III was up-gunned with a 6-pounder. The Churchill proved rugged and reliable in service and its cross-country capability was remarkable. Its armour was effective against the German 5cm Pak anti-tank weapon but ineffective against the dreaded 88.

W. E. Bowles MC who served in 10th Armoured Division recalled perhaps the most significant crisis point of the Alamein battle:

> I think the most 'telling' event of the whole battle, from a tank soldier's point of view, was that after about ten days of the crumbling dog fight, Monty, at an 'Order group', said that the final breakthrough would be achieved by 9th Armoured Brigade crashing through the anti-tank screen, regardless of losses. When the brigade commander ventured an estimation that this would cost 75% casualties, Monty replied that if it cost 100% it would still go in ... and I saw the remnants of that charge of the Heavy Brigade coming back in dribs and drabs – shades of Balaklava.[11]

If German armour was initially superior in design then German tactics were equally superior in execution. The élan of the cavalry was not an element in German tactical thinking. Rommel did not expect his panzers to engage in Homeric duels with their enemies. Killing Allied tanks was primarily the function of anti-tank guns leaving the armour free to punch through and wreak havoc. When the panzers did take on Allied tanks, their superior armour and armament told. British cruisers might sweep forward in a gallant but doomed charge but well sited anti-tank weapons exacted a fearful toll. The issue was decided before the panzers discharged their first round. Indeed the German armour might be nothing more than bait to tempt British opponents into pelting towards a well-concealed gun line:

> Psychologically crew members felt they should engage the enemy tank, a similar beast, a larger and apparently more dangerous target. They did so to their detriment, for the ground anti-tank gun was the more effective and being unobserved took its toll of British armour.[12]

Harsh and brutal as the realities of the Desert War undoubtedly were the tank men still found relief in humour:

> ... let me tell you about the mess tins. In those days we had no plates and ate all of our grub out of these mess tins and even drank our tea out of them, too, if we lost our mugs. Well, mine were getting a bit rusty and rumour was that the stores had just received a batch of new ones. So I put them down on the sand and ran over them with the tank. But,

of course, when I got round to the stores the rumour was false and so I had to straighten them out again. And what a job that was.[13]

Despite their technical superiority the Germans found tank warfare every bit as bloody and bruising as their Allied counterparts. Rolf Volker of the DAK recalled how hard Rommel drove his panzers and the toll this relentless pressure exacted:

We didn't have any rest for weeks. We didn't have time to think. When we stopped for one day we would fall asleep sitting in the vehicles. In the week of 26 May onwards when things really got going we got three or four hours sleep. Every night we were completely exhausted. We had only one thought – let's get to Cairo! Let's get to Alexandria – this is where we really wanted to go.[14]

Poor Bloody Infantry

Regulars and their TA contemporaries both served in the desert campaigns:

I should like to emphasise the value of the TA soldier. All ranks were volunteers and the officers were hand-picked. I believe they were all steeped in the 300-year-old tradition of the regiment. They used their brains the whole time and were not able, as regular soldiers are, automatically to carry out their tasks as a result of long training.[15]

War for the footslogger was never an affair of strategy or grand tactics. It was a daily grind of discomfort and tedium, poor and monotonous rations, dirt, squalor and the odd burst of sheer terror. His basic tactical unit was the infantry section of ten men, led by an NCO. Second and third men in the file were jointly responsible for the Bren. Three riflemen followed, two bombers and a lance corporal completed the section file. This composition would have been recognisable to veterans of the later battles of the Great War. Three sections with the Lieutenant's three-man HQ function formed a platoon. Three of these constituted a rifle company, led by a major with a captain as 2/ic and his HQ group including CSM, medics, signallers and company runners. Four rifle companies with a specialist HQ company completed the infantry battalion. The battalion HQ Company included the tactical support units, mortar platoon, the carrier platoon, equipped with Bren carriers, an MT platoon and, latterly some anti-tank weapons. The transport platoon had a single three-ton truck per company. The battalion could be a self-contained unit with its medical, signals and pioneer complement. Arrival in this alien and overpowering environment was generally challenging:

> My first meeting with the Desert Rats was before the main battle when I went forward with the Divisional Commanders Reece Group. As taught in England I was in full battle order complete with tin hat and gas mask: I had, of course, very white knees. I felt a complete fool to see the officers of 7th Armoured Division in jerseys, corduroy trousers, flowing scarves, berets and desert boots: their only weapon in a few cases being a revolver strapped around the waist. I never wore a tin hat again![16]

Bill Winchester served with the 4th Bn Royal Sussex; he had no illusions about the reality of conflict and experience merely confirmed his worst fears:

> Well sure enough there we were with our little pop guns when the first German tank with a dirty black cross on it came rumbling up the road towards us. My knees turned to water as I waited for the hell that I knew was now going to be let loose. The tank stopped and fired its machine guns at us and plastered the road behind us with several rounds of HE.[17]

Influenced by the dire experience of the battle for France in 1940 and subsequent experience in the desert, infantry rightly dreaded the onslaught of German panzers. Hence the constant cry for armoured support. Infantry officers were aware of the shortcomings of the 2-pounder anti-tank gun and the Boys AT rifle. A company or battalion strongpoint would be constructed for defence against the enemy's infantry and guns, with the ability to call down supporting fire. Platoons would deploy in slit trenches with pits for the Bren guns which, with rifles and grenades, would supply the immediate firepower. Separate positions for the heavier Vickers MGs would be dug behind the infantry line and sited so as to provide interlocking fields of fire. It was customary, as the war progressed, to gird defensive positions or 'boxes' with minefields and wire, forming mini-fortresses or redoubts. An obvious weakness, amply demonstrated during the Gazala battles in the spring of 1942, was the vulnerability of widely dispersed brigade boxes. These could be eliminated in turn and were not so placed as to provide mutual support. In the featureless terrain, vehicles could not easily be accommodated within the box so were parked, as a rule, well to the rear. This protected the valuable transport but meant that the infantry were denied a quick means of escape if the box was overrun.

Bill Winchester continues his story of an unequal struggle:

> I was lying there feeling sort of helpless with bullets buzzing past my ears, like a swarm of bees. Two of the chaps were firing at the tank with a Bren gun, like David taking on Goliath, and then the incredibly brave, stupid Corporal Wright got up and walked towards the tank, his rifle held at the correct 'high port'. He fell dead riddled with bullets before he had got many yards, such a useless way to die.[18]

Digging slit trenches might, depending on the composition of the desert floor, be relatively easy but in areas where the relentless wind had scoured down to the unyielding bedrock, pick and shovel would not avail and trenches had to be bludgeoned or blasted through by sappers. 'Real' mines would be interspaced with fields of dummies and safe paths through defined. Platoon trenches would be sited in approximate oval patterns with the HQ element located centrally. Company HQ would be slightly to the rear to give the CO an overview of the fight as it unfolded.

The Gunner's War

In some ways the deadly German 88mm gun is that most associated with the Desert War yet the RA achieved considerable successes. Chief among its arsenal was the 25-pounder gun/howitzer. This inspired a similar degree of terror in DAK as their 88mm did for 8th Army. Such was the gun's rate of fire that the Germans came to suspect the weapon was belt fed! The 25-pounder could throw a shell 13,400 yards on a low trajectory or rather less for higher. It weighed only 1.75 tons which made it both light and easily manoeuvrable. It could fire both HE and AP so it possessed a tank-killing capacity. If its range was less than that of the 88mm it had a far lower profile and worn out barrels could be changed with relative ease. Serving the guns in desert conditions was gruelling work, as R. G. W. Mackilligin MC remembers:

> The prelude to the battle was a nightmare period of dumping ammunition at the gun position we were to occupy, on the eve of the battle. Gun-emplacements had to be dug and sandbagged, and vast quantities of ammunition transported forward and dumped

ready on the gun position. All this was done at night and the whole area of the gun position thoroughly camouflaged to look like empty desert and vacated by first light.[19]

British gunners also fielded the 4.5-inch gun and 5.5-inch gun/howitzer and the RA constantly displayed magnificent skill in gunnery. One deficiency which was not remedied by the time of Second Alamein was for greater range and increased weight of shot. It would not be until the campaign in Tunisia that the 7.2-inch howitzer partially satisfied this need and the fearsome US 155mm howitzer would not be provided to UK forces until after the end of the North African campaigns. Air-burst HE shells were increasingly perceived as having both a deadly and morale-shaking effect. Problems with suitable fuses were not, however, resolved until later in 1943. A direct competitor for the 88mm was the British 3.7-inch anti-aircraft gun which was a first class weapon though one which was not generally deployed in an anti-tank role. There were several reasons for this: correct sights for the job proved problematic, the gun was heavier, slower to deploy and had a dangerously high profile by comparison. There may have been some reluctance to deploy these weapons for an offensive role when it was felt they were more needed to defend base areas and fixed installations. With suitable air-burst HE fuses for most artillery unavailable or unsuitable, the 3.7-inch gun was increasingly used as a stop gap.

A limitation affecting all of the British ordnance discussed above was their dependence on a towing vehicle or tractor. Gunners constantly sought a form of gun that was self-transporting, the self-propelled or SP gun. One expedient on which opinions differ was the US 'Priest'. This mounted the potent 105mm gun on a Grant chassis. The gun was formidable but not as effective or durable as was hoped and the Grant was not entirely suitable, nor outstandingly reliable. The requirement was for a suitably modified 25-pounder mounted on a compatible tank chassis but no such variant was available for the period under consideration.

Much has been said of the failings of the British 2-pounder anti-tank gun. The weapon was still one of the best in its class, superior to the German 3.7cm Pak 36, stable and with a full 360-degree traverse. It was simply not powerful enough to dent Axis tanks and was never used with an HE round. Redoubtable Sergeant Grey DCM, MM of the Camerons witnessed British anti-tank guns in action and doing good service:

About 2530 they arrived. An armoured car and a tank, followed by lorries came streaming over the top. Twenty Kittyhawks paid no attention and cruised above us, as if on a Bank Holiday. The lorries stopped on the top and the tank and armoured cars came on, watched breathlessly by everyone, until they got neatly picked off by an anti-tank gun as they came round the last corner – nicely within Bren range. The crews only ran a yard or two! Then the party started. The Germans deployed well out of range, got their mortars, machine-guns and a battery going, and rushed stuff over and into our hill without stopping.[20]

The German 88mm FlaK 18, 36 or 37 (the 'eighty-eight') began life in an anti-aircraft role. Its usefulness as an anti-tank gun was handy improvisation but one which proved devastatingly effective. This was an exceptionally fine weapon with extremely high muzzle velocity. It could punch through 150mm of armour at 2,000 metres and, with excellent sights, was in its element deployed over the flat terrain of the desert. Rommel, from his early days as a field commander in the battle for France, was an advocate of massive and ruthless firepower, believing that a first and decisive strike by artillery was a key component of tactical success. Mortars are the infantryman's artillery and if inferior in range and accuracy to their large siblings in the gun line are highly effective at closer quarters. In general terms the British 3-inch mortar was a useful weapon, capable, at least in theory of dropping some 200lb of bombs in a mad minute of rapid fire. Its principal failing was its short range. In this it was thus markedly inferior to the Axis equivalents.

Once battle was joined the gunners could count on being fully employed throughout:

We fired an average of five hundred and fifty rounds or about seven tons of steel-clad high explosive per gun that night, and at first light next day when the firing stopped, we just dropped in our tracks ... The next day we moved forward through a narrow gap cleared through the enemy minefields and took up a new position, from which we fired another formidable box barrage that night.[21]

Sappers
Lieutenant-Colonel B. S. Jarvis served with 3 (Cheshire) Field Squadron:

Then came the move to the front [written on 27 November 1942]. It was done with the utmost secrecy and for a few days we lay a few miles behind the lines, only going up now and again to peep from gunner's Ops. The latter revealed a very lonely battlefield and taught us nothing. The day before full moon we received our orders.[22]

Both the complexity and depth of minefields grew exponentially as the campaign unfolded. Initially, it was the British who made use of defensive belts at Gazala, First Alamein and Alam el Halfa but, as the advantage in material strength swung toward 8th Army, the Axis began to sow mines in earnest. Mine-clearing operations on the British side were directed by Brigadier Frederick Kisch who significantly improved on existing techniques hitherto both laborious and hazardous. The tally of mines laid across the front ran to hundreds of thousands and dense belts were sown as far eastwards as the shadow of the Pyramids, should the Axis advance penetrate that far.

Mines were attractive for dense fields created a kind of Great War defensive system enabling a commander to exercise sway of great tracts of landscape, channelling attacks into gaps covered by his guns. The British found themselves, at the outset, desperately short of effective tactical mines which produced an unexpected windfall for local engineering companies called upon to produce large numbers of what became known as the Egyptian Pattern Mark 1 mine ('EP1'). These were crude and unstable, dangerous both in the laying and in the lifting. Gelignite, the explosive compound used had a nasty habit of 'sweating' in the intense heat and this deadly perspiration was raw nitro-glycerine!

Colonel Jarvis continues:

Every sapper was told the Army Commander's plan and every sapper was thrilled to the teeth. We felt we had finished with half measures and half-chances and that this time we would fix the job once and for all. It was worth dying for.[23]

Montgomery established a training school, initially for sappers but then extended to draw in all arms. Though techniques might vary from army corps to army corps, the formation of specialised minefield task forces was common. The Axis were both thorough and ingenious. One of the principal DAK devices was the Tellermine (model T.Mi.35), about the circumference of a dinner plate and packed with several pounds of explosive. Intended primarily to disable vehicles, the fuse could be fitted so the foot passage of an unwary infantryman would not dissipate the blast on an unworthy target. Mines could be linked in tandem by attaching wire to the fuse-ring. The devices could be laid one on top of the other so the lifting over the uppermost triggered the detonation of the second. Mine clearance was nerve-wracking and immensely dangerous; it demanded knowledge, skill, dexterity, thoroughness, nerve and judgement.

> The day came and we were dumped at the front. I remember those last few hours before
> zero hour. I had finished my work, briefing my recce party and testing the equipment
> and didn't know how to pass the time. I recall changing my socks over very slowly and
> thoroughly for want of something to do.[24]

Latterly, the more specifically anti-personnel or 'S' mine (model S.Mi.35) appeared and these were laid in vast quantities in the German defences before Second Alamein. A very nasty 'jack in the box':

> ... the whole thing looked like a tin of baked beans with a nozzle on top, but of course
> all that were visible were the three prongs of the detonator. When a foot trod on the
> detonator there were two distinct explosions. The first flung the mine up into the air and
> the second explosion was at waist height and it spewed out hundreds of ball bearings
> horizontally. You can guess how we felt about those things.[25]

An added peril was the likelihood of 'de-lousing' being carried on under enemy fire. The sapper cannot concentrate upon his specialised task and fight as infantry at the same time. Engineers therefore had to be protected by a screen of infantry and, if necessary armour, a bridgehead into enemy territory. Obviously it was not necessary to lift the entire enemy minefield. What was required was a systematic clearance of roads or lanes which would enable the attacking troops and AFVs to pass through unharmed. The infantry vanguard advanced ahead of the sappers, through the live mines: 'Speaking from personal experience, it was a horrible feeling.' This nerve-wrenching chore was accomplished by sappers crawling crablike across the ground, feeling for the tell-tale trip wires. Behind them a further dispersed group prodding with bayonets, moving foot by foot, dreading the feeling of contact as the point of the Lee-Enfield sword bayonet glanced from a solid object. The mine had to be painstakingly exposed and checked for booby traps after which it was lifted, stacked and possibly defused.

An hour before zero we marched up to the FDLs and lay down behind the starting tape. At zero precisely (I knew by my watch!) it started. I saw the horizon spring into flame behind me and a few seconds later the first crash reached my ears. 'Hell let loose' I believe, is the term they use and it certainly fits. Such a noise I could never have imagined.[26]

Despite the weight of the challenge the RE rose heroically to the occasion and the products of the training schools became, in due course, consolidated into training manuals. 'Gapping' was the essential precursor to any successful attack, beginning with the relatively easy job of clearing lanes through the British defensive belt. Then the attackers advanced into the uncharted and heavily infested areas of Axis minefields, many of which were consolidated on old British positions:

The first party got cracking with their work of clearing the gap. I went off with half a dozen sappers to find the next minefield. We passed through masses of infantry consolidating in their bounds. The paces were getting into the thousands when suddenly the success signal went up. A few minutes later it went up on the left, then again on the right. Nice work! Our job should be easy now.[27]

Obviously, traditional mine-clearing techniques were far too slow to facilitate a fast moving advance yet the sappers were the vanguard of the army, unless the defender's fields were gapped there could be no offensive. At Second Alamein, the forlorn hope would not comprise purely infantry but of engineers with infantry supports. Polish officers had devised an electronic mine detector which worked through electrical impulses and was operated like a vacuum cleaner sweeping the ground. This was quicker and easier but by no means safer for the operator was obliged to remain standing, wielding his cumbersome equipment and thus presenting a most attractive target. Detectors worked in pairs with the second man marking the mines located by the first, sowing a trail of improvised cones. The detector teams were literally at the front, either with or even in front of the supporting infantry and with certain knowledge enemy artillerymen knew the ranges most exactly.

I reached the forward infantry and spoke to the company commander. He pointed to a trip wire on the crest in front. The second minefield was in front of the objective! Our company commander appeared from nowhere and quite unperturbed, said we were to carry on a clear a gap. The infantry provided a covering party and on we went. I kept my

eyes on the ground and by good fortune saw the anti personnel mines just showing above
the ground before anyone stepped on one.[28]

One device which could ensure the process was both quicker and, for
the sappers, safer was the 'Scorpion' or flail tank. This was a standard
chassis and tracks with projecting arms or boom fitted to the front which
supported a revolving drum fitted with chains which literally flailed the
ground to detonate mines. These could be effective but were of course
very noisy and created a vast khamsin of tell-tale dust in their wake. In
the vanguard of the Scorpions was a lead or pathfinder lorry, fortified
by sandbags, which drove forward till it struck a mine; thus indicating
a further belt. Behind these flail tanks came the 'snails' – more transport
spewing out a trail of diesel to leave a trammelled track-way in the desert
sand.

> As we topped the crest the enemy opened up. The covering party rushed the post. Half of
> them were hit before they got there, but they captured the chaps causing all the trouble.
> Whilst they were doing this we probed for mines. Yes, there they were, our own, captured
> in June and relaid by the Boche. That was a good start. I found the far end of the field and
> placed my light. I went over to the infantry and told the dazed corporal to get back. The
> prisoners carried their officer – shot in the stomach. They told me he had led the charge
> waving an empty pistol.[29]

When the sappers and their escorts had accomplished their task there
would be three clearly marked lanes cleared through the British minefields
with a fourth, reserve track provided for contingency use. Attacking units
would queue in orderly columns at each passage, ranked in order of their
deployment in the coming action. Clearing the lanes was a vital curtain
raiser but the job was not done yet for traffic had to be controlled. No
reckless 'balaklavering' but a disciplined, controlled and steady progress.

Transport & Rear Echelons

In the Desert War transport and logistics were absolutely vital to the
ability of combatants to maintain their effort. Without the vast trail of
second and third echelons neither side could even maintain the defensive,
far less mount an offensive. Transport thus was the key. Throughout the
course of the war Germany suffered a chronic lack of motor vehicles.
She looted and requisitioned all available stocks from the subject nations

but was chronically deficient. Thus an attack on Rommel's soft-skinned supply vehicles constituted a potent threat, more damaging than a head-on assault on his armour.

One well qualified to comment from experience was Corporal Norman Berry OBE BSC, who served as senior mechanical engineer in 13 Corps:

> It was my responsibility to organise the repair and recovery of all the tanks, guns, vehicles etc., in whichever formation to which I was posted. Starting in October 1935 with the 8th Hussars, I had been doing this work with a wide range of units in all the desert campaigns and probably saw more of the technical problems that arose than most.[30]

It was also axiomatic that, as the campaign see-sawed back and forth across the open expanses, the side that was nearest its base areas had a significant logistical advantage. For 8th Army therefore retreat to El Alamein, a bare sixty miles west of Alexandria, helped rather than hindered supplies. Rommel was continually at odds with his nominal Italian superiors who faced his considerable wrath when they repeatedly fell short of promised targets. This was not entirely a consequence of their incompetence. Ultra and the broken Italian naval code (see below) provided the RN and RAF with good intelligence which resulted in many sinkings. The failure of the Axis to conquer Malta was a significant defeat.

Corporal Berry was one who struggled to keep the British armour in motion:

> The basic trouble with all our tanks in the early stages of the war was that no engines were designed for them. Presumably this was due to lack of money, but the fact remains that in the case of the Matilda tank which was designed as an infantry tank, the power unit was two London bus engines geared together giving a total of 180 bhp. This may have been acceptable on Salisbury Plain but was not acceptable in the soft, sandy conditions that were often encountered in the desert. The poor Matilda which had been Queen of the Battlefield against the Italians who had no anti-tank weapon that could touch its four and a half inch armour, became a sitting duck to the Germans with their 88 mm high velocity converted anti-aircraft gun.[31]

Alarums in the desert could, in the worst cases, produce a form of mass-panic in exposed transport columns. Such incidents of 'scarpering' were variously dubbed 'the Gold Rush', 'Gazala Gallup', 'Msus Stakes'.

They were more decorously described in official communiqués as 'an unnecessarily rapid movement of transport'. Where the featureless terrain, largely devoid of cover, exposed soft-skinned transport of both sides to the hostile attentions of enemy armour, drivers and other rear echelon 'wallahs' could be excused for feeling apprehensive. In such circumstances a rapid relocation elsewhere, taking shelter in the vast natural dust cloud thrown up, seemed a sensible tactic. Preserving the precious vehicles was also important. The British army had suffered massive haemorrhages of soft-skinned vehicles in the withdrawal from France, the debacle in Greece and defeat on Crete.

Corporal Berry continues:

It must be very difficult for anyone who has not lived there to begin to understand what life in the desert during a campaign is all about. One reads about Eighth Army Headquarters, 7th Armoured Division workshops or some such but all these different units consist only of vehicles, tents and people. There are no buildings, factories or offices of any kind.[32]

War in the Air

The DAF variously known as Air HQ Western Desert, the Western Desert Air Force and First Tactical Air Force performed a vital role during the Desert War. Formed in 1941 to provide close air support to 8th Army, DAF comprised squadrons drawn from the Royal Air Force, its South African and Australian counterparts and latterly the USAAF. Prior to the formation of a united air arm, RAF Middle East Command, then under Air Chief Marshal Sir William Mitchell, was responsible for a quartet of different regional functions: Egypt, Malta, Iraq and Aden. When war broke out in the Mediterranean theatre the RAF, now under Air Vice-Marshal Sir Arthur Longmore, had some twenty-nine squadrons with no more than 300 machines spread over this vast canvas.

As ever, the hostile desert was an accomplished if impartial enemy. Group-Captain Sir Frederick Rosier commanded a fighter wing:

It was the aeroplanes that suffered, above all from the sand. We eventually got these filters, called Vokes filters, to stop the ingestion of sand but they affected the performance of the aeroplane. Hurricanes fitted with Vokes filters were awful compared, for example, with the German Messerschmitt 109Es and 109Fs.[33]

Re-supply of aircraft was a major difficulty and this spurred the long flight via Takoradi on West Africa's Gold Coast. By the end of November 1941 the RAF had received two Hurricane and two Wellington bomber squadrons. Consequently air support for Operation 'Compass', if stretched was adequate. However urgent the demands of the Desert War, the RAF here tended to be the poor relation and usually received those machines not required for or suited to defence of Britain. At the end of July 1941 Collishaw handed over to Air Vice-Marshal Coningham. But, by the end of the year, the whole of Middle East Air Command came under the aegis of Air Marshal Arthur Tedder, destined to be one of Montgomery's most bitter opponents. Three wings were deployed in the skies over North Africa: 258 and 269 Wings covered the front with 262 Wing held in reserve over the Nile Delta. As the direct threat to the homeland receded, more and newer machines were sent to the Mediterranean, more Hurricanes and the Douglas Boston medium bomber. A further, useful addition was the P-40 Tomahawk/Kittyhawk.

Despite the danger, discomfort and general hardship of life in the desert some airmen, like Richard de Yarburgh-Bateson, serving as a sergeant-observer on night ops, found beauty and wonder in their outwardly harsh surroundings:

[6 December 1942]... it is certainly cooler now. I sit on my bed wearing long khaki-drill trousers, battle-dress jacket and desert shoes. An Irvin jacket is spread over my knees. Outside the sand is the same ruddy yellow, but the sky is a paler blue than in mid-summer and partially screened by cirrus and stratus clouds. The mountains raise their rugged grey-brown flanks in the middle distance, while the monotony in the foreground is only relieved by the sandbagged bays and numerous aircraft, some of whose engines are roaring angrily, their propellers blowing clouds of sand dust behind them; some are black with the sinister intent of the night bomber, their bellies bulging earthwards, pregnant with destruction.[34]

Throughout 1942, DAF provided long-range interdiction and tactical support to 8th Army though its fighters were significantly outclassed by the German Messerschmitt Bf109 E & F variants which inflicted heavy losses, even if their Italian counterparts were outdated and outclassed. It was not until August, with the arrival of Spitfires, that the strategic balance in air-to-air combat shifted in the Allies' favour. In part, this was due to a shift in tactical doctrines, utilising the Luftwaffe concept of close army cooperation through the deployment of forward air controllers, the DAF's answer to the gunners' FOO. DAF then began to deploy 'cab-ranks' of fighter-bombers, waiting to be directed onto specific targets. By this means DAF won control of the desert skies and provided significant and highly effective tactical support to 8th Army during Second Alamein, the pursuit and Tunisian campaign.

Though DAF was frequently outnumbered and outgunned the pilots never shirked a fight, as this anonymous account confirms:

> Today we were rewarded for the hours we've spent sitting around waiting for the Hun to take the plunge and pay us a visit. Pilots representing every country in the Empire got away to a good start and caught the Hun as he beat it for home. There were equal numbers of fighters on either side but for a change the Hun was tied down, having had to escort his Stukas ... Then began a dogfight such as I have rarely ever been lucky to know. It was shades of the last war; the greatest fun in the world. The Hun was forced to fight at our level – there were 109s, Tomahawks, Stukas and Kittyhawks going spare in all directions. It was a wonderful sight with plenty of action; aircraft crash landing on the coast, parachutes floating down and aircraft diving into the sea only added to the excitement.[35]

Unquestionably the most famous and successful Axis air formation engaged in the Desert War was Jagdgeschwader 27 'Afrika'. I Gruppe was first deployed to support Rommel in the Gazala battle in April 1941, led by Hauptmann 'Edu' Neumann. On 19 April, JG27 claimed its first four combat 'kills', more would soon follow. German fighter formations, prizing the 'Red Baron' spirit of competitive aces, flew their superior Bf109Es ('Emils') and latterly the F or 'Friedrich' types with great skill, technically and often qualitatively superior. II Gruppe arrived in theatre in September and then III Gruppe was sent from the Eastern Front in November. Now synonymous with DAK on 24 March 1942 JG27 claimed its thousandth victim, a Boston bomber. The Bombay carrying General Gott was a 'celebrity' kill on 7 August. Though highly effective against inferior Allied fighters, JG27 did not score many successes against bombers. There is a suggestion the fighter aces were more concerned with adding to their tally than strategic intervention. By the time of Second Alamein more and better Allied fighters, Spitfires, were beginning to have an effect. A trio of German aces swiftly fell and, in December 1942, the remnants of JG27 were withdrawn from theatre; the tide had irrevocably turned.

The Ultra War

Ultra, Britain's best kept secret in 1941, was born of Enigma and this was the brainchild of a German inventor Arthur Scherbius whose objective had been to design a machine that could both encipher and decipher automatically. The concept was not a novel one. The machines all worked on a rotating disc principle and Scherbius was not the first to attempt a mass-produced version. His design came onto the market in 1923 and was adopted by the German army five years later. Its capabilities were sufficient to also enthuse the Navy and, latterly the Luftwaffe. Its value was for usage in all secret messaging that was vulnerable to interception, primarily radio traffic. What, in modern business parlance, would rank as the Engima's unique selling point 'USP' was its reflector disc which empowered the machine to both encrypt and decrypt. Powered by dry cell batteries, it was also lightweight and easily portable. In appearance it seemed as innocuous as a contemporary portable typewriter. Its potential in the field of modern warfare was immense.

Because of its ability to multiply possible encryptions to such an infinite degree, it was thought utterly impregnable to 'cracking' by even the most gifted of cryptanalysts. The Germans believed that hundreds or even thousands of mathematicians could labour for generations without success. This belief persisted even once the codes had been thoroughly penetrated. It was not in fact the 'boffins' at the British Government's Code and Cipher School (GCCS) at Bletchley Park who first began to fracture the Enigma but the cryptanalysts of the Polish army who achieved miracles by means of pure applied mathematics with some 'mechanical aids'. The latter, which were to assume increasing importance at Bletchley, were electro-mechanical devices that tested the solutions of encrypts much faster than could be achieved by pure manpower, 'bombes' as they were known.

In July 1939 as the threat of war loomed, British and French Intelligence officers attended their Polish counterparts in Warsaw where they were presented with a facsimile of the Engima the ingenious Poles had constructed. However, they had been beaten by the Enigma designers who had now added two additional discs thus multiplying the complexity. Room 40 at Bletchley continued on the Polish model with the recruitment of civilian academics, an eccentric and eclectic mix of genius whose existence became the stuff of legend. The most outstanding of these was Alan Turing, whose Olympian intellect stood out even in such

ıy. He could be described as the originator of the computer
e who designed the bombes at Bletchley.

ınt of operator laziness and, in the case of Luftwaffe personnel,
inexₚ ıce, greatly facilitated the cryptanalysts' work as did the use of
some partial guessing or 'cribs' as they were known. The great intellectual
powerhouse that was Hut 40, where operators put in thousands of hours
of painstaking work, saw them achieve miracles. Firstly the Luftwaffe
codes were broken and then others. Some of the naval codes and that
used by the Gestapo were never cracked. 'Shark' the Atlantic U-Boat key
remained inviolate all through the murderous months of 1941–42, when
the Battle of the Atlantic hung in the balance and thousands of seamen
with hundreds of thousands of tons of merchant shipping succumbed
to U-Boat attacks. One of the limitations with Ultra as the Enigma
intelligence was designated was that officers in the field never saw the
original decrypts.

These were frequently unintelligible and needed to be translated and,
effectively, interpreted, so that which was passed on was in an edited
form. In the early days this fine art of interpretation was left to linguists
rather than IOs with the risk that a competent IO might have read the
decrypt in a subtly different way. As Ultra was Britain's most closely
guarded secret, perceived as the trump that could tip the finely wrought
scales between survival and defeat, entry to the circle of initiates was
restricted. The source of the intelligence had to be concealed so that the
Germans would not come to suspect Enigma had been broken. Field
commanders were generally told that information had been gleaned from
well-placed agents or detailed reconnaissance.

For this reason Bernard Freyberg, when he commanded on Crete
was not within this charmed circle. Ultra intelligence was thus filtered
through Cairo and, as early as 1 May 1941 there was an intimation of the
intended attack on Crete. Four days later further intercepts revealed the
main targets and set a date of the 17th when the assault would begin. This
signals traffic, crucially, mentioned seaborne elements and made reference
to 5th Mountain Division. Creforce HQ had been set up in a disused
quarry above Souda Bay, utilising a network of caves that offered good
protection from aerial bombardment. Freyberg's staff was somewhat
makeshift, with a chronic shortage of signallers and reliable wireless sets.
His predecessor Weston, huffed at his removal from overall command,
retained a separate and well-equipped HQ. Freyberg was too punctilious

to 'pull rank'. In the troglodyte world of Creforce HQ, Captain Sandover was the IO responsible for decrypting the ULTRA intercepts.

It must, therefore, be borne in mind that Freyberg was not in the 'know' where this marvellous intelligence was coming from. The signals were codenamed 'OL' for 'Orange Leonard' the usual fiction about agents in place being employed. The key Engima decrypt (OL 2/302) was passed to Creforce at 5.45 p.m. on 13 May and, on the surface, was pure gold. This confirmed that the date of the attack was to be the 17th as previously understood (this was moved to the 20th subsequently). It specified the first day's targets for the paratroops as Maleme, Chania, Rethymnon and Heraklion. It revealed the extent of the air support that would be thrown into the fight, that additional troops would be brought in by glider and, latterly, once an airstrip was secured, by transports. It finally confirmed that elements of the projected invasion force would arrive by sea, together with AA batteries.

Although the units to be employed in the assault were listed there was no specific mention of which units would appear where or how, precisely, they were to be landed. Ultra, despite the very precision of the intelligence actually misinformed Freyberg or allowed him to form a wrong assessment – that a substantial element of the attacking force would be amphibious. Given that Crete was an island and that, as mentioned, the concept of vertical envelopment was untried this was not an unreasonable conclusion. Had the fine detail shown that only relatively minor elements of the force would be coming in ships then the General might have re-considered his defensive strategy. The decisions made during the critical period of 21–22 May need to be considered in the light of this. Freyberg was convinced that the initial airborne landings were merely an overture and that the more solid threat would come over the water. This assessment was fatally flawed and the Ultra intelligence in fact created a fatal obfuscation despite the accuracy of the material.

The arrival of Rommel in the North African Theatre coincided with the establishment of a Special Signals Link to Wavell and Middle East Command in Cairo. Hut 3 at Bletchley could now transmit reports directly to the GOC. Ultra intelligence was not able to identify Rommel's immediate counter-offensive but Hut 6 had broken the Luftwaffe key now designated 'Light Blue'. Early decrypts revealed the concern felt by OKH at Rommel's maverick strategy and indicated the extent of his supply problems. Though the intercepts were a major tactical gain in principle, the process was new and subject to delay to the extent that they rarely arrived in time to influence the events in the field during a highly mobile campaign. Equally Light Blue was able to provide some details of Rommel's seaborne supplies but again in insufficient detail and with inadequate speed to permit a suitable response from either the RN or RAF.

Then, in July 1941 a major breakthrough – an Italian navy cipher, 'C38m', was also broken and the flood of detail this provided greatly amplified that gleaned from Light Blue. Information was now passed not just to Cairo but to the RN at Alexandria and the RAF on Malta. Every care, as ever, had to be taken to ensure the integrity of Ultra was preserved:

> Ultra was very important in cutting Rommel's supplies. He was fighting with one hand behind his back because we were getting information about all the convoys from Italy. The RAF were not allowed to attack them unless they sent out reconnaissance and if there was fog of course they couldn't attack them because it would have jeopardised the security of Ultra, but in fact most of them were attacked.[36]

Ultra thus contributed significantly to Rommel's supply problem. On land a number of army keys were also broken; these were designated by names of birds. Thus it was 'Chaffinch' which provided Auchinleck with detailed information on DAK supply shortages and weight of materiel including tanks. Since mid-1941 a Special Signals Unit (latterly Special Liaison Unit) had been deployed in theatre. The unit had to ensure information was disseminated only among those properly 'in the know' and that, vitally, identifiable secondary intelligence was always available to mask the true source. Experience during the Crusader offensive indicated that the best use of Ultra was to provide detail of the enemy's strength and pre-battle dispositions. The material could not be decrypted fast enough nor sent on to cope with a fast changing tactical situation. At the front, information could be relayed far more quickly by the Royal Signals mobile Y-Special Wireless Sections and battalion intelligence officers, one of whom, Bill Williams, recalled:

> Despite the amazing speed with which we received Ultra, it was of course usually out of date. This did not mean we were not glad of its arrival for at best it showed that we were wrong, usually it enabled us to tidy up loose ends, and at least we tumbled into bed with a

smug confirmation. In a planning period between battles its value was more obvious and one had the opportunity to study it in relation to context so much better than during a fast moving battle such as desert warfare produced.[37]

Wireless in the vastness of the desert was the only effective mode of communication but wireless messages are always subject to intercept. Jews from Palestine, who had temporarily buried the hatchet in the face of a greater foe, provided specialist skills. Many were German in origin and understood only too well the real nature of the enemy they faced. The Germans had their own Y Dienst and the formidable Captain Seebohm, whose unit proved highly successful. The extent of Seebohm's effectiveness was only realised after his unit had been overrun during the attack by 26th Australian Brigade at Te-el-Eisa in July 1942. The captain was a casualty and the raiders discovered how extensive the slackness of Allied procedures actually was. As a consequence the drills were significantly tightened. If the Axis effort was thereby dented Rommel still had a significant source from the US diplomatic codes which had been broken and regularly included data on Allied plans and dispositions, the 'Black Code'.

Reverses following on from the apparent success of Crusader were exacerbated by 'a serious misreading of a decrypt from the Italian C38m cipher'. Hut 3 could not really assist the British in mitigating the defeat at Gazala or, perhaps worse, the surrender of Tobruk. This was one which Churchill felt most keenly: '... a bitter moment. Defeat is one thing; disgrace is another.' Until this time it had taken Bletchley about a week to crack Chaffinch but, from the end of May, the ace code-breakers were now able to cut this to a day. Other key codes, 'Phoenix' and 'Thrush' were also broken. Similar inroads were made against the Luftwaffe. 'Primrose' that was employed by the supply formation and 'Scorpion' the ground/air link were both broken. Scorpion was a literal Godsend. As close and constant touch with units in the field was necessary for supply German signallers unwittingly provided a blueprint for any unfolding battle.

On the ground 8th Army was increasing the total of mobile Y formations while the Intelligence Corps and RAF code-breakers were getting fully into their stride. None of these developments could combine to save the 'Auk' but Montgomery was the beneficiary of high-level traffic between Rommel and Hitler, sent via Kesselring – as the latter was

Luftwaffe. The Red cipher, long mastered by Bletchley, was employed. Monty had already predicted the likely genesis of the Alam Halfa battle but the intercepts clearly underscored his analysis. By now the array of air force, navy and army codes penetrated by Bletchley was providing a regular assessment of supply, of available AFVs and the dialogue of senior officers. The relationship between Rommel and Kesselring was evidently strained. Even the most cynical of old sweats had cause to be impressed:

> ... he [Montgomery] told them with remarkable assurance how the enemy was going
> to be defeated. The enemy attack was delayed and the usual jokes were made about the
> 'crystal-gazers'. A day or two later everything happened according to plan.[38]

Ultra was dispelling the fog of war.

In some ways the Desert War provided the coming of age for the Bletchley Park code-breakers:

> ... Until Alam Halfa, we had always been hoping for proper recognition of our product
> ... Now the recognition was a fact and we had to go on deserving it. I had left as one of a
> group of enthusiastic amateurs; I returned to a professional organisation with standards
> and an acknowledged reputation to maintain.[39]

Certainly nothing in the Western Sahara's previous history could compete with the great dramatic vortex of violence which roared back and forth for two and a half years. For all too many the barren expanse would become a final, desolate resting place:

> For most of them there is a grave in the sand, perhaps a few rocks piled over them, their
> names in a hurried pencil-scrawl upon a cross made of petrol cases. For some there is no
> cross: only a mound of sand that the wind will soon soften and gently erase.[40]

2
'Compass':
June 1940 – March 1941

Today we have naming of parts, Yesterday,
We had daily cleaning. And tomorrow morning,
We shall have what to do after firing. But today,
Today we shall have naming of parts. Japonica
Glistens like coral in all of the neighbouring gardens,
And today we have naming of parts.

Henry Reed

On the balmy evening of 10 June 1940 the Italian dictator preened from the central balcony of the Palazzo Venezia in Rome. To a roaring crowd he announced that Italy was now at war with 'the sterile and declining nations of Britain and France' – pure mummery which would cost his country dear. Mussolini had greater faith in his own potential than his ally Hitler. If Britain, by comparison, was equally unprepared for war there had been some efforts made to link both strategic and tactical thinking in the vital Mediterranean Theatre. As early as June of that year the joint commanders had established a liaison group; Lieutenant-General Archibald Wavell, Admiral Sir Andrew Cunningham and Air Marshall Sir William Mitchell. These senior officers saw quite clearly that there was a need to closely coordinate their respective arms where they were jointly responsible for so vast a territory, over 2,000 square miles with Wavell, following his appointment on 2 August 1939, as Commander in Chief. His task was an unenviable one.

Il Duce's White Charger
Marshall Graziani, with other senior officers, had extreme doubts

about the capacity of the Italian army, despite the apparent superiority in numbers, to mount a successful offensive. General Giuseppe Mancinelli had seen the Wehrmacht in action and gloomily noted the contrast:

> In 1938, the division, through the unhappy initiative of the then Chief of Staff ... had been transformed from 'ternary' to 'binary': this meant that the infantry component had been reduced from three to two regiments. This was a strange operation which certainly did not do any good to the general efficiency of the army. In the new units, the infantry-artillery ratio had been raised but the result could not be considered satisfactory since the division became too small a unit to be able to undertake and successfully terminate a tactical action of any importance; it was subject to quick deterioration and was incapable of any prolonged effort ... In general the problem of mechanisation, or more appropriately non-mechanisation, of our army, represented one of the largest gaps in our organisation, a canker which excluded any capacity for large manoeuvres ...[1]

To forestall Mussolini, defensive action alone would not avail. Wavell saw both the need and the opportunity to trounce the Italians and then secure a foothold on the European mainland. If the Mediterranean theatre could not encompass the defeat of Germany, it might be the means and the place whereby that process could begin. Wavell identified four clear strategic aims:

1. To secure control by an advance into Italian held territory.
2. To secure control of the Eastern Mediterranean.
3. To clear the Red Sea.
4. To develop land action in South-East Europe.

Hitler, for his part, was poised to make a major strategic blunder by diverting his attention eastwards and focusing on the forthcoming trial against Soviet Russia. Though his position in the west seemed secure this was rank folly while Britain remained undefeated:

> But if there were no prospect of a successful decision against Germany herself there was a subsidiary theatre where British forces could be employed to harass the enemy and perhaps inflict serious damage. Italy's entry into the war had turned the Middle East into an active theatre of operations; as a centre of gravity of British forces it was second only to the United Kingdom itself.[2]

Even as France was about to fall Wavell, in a further study, had spelt out how the Middle East had become the 'centre of strategic gravity':

1. Oil, shipping, air power and sea power are the keys to this war and they are interdependent. Air power and naval power cannot function without oil. Oil, except very limited quantities, cannot be brought to the destination without shipping. Shipping requires the protection of naval power and air power. Shipping requires the protection of naval power and air power.

2. We have access to practically all the world's supply of oil. We have most of the shipping. We have naval power. We have potentially the greatest air power when developed.

Therefore we are bound to win the war.[3]

In 1945, Goering admitted that 'not invading Spain and North Africa in 1940 had constituted a fatal blunder'.[4] Wavell's resources were stretched perilously thin and he was palpably short of materiel. These difficulties notwithstanding General O'Connor, when he assumed command of Western Desert Force in June 1940, found the Commander in Chief already had ideas for an offensive. To create a viable infrastructure to fuel such an enterprise it was necessary to construct port, rail and road facilities, lay hundreds of miles of water piping, lay out desert airstrips, establish supply dumps and depots, stockpile vast quantities of petrol, foodstuffs, clothing, tentage and all manner of supplies. Hospitals, workshops, tank repair facilities all had to be planned and constructed.

This vast logistical effort was underpinned by supplies from the UK, USA, Canada and India. British shipping could not move freely in the Mediterranean while the Axis, sailing from Brindisi or Taranto, had easy access to Tripoli or Benghazi. Easy but not secure as British submarines, warships and planes could issue from Malta and Alexandria. The passage from Britain, around the shoulder of Africa, past the Cape of Good Hope and then via the Red Sea to Suez was 12,000 miles, a huge distance but less perilous than the Mediterranean; even India was 3,000 miles away. The small and constricted port of Suez was not the end of the chain; supplies still had to reach the front:

If you cabled for something, it might and usually did, take two or three months to manufacture and collect at an English port, a week to load (if bombing did not interfere), ten weeks at the lowest at sea, another two weeks perhaps to unload it at a small and most congested port, a day or two at a Base Depot, and from there four or five hundred miles by rail or road to the fighting troops in the desert.[5]

First Swing of the Pendulum

Marshall Balbo, when writing to Il Duce after the fall of France, put his finger on the difficulties confronting an Italian army preparing for offensive operations in the Western Desert:

> It is not the number of men which causes me anxiety, but their weapons. With two big formations equipped with limited and very old pieces of artillery, lacking in anti-tank and ant-aircraft weapons, I need to be able to depend on the closing of ways of access to Tripolitania, and on the perimeters of Tobruk and Bardia. To have fortified works without adequate weapons is an absurdity. Another urgent necessity is anti-aircraft defences – batteries and organisation. It is useless to send more thousands of men if then we cannot supply them with the indispensable requirements to move and fight.[6]

Marshall Graziani confined his deployment to a slow build-up of forces between Tobruk and Bardia. On 10 August, he received a communication from the Dictator intimating that the invasion of Britain 'has been decided upon'. Not wishing to be yet again sidelined and outshone by his Teutonic allies, Mussolini gave his General most specific instructions:

> Well, the day on which the first platoon of German soldiers touches British territory, you will simultaneously attack. Once again, I repeat that there are no territorial objectives – it is not a question of aiming for Alexandria, nor even for Sollum. I am only asking you to attack the British forces facing you.[7]

O'Connor was an officer of known dash and initiative, undaunted by the task which confronted him. Indeed offensive operations had already commenced; 11th and 7th Hussars with the élan of their light cavalry forbears had been enthusiastically 'biffing' the enemy. At home in the desert, the cavalrymen used their armoured cars as the eyes and ears of O'Connor's army. In a succession of raids they beat up enemy quarters at Forts Maddalena and Capuzzo. The former fell virtually without a fight though the latter proved a much harder nut. In Churchill's words the Hussars typified the romantic notion of the desert soldier: 'lean, bronzed, desert-hardened and truly mechanised'. General O'Connor was aware of the potential for offensive action and had the wisdom to remain flexible as to the manner and extent whereby success could be exploited:

> I hoped our raid would be successful and that if it was so we might be able to exploit it. But it was a complicated affair and I couldn't be certain what use we could make of the success we gained. But I was fully prepared, that if we did get a success that we could make full use of it.[8]

The Raiders

It is fair to assert that the British, despite the innumerable discomforts, were always more at home in desert conditions. By late June, the LRDG had been established. This and the later Special Air Service, would prove not only invaluable as information gatherers but a potent thorn in the side of the Axis armies. Their epic marches and daring raids meant LRDG punched well above their weight. They became in the popular mind the very breath of romance with which safe distance cloaked the realities of desert fighting:

> They sit like shrubs among the cans and desert thistles
> in the tree's broken shade and the sea-glare
> strange, violent men, with dirty unfamiliar muscles,
> sweating down the brown breast, wanting girls and beer.
> The branches shake down sand along a crawling air,
> and drinks are miles toward the sun
> and Molly and Polly and Pam are gone.

> Terence Tiller[9]

Count Almasy's former desert companion Ralph Bagnold conceived, at a very early stage the need for a deep penetration force able to operate behind enemy lines:

> When the Italians declared war I took my courage in my hands and asked a friend of mine to send a note to the Commander-in-Chief. Within an hour I was sent for by Wavell and I told him that we needed a small, mobile force able to penetrate the

desert to the west of Egypt to see what was going on. Wavell said: 'what if you find the Italians are not doing anything in the interior at all?' I said without thinking: 'How about some piracy on the high desert?' At this his rather stern face broke into a grin ...[10]

The LRDG and its exploits swiftly became the stuff of legend, their derring-do and swashbuckling provided a welcome diversion from the desperate fighting and string of defeats which followed Rommel's arrival. Bagnold was in his perfect element:

The creation of a completely unorthodox force in six weeks was quite a feat. And it was great fun. There was an awful lot to do. Everything was new. Clothing and footwear had to be redesigned. Army boots were no good at all because they got filled up with sand. So I had sandals made – the Indian North West Frontier chappali which was very tough with an open toe so that if sand got into it you could shoot it out with a kick.

Uniform became both very informal and highly practical:

All we wore was a shirt and shorts and Arab headgear. The advantage of wearing a shemagh or shawl which goes round the head, was that it flaps in the wind and keeps the face cool.[11]

In the absence, at this early date, of four-wheel-drive vehicles, the 30-cwt Chevrolet truck (a fine example recently uncovered by desert sands may be viewed in the Imperial War Museum, London) was pressed into service, bristling with arms in best buccaneering style. Bagnold was nothing if not infinitely resourceful:

If one was bogged down, the nose of the car would tip right forward, axle deep in the sand. The problem was to get it out. Going round the junk shops in the slums of Cairo we found these heavy metal channels which had originally been used in the First World War for roofing dugouts. They were about five feet long and you could carry one under each arm, just. You scooped the sand away from the back wheels and pushed the channel under the wheel; directly it gripped the car the car would be shoved forward and hopefully you'd get out of the soft patch onto harder ground.[12]

'Compass'

Wavell, consistently badgered from Whitehall, used those elements of Churchill's instructions which made tactical sense and disregarded the rest, 'a good deal of it'. His thinking was already more aggressive than that of his political superior and he was actively planning a thrust into Cyrenaica. O'Connor was assisted in his detailed planning by Major-General Eric Dorman-Smith ('Chink') one of the most interesting commanders of the desert campaigns. The forthcoming offensive, Operation 'Compass', had four clearly defined objectives: the capture of Sidi Barrani, the capture and occupation of Bardia, the capture of Tobruk and an advance on Derna.

O'Connor's forces were mainly dug in around Mersa Matruh as, on 13 September 1940, Graziani finally lumbered into action. 10th Army advanced some sixty miles into Egypt to reach Sidi Barrani and Sofafi. No major clashes occurred and the Italians seemed, having reached their objectives within three days, in no hurry to advance further. From the British perspective this loss of ground was trifling except that the forward air bases were forfeit. This was serious in that British fighters would no longer be able to reach Malta. Graziani now proceeded simply to dig in, constructing a series of forward camps and establishing his HQ and administration. Wavell meanwhile, continued with his planning, favouring a short, sharp offensive of perhaps five days' duration to eject the enemy from the Sidi Barrani, Buq Buq, Sofafi area. His subordinate was, however, already thinking in terms of a more decisive blow:

> General O'Connor had already been thinking on these lines but had come to the conclusion that to attack the strongly held Sofafi group of camps simultaneously with the coastal group would involve too great a dispersion of the available forces. He proposed instead to attack first the centre group of camps, leaving those on the extreme flanks to be watched and dealt with later. The important supply and water centre of Buq Buq would be a profitable objective for raids; and when the enemy's administrative arrangements were thoroughly dislocated would be the moment to encircle Sofafi. This plan meant that the main attacking force must pass through the gap, fifteen miles wide, which existed between Nibeiwa and Rabia; from now on it would be necessary to ensure this gap was kept open.[13]

The plan was indeed bold, '... the Western Desert Force was to be thrust into the heart of the enemy's position. There was a risk of discovery and heavy loss from air attack.'[14] Italian forward defences at Nibeiwa were overrun in fine style though elements of the garrison, including its gallant commander, fell at their guns; 4,000 prisoners were taken.

> The whole 'Compass' plan showed not only great imagination but a firm determination to do the utmost with the resources available; the role of 7th Armoured Division was not, of course, a new one to them; but to 4th Indian Division the operation had several novel features, yet the confidence and enthusiasm of the troops, when they learned what they had to do, could not have been greater.[15]

So swift was the Italian collapse as the British chased them down their own newly constructed highway, the Via della Vittoria, that comparisons to the hunt seemed justified. As one Guards officer famously remarked: 'We have about five acres of officers and 200 acres of other ranks.'[16] It was not all one-sided, the Italians could fight hard and well. Captain Rea Leakey recorded the carnage when one of his cruiser tanks took a hit, its radio still functioning:

> The driver was killed by the first shot and the commander, our newest young officer, had one of his hands shattered. The driver's foot still rested on the accelerator and the tank continued ... Suddenly [the commander] yelled, 'The tank's on fire' ... Before the two in the turret could bale out they had to open the hatches ... [They] were stuck fast. Then all we heard were the most terrible screams of agony; they were being burned alive while their tomb of fire still went on towards the enemy.[17]

The campaign was one of a series of sweeping encirclements and successful assaults on defended positions unable, due to their siting, to provide mutually supporting fire. Here was a lesson for the British. On 5 January 1941 Bardia fell; 40,000 further prisoners were taken. Not even the determined commander of the doomed garrison Lieutenant-General Annibale 'Electric Whiskers' Bergonzoli could delay the collapse. On the 22nd Tobruk was stormed, netting a further 25,000 Italians. The hunting metaphors, of which Wavell was so fond, were by no means inappropriate: '... Hunt is still going but first racing burst over, hounds brought to their noses, huntsmen must cast and second horses badly wanted; it may be necessary to dig this fox.'[18] O'Connor had made good use of his Infantry ('I') tanks. These Matildas were slow and, as with all British tanks of this time, under-gunned but they were heavily armoured and impervious to much that was thrown at them.

One of the British gunners in action during 'Compass' was L. E. Tutt of 414 Battery, Essex Yeomanry:

> Our first position on enemy soil was near Fort Capuzzo and we dug in with a real sense of urgency, hastened by some desultory enemy fire. We were nearly frozen to death during the night. We were still in khaki drill and the shortage of transport had meant that essential clothing, blankets, cookhouse equipment and the like had been left behind. We were sited on solid rock, but I genuinely believe we wouldn't have changed places with anyone ... At first light we fired our first shells in anger. These early rounds gave everyone immense satisfaction. I think that a sigh went up from the whole regiment. Like the elderly spinster we hadn't wanted to die wondering ...[19]

The general had also established all-arms coordination and, having taken and kept the initiative, he now he had the opportunity to destroy the fleeing remnants of 10th Army. 7th Armoured, with the dashing 11th Hussars, led a flanking charge through Mechili, Msus and Antelat towards Beda Fomm and Sidi Saleh while the Australians, who had replaced 4th Indian Division, pushed forward along the coast. The Italians appeared to have a particular horror of these Australian 'barbarians' whom the British had 'unleashed' into the desert. These 'barbarians' were certainly astonished at the level of creature comforts their enemies had enjoyed till their rude awakening. War correspondent Alan Moorehead observed:

> Officers' beds laid out with clean sheets, chests of drawers filled with linen and an abundance of fine clothing of every kind. Uniforms heavy with gold lace and decked with the medals and colours of the parade ground ... pale blue sashes and belts finished with great tassels and feathered and embroidered hats and capes ... great blue cavalry cloaks that swathed a man to the ankles, and dressing tables ... strewn with scents and silver mounted brushes.[20] [Or, as one digger more earthily commented:] The Tel Aviv police gave us a better fight.[21]

O'Connor had at first been unhappy to lose his superb Indian Army division: 'It came as a complete and unpleasant surprise.' Nonetheless, the Aussies very quickly showed their mettle. Gunner Tutt and his comrades were deployed in support:

We moved our guns to a new position for our attack on Bardia. Details of the assault
are more properly documented in the official war diary of our unit, but I have a jumble
of impressions of the things that affected me personally. There was the visit of our
colonel just before zero hour. His exhortations to battle were so peppered with Tally
Hos and talk of flushing out the fox and making a good kill that in the end we were
not sure whether to put on our tin hats or our hunting pinks. I think, had we raised a
fox in the course of the battle, we would have lost half the battery after it.

As a gunner Tutt did not share the common disdain for the Italians.
'Their bodies were scattered close to their firing positions and they must
have remained in action until our infantry tanks and the Australians
had overrun their gun sites.'[22]

'Fox Killed in the Open'

By 22 January Tobruk had also fallen. A British tank commander,
Captain Barker participated in the assault:

Approaching a wadi we'd been shelled for about three miles without being able to tell
where the fire came from. I spotted a gun flash from behind stones on the wadi edge. I
ordered my troop to attack, ignoring machine guns and anti-tank fire from the flank.
It was the guns we were after ... Then I heard a whoof of shells passing at point blank
range. It was a question of which would knock out the other first. I just kept straight
on and told the gunner to let go when we were near. Although we were yawing and
pitching all over the place, he hit the emplacement with his first shot ... Then we went
for three other guns. I turned quickly which threw up a cloud of dust, drove round the
cloud and took them by surprise. When we were only yards away we could see the
men in their dark green uniforms with their coats open, sweating as they tried to hump
their guns round and train them on us. We simply went straight towards them, firing;
we would have gone straight over them if we hadn't knocked their guns out. Then we
drove the loaders and odds and sods into the dugout. And the next thing I saw was a
white flag emerging.[23]

By noon on 5 February, the galloping Hussars had interdicted the
enemy's line of retreat firmly astride the road over which the Italians
must pass. The odds were formidable, at least ten to one, but the light
cavalry held their ground in bitter fighting till the 7th Hussars came
up and the jaws of the trap closed inexorably. Next day witnessed
more desperate attacks to break the ring and 100 light Italian tanks

were knocked out. Their frantic attacks continued in darkness and into the following day before white flags began to appear, steadily and then in droves. The battle was over and, as O'Connor with suitable understatement reported: 'I think this may be termed a complete victory as none of the enemy escaped.'[24] Or, as he wrote to the Commander in Chief, still firmly posted in the hunting field, 'fox killed in the open' – colourful perhaps but largely justified.

Even in defeat some aspects of the conduct of the Italians smacked of comic opera:

Fascist flamboyance was exhibited by a captured major in a column of prisoners. When it had reached a safe spot he rushed to the head of the column and baring his chest to them, cried (in Italian): 'Shoot me ... and save my honour.' This brave Roman exhortation must be read with the obvious knowledge that whatever the prisoners had, they certainly had nothing with which to shoot anybody. The 'suicidal' major repeated his gesture of honour several times until an Australian sentry approached with bayonet levelled at the seat of his pants and said: 'Get back you mug, before I shoot you.' The terrorised Fascist major skipped back into line at the double.[25]

What did I see in the desert today,
As the sun dropped, angry, red,
Out of the golden western sky?
The smoke still rose ahead,
And the last of the fighters from patrol
Over our lines had sped,
And the sands had folded into their void
The last of the unknown dead

L. Challoner[26]

British troops, surveying the ground, could swiftly appreciate the scale of the disaster which had befallen their enemies:

After we had gone a few miles south ... we came upon the scene of the campaign's last great battle ... an imposing mess of shattered Italian tanks, abandoned guns and derelict lorries. There was the familiar sight of hordes of prisoners being rounded up; processions of staff cars, containing General Bergonzoli and his entourage, passed up the road towards Benghazi.[27]

At last after a string of dismal defeats and hurried evacuations, Britain had a victory, a complete and magnificent triumph over vastly superior odds. Il Duce's dreams of empire crumbled in the desert wind:

> In the three days from 9th to 11th December the Western Desert Force captured no fewer than 38,300 Italian and Libyan prisoners, 237 guns and 73 light and medium tanks. The total of captured vehicles was never recorded, but more than a thousand were counted. The British casualties were 624 killed, wounded and missing.[28]

In the two months' duration of 'Compass', British and Dominion forces had advanced over 500 miles, captured a staggering total of 130,000 of their enemies, taken 400 tanks, twice as many guns, had destroyed 150 enemy aircraft and secured all of their objectives. Total losses were around 2,000 killed, wounded and missing. Tutt had already seen evidence of Allied losses at first hand:

> I stumbled on my first casualty in this campaign. He was an Australian private, new to action because he was dressed in full kit, including a gas mask haversack strapped in position on his chest. A veteran of only a few weeks active service would have discarded that. I noticed that his rifle was new too; the stock honey colour, unlike our oil-blackened relics of World War One and earlier. It was difficult at first to see how he had died, until one saw the neat, bruise-fringed hole in his temple. He seemed to have assumed heroic proportions in death.[29]

As Churchill himself phrased it after the initial successes: 'It looks as if these people [the Italians] were corn ripe for the sickle.' O'Connor was desperate to capitalise on the moment and sweep onward to Sirte and Tripoli but the emerging demands of Greece and the Balkans acted as a brake. This must be the great 'what if' of the Desert War. Rommel for one was in no doubt:

> If Wavell had now continued his advance into Tripolitania, no resistance worthy of the name could have been mounted against him – so well had his superbly planned offensive succeeded.[30]

O'Connor was equally adamant:

In my opinion the operation would not only have been possible, but would have had every chance of success provided all three Services gave their maximum support and were not deflected by other commitments.[31]

Whether this would in fact have been possible and how such gains might have been sustained remains a matter of conjecture. A very new breed of fox was, however, set to emerge, one whose presence would transform the nature of the Desert War. Corelli Barnett has dubbed O'Connor as the 'Forgotten Victor' – fittingly so for whatever came after should not obscure the worth and achievement of 'Compass', a very signal triumph.

By the time the dust had settled over Bardia on 5 January, Hitler had taken the decision to intervene on behalf of his crumbling ally. He could not countenance a total collapse of the Italian position in North Africa. Major-General Hans von Funck was sent to carry out an analysis and gloomily reported that the proposed injection of German forces would not suffice to stem the rot. Hitler had already issued Directive No. 22 of 11 January determining that Tripolitania must be held and that a special military 'blocking force' would be deployed, Operation 'Sunflower'. This infusion of German troops would enjoy air support from Fliegerkorps X which was to be moved to Sicily. This formation was already trained in air attack upon shipping and quickly made its presence felt, inflicting considerable damage on the aircraft carrier *Illustrious*. The Luftwaffe squadrons could also strike at British depots and targets in North Africa. If the British could strike at the Axis in the Eastern Mediterranean then, deprived of any other opportunities in the west, Hitler could riposte:

On December 10th a formal order was issued allotting air units to bases in southern Italy for operation 'Mittelmeer'. (It is to be noted that there was no intention of sending any German units to Egypt or Cyrenaica until the Italians should have secured the use of Matruh.) The force selected was Fliegerkorps X from Norway, many of whose units had specialised in operations against shipping.[32]

The Führer had decided to send 5th Light Motorised Division, replete with anti-tank guns and later added 15th Panzer to the deployment to beef up its offensive capabilities. A further two Italian divisions, Ariete Armoured and Trento Motorised, were to be dispatched to make up, at least in part, the Italians' catastrophic losses during 'Compass'. In

February, the Führer appointed Lieutenant-General Erwin Rommel to command. The Desert Fox thus enters stage, a player who would tax the hounds rather more sorely than his predecessors.

Cratered the land, unploughed, unsown, unfamiliar as a star

Libyan Front

Routine and dirt and story telling are triggered to something far

Night is death's day when he sees best and when his appointments

are

Libyan Front

Sand, our metaphor for time and waste, is all the world and its springs

Libyan Front

Very distant the feet that dance, the lifted silver and the strings

Poets and lovers and men of power are troops and no such things

Bernard Spencer[33]

3
'Brevity' & 'Battleaxe':
May – July 1941

The sea at evening moves across the sand,
Under a reddening sky I watch the freedom of a band
Of soldiers who belong to me. Stripped bare
For bathing in the sea, they shout and run in the warm air;
Their flesh worn by the trade of war, revives
And my mind toward the meaning of it strives

F. T. Prince[1]

As Mr. Churchill stated in his review of the campaign, the military authorities considered that there was a line which, given certain circumstances, could be successfully defended. The Greek campaign was not undertaken as a hopeless or suicidal operation. It turned out to be a rearguard action only …[2]

Given certain circumstances; the Official History does not define what these circumstances might have been and there has, with the inestimable benefit of hindsight, been a common perception among historians that the Greek adventure was a hare-brained notion from the start. Wavell was, from the outset, far from sanguine about Allied prospects in Greece. Supply was by convoy taking the long route around the Cape of Good Hope and through the Red Sea, prone to attack by swift Italian destroyers and submarines. An overland air supply route over the trackless wastes of the Sahara was opened from Takoradi, each run an epic in itself.

A New Thermopylae

General O'Connor, in his later assessment, stressed that the opportunity to take Tripoli and effectively conclude the desert campaign was squandered:

We completely liquidated the enemy and there were no other troops in the way –
nothing to stop us really. I felt that we should have got there; especially looking back in
hindsight, after Hitler had said to Rommel of the campaign 'Don't for one second relax
your determination to follow up, whatever the odds; don't be like the British who had a
chance of getting to Tripoli and didn't take it.'[3]

In his directive of 16 August 1940 the Prime Minister stressed the vital
importance of defending Egypt. Wavell certainly would not demur but
he identified the overriding need, not for men but materiel, aircraft,
trucks and tanks. Quite correctly he had judged that the war in the desert
would be one that was decided by firepower and mobility, supported
by superiority in the air. The General's conclusions were accepted and
the supply of equipment stepped up accordingly. Churchill's bold idea
of sending a convoy through the Axis-infested waters of the western
Mediterranean, while extremely risky, paid off.

With the Italians seemingly eliminated the Australians were seen to
be sporting 'Italian pistols and revolvers at their belts, binoculars round
their necks, and some even discarded their own jackets in preference to
the gilded majesty of an officer's gold-braided ceremonial tunic'. Such
sartorial liberties earned a swift upbraiding:

… there is a tendency towards a picnic spirit, evidenced by the promiscuous firing of
enemy rifles and pistols and the exploding of bombs, the 'showing off' of units and
drivers in possession of captured vehicles, dressing in articles of Italian uniform like
clowns and not like soldiers …

Not everything Italian was so innocuous, they had scattered a quantity
of 'Thermos flask' bombs – so called because that is what they
resembled. The contents, however, were very much less agreeable and
easily detonated:

One afternoon I was surprised by a nearby explosion and looking round saw a drifting
haze and a figure on the ground; it turned out to be a Thermos bomb about which an
aircraftman had been unduly inquisitive.[4]

The overwhelming weight of military advice was therefore, and from
the outset, against any intervention in Greece. Britain's stock of military
capital was simply too slender to face a fresh division of resources.

Churchill, writing later, and with a fine eye for the useful benefits of hindsight, gives the wider political view:

> We often hear military experts inculcate the doctrine of giving priority to the decisive theatre. There is a lot in this. But in war, this principle, like all others, is governed by facts and circumstances; otherwise strategy would be too easy. It would become a drill book and not an art; it would depend upon rules, and not on an ever changing scene.[5]

Wavell, as GOC, had already reiterated his earlier misgivings in a cable dated 2 November:

> As hostilities develop between Italy and Greece we must expect further, persistent calls for aid. It seems essential that we should be clear in our minds on this main issue now. We cannot from Middle East resources send sufficient air or land reinforcements to have any decisive influence on the course of the fighting in Greece. To send such forces from here or to divert reinforcements now on their way or approved would imperil our whole position in the Middle East and jeopardise plans for offensive operations. It would surely be bad strategy to allow ourselves to be diverted from this task and unwise to employ our forces in fragments in a theatre of war where they cannot be decisive ... [and later in a further communication of the following day] ... in general all Commanders-in-Chief are strongly of the opinion that the defence of Egypt is of paramount importance to our whole position in the Middle East. They consider that from the strategical point of view the security of Egypt is the most urgent commitment and must take precedence of attempts to prevent Greece being overrun.[6]

It is beyond the scope of this current work to consider the Greek campaign in detail but, from a military perspective it was an unmitigated disaster. The campaign is aptly summed up in Aussie soldiers' doggerel:

> We marched and groaned beneath our load,
> Whilst Jerry bombed us off the road,
> He chased us here, he chased us there,
> The bastards chased us everywhere.
> And whilst he dropped his load of death,
> We cursed the bloody RAF,
> And when we heard the wireless news,
> When portly Winston aired his views –
> The RAF was now in Greece

Fighting hard to win the peace;

We scratched our heads and said 'Pig's arse',

For this to us was just a farce,

For if in Greece the air force be –

Then where the Bloody Hell are we?[7]

On 22 April the Greeks formally surrendered and by the 30th, evacuation by sea from the beaches was largely complete despite a successful attempt by German paratroops to seize a vital crossing at Corinth by a coup de main. At 17.54 hrs on 25 April some 5,000 men from the 19th Brigade were landed at Souda Bay; the first contingent of 'Jumbo' Wilson's battered evacuees: 'They had very little in the way of arms or personal equipment; they were dirty, ill organised, with no proper chain of command existing, 'bomb-shy' and conscious of their recent defeat.'[8] Crete; the backwater, ill manned, barely considered was about to become the new front line.

Bernard Freyburg had been persuaded to command the garrison which, overall, was in a poor state of readiness and fatally hamstrung by the total Axis air superiority. Hitler, for his part, was anxious to get the business done so that he could direct resources eastwards for Barbarossa. Axis intelligence was faulty in the extreme and the opening phases of the attack, on 20 May, resulted in heavy loss. Though victory had been in the Allies' grasp it was thrown away and the battle ended with a nightmare trek over the spine of the mountains and down the precipitous gorge to Sfakia on the southern flank where the RN, once again, came to the rescue and evacuated many thousands of survivors.

Who for some vague thought

Of honour fell,

Nor why he fought

Could clearly tell

Patric Dickinson[9]

A New Breed of Fox

Erwin Rommel owed his appointment to a personal relationship with the Führer and the perceived charisma observed by Josef Goebbels. Both Von Brauchitsch and Halder had made it perfectly plain his role was defensive and subordinate to the Italian C in C, General Gariboldi. The forces he had were all that he would get. There would be no more and he must not consider plans for an offensive until 15th Panzer were deployed in theatre. His superiors, unlike Rommel himself, were privy to plans for Barbarossa – the invasion of Russia, compared to which North Africa was the merest of sideshows. The deployment was strictly a blocking move. Despite these stern admonitions the Fox was keen to make his bite felt and had already determined 'to depart from my instructions to confine myself to a reconnaissance and to take the command at the front into my own hands as soon as possible'.[10]

Rommel was not destined to enjoy good relations with the Italians. That necessary talent for patient diplomacy was simply not in his nature. Gariboldi, who had succeeded Graziani, was not in favour of early offensives and chided Rommel on his lack of desert experience. Nonetheless, his position was strengthened when Il Duce instructed that all motorised Italian units should be placed under Rommel's immediate command. The General's newly appointed aide de camp, Lieutenant Schmidt, witnessed the disembarkation of the first formations which would finally form the Panzerarmee. Pressed, brushed and gleaming, the soon-to-be desert veterans drove through the streets of Tripoli. As Schmidt noted, their Italian hosts showed little enthusiasm:

> It was a bright sunny day, but the Italian population did not seem to show a great deal of interest in this display of might ... Singly and at regular intervals the Panzers clattered and rattled by. They made a devil of a noise on the macadamized streets ... I began to wonder at the extraordinary number of Panzers passing, and to regret that I had not counted them from the beginning. After quarter of an hour I noticed a fault in one of the chains of a heavy Mark IV Panzer, which somehow looked familiar to me ... Only then did the penny drop ...[11]

The Fox was already in action, parading his armour in a caracole around the streets to convince British eyes that he was stronger than he was. Soon, he had Volkswagen cars padded and disguised to fool aerial observers. The three divisional formations, 15th and 21st Panzer (forming DAK), with 90th Light Division, were already fully mechanised all-arms units and blessed with the inestimable advantage of superb communications. As OKW had cautioned Rommel not to contemplate serious offensive action until 15th Panzer arrived in May, Wavell too believed no attacks could be launched just then. In this both he and Halder were mistaken. Both had equally underestimated Rommel. While he had clear respect for Wavell as an opponent this did not extend to his superior whom Rommel regarded as a mere pen pusher. Relations between him and Halder were always strained; when the latter subsequently dispatched Von Paulus to report on the alarming developments in Africa he observed that this was 'perhaps the only man with enough influence to head off this soldier gone stark mad'.[12]

General O'Connor had been evacuated from the front to undergo treatment in Egypt for a stomach condition and his replacement was Sir Philip Neame VC. As he did not expect an attack before May, Wavell considered that a single infantry division, supported by one armoured brigade, should be sufficient to consolidate the British grip on Cyrenaica while forces were diverted to Greece and Abyssinia. Wavell's chief difficulty was the vast sphere of his fiefdom where demands were coming in from so many quarters. The debacle in Greece had led to further catastrophe in Crete. The campaign in Abyssinia was followed by others, firstly in Iraq and then in Syria.

> He [Wavell] had had to decide upon the least strength required to make the western front of Egypt secure, and then to provide the largest possible force for Greece or Turkey. Naturally the one requirement directly affected the other. The decision had to be made quickly, soon after the middle of February, and the consequent moves and reorganisations began at once. At that time General Wavell thought that the force he was allotting to Cyrenaica could deal with anything the enemy was likely to do before May; thereafter the Germans would become appreciably stronger, but so also would the British.[13]

In March then Neame had 2nd Armoured Division's support group around Mersa Brega, with 3rd Armoured Brigade stationed some five miles north-east. The British tanks were in poor shape, worn out by the rigours of earlier fighting. Two brigades of infantry from 9th Australian Division were dug in east of Benghazi while a third occupied Tobruk. An Indian motorised brigade held Mechili. Rommel was poised to strike. He had 5th Light Division with eighty PzKw Marks III and IV, the Italian Ariete Armoured Division, additional Italian infantry and support from advance squadrons from Fliegerkorps X.

Teeth of the Fox

Wavell was convinced Rommel would not be in a position to attack before May. His trust in Neame's abilities was limited:

I found Neame pessimistic and asking for all kinds of reinforcements which I hadn't got. And his tactical dispositions were just crazy; he had put a brigade of Morshead's 9th Australian Division out into the middle of the plain between El Agheila and Benghazi, with both flanks exposed ... I came back anxious and depressed from this visit, but there was nothing much I could do about it. The movement to Greece was in full swing and I had nothing left in the bag. But I had forebodings and my confidence in Neame was shaken.[14]

On 24 March Rommel launched a probing raid on the British positions at El Agheila. This was entirely successful and justified his confidence in a more ambitious undertaking. Churchill sent a tremulous cable to Wavell:

We are naturally concerned at rapid German advance to El Agheila. It is their habit to push on whenever they are not resisted. I presume you are only waiting for the tortoise to stick his head out far enough before chopping it off ...[15]

Rommel could be described as many things but never as a tortoise; this was not an analogy likely to be applied again.

By 31 March, Rommel was about to confound both Neame and his own superiors at OKW. His advance began on that day, columns sweeping along the coastal route in the north, striking for Mechili through Andelat and Msus in the centre, and with Ariete cruising to the south in a wide flanking movement converging on Mechili. These dispersed, all-arms groups were ideally suited to desert warfare and their deployment gave the lie to any assertion Rommel did not understand the nature and demands of the terrain. Like a battlefield conductor, he led from the front, flying overhead in his Fiesler Storch light spotter, constantly urging his formations to 'push on'. His style was one of relentless insistence backed by personal leadership and intervention.

Gunner Tutt was one of those who experienced the dash and energy of the new Axis commander:

Our battery position was shielded by some low hills. We saw tanks coming over them, wireless aerials with pennants atop like a field full of lancers. They assumed hull down positions and blasted the thin screen of recovered tanks which were deployed to face them. The men of the Tower Hamlets went forward to face them in Bren carriers and were virtually destroyed in a mater of minutes; their bravery was unquestioned but they should never have been asked to face such odds. Both our batteries fired a heavy concentration on the German Mark IIIs and some Mark IVs and they were forced to withdraw slightly, but it was only a temporary respite as their infantry moved against the flank exposed by the withdrawal of the Free French.[16]

Such close and constant contact enabled Rommel to direct the flow of battle to exploit opportunities. By 5 April he had decided to concentrate his drive upon Mechili. On the day before his troops entered Benghazi, Neame was focusing upon withdrawal. This at least was sound, there was more to be gained from keeping forces intact than clinging onto ground. As Benghazi fell, Wavell had sent the recovering O'Connor to bolster Neame:

During the evening of 2nd April the Commander-in Chief sent for General O'Connor from Egypt with the intention of placing him in command in Cyrenaica because of his great experience of desert warfare. General O'Connor arrived by air next day, bringing with him Brigadier J.F.B. Combe, who had commanded the 11th Hussars and whose knowledge of the desert was unexcelled. After discussion with General O'Connor, who shared General Neame's view that the enemy was likely to make a move by the desert route, General Wavell decided to leave General Neame in command.[17]

On 7 April, a fresh reverse detonated when both generals, together with Brigadier Combe, were captured along with O'Connor's ADC 2nd Lieutenant Lord Ranfurly:

9 April 1941

Jack Dent, General O'Connor's ADC came to see me. He'd just returned from the Desert. He told me that Dan [Ranfurly] and several Generals had set off in two cars and were last seen heading for a short-cut track behind Derna en route for Tobruk. He said an Australian who had gone that way had doubled back after finding a lot of cars stationary and hearing shouts. It was dark. For two days a big search was made for the Generals, to no avail. He told me Germans are now in the area and he thought it probable that a German commando had captured Dan and the Generals.[18]

O'Connor himself wrote of the moment of his capture:

> It was a great shock and I never thought it would ever happen to me; very conceited perhaps but it was miles behind our own front and by sheer bad luck we drove into the one bit of desert in which the Germans had sent a reconnaissance group, and went bang into the middle of them.[19]

Also on 7 April, Wavell reported gloomily to London and Churchill was quick to pick up on the Commander in Chief's earlier and outwardly more confident briefings – 'the War Cabinet decision regarding assistance to Greece had largely been founded on this appreciation'. Purest tosh of course; Wavell had opposed the Greek fiasco from the start and the Prime Minister was now preparing to offload responsibility for defeat in Cyrenaica. Churchill and Wavell were in accord, however, that the place which must be held was Tobruk; 'if we could hold the advance at Tobruk we would be well satisfied ... Tobruk therefore seems to be a place to be held to the death'.[20] The Chiefs of Staff were in full agreement and Morshead, with 9th Australian Division, was entrusted with the defence while the shaken British regrouped around Mersa Matruh.

The Official History's account is a good deal more considered:

> General Wavell blamed no one but himself for the miscalculation ... The truth is that the force allotted to the desert front could only have proved reasonably adequate if it had been up to strength in men and weapons – particularly serviceable tanks – and fully backed by the necessary transport, supply, and maintenance services to give it the freedom of action appropriate to its role ... it was here that the simultaneous dispatch of an expedition to Greece had such serious consequences, for Greece was an under-developed country exhausted by war, and the British had to take with them every single thing they wanted.[21]

The Great Siege

Rommel too, was aware of the significance of Tobruk and determined upon its capture. His own supplies were becoming a matter of acute concern and he could ill afford to permit a major Allied garrison to remain and threaten his rear. To maintain current efforts the Axis required some 50,000 tons of supplies every month. These were shipped by sea through Tripoli but less than 30,000 tons were arriving. British activity from Malta and raids by the Royal Navy were taking their toll.

The use of Tobruk and the elimination of the garrison would greatly ease this burden:

> On 6th April Mr. Eden and Sir John Dill ... and the three Commanders-in-Chief met ... They decided it was essential to stabilise the battle as far west as possible, mainly to reduce the air threat to the naval base at Alexandria, and because of the moral effect in Egypt. The best chance of holding the enemy was at Tobruk. Here there were large stocks of stores, a supply of water, and a port whose use would be invaluable to the enemy and should be denied to him.[22]

In attacking the Australians, well dug in and equally well prepared, Rommel discovered this was a new type of warfare, where mobility and firepower were not the determining factors. Each attack was repulsed in turn: 'In this assault we lost more than 1,200 men killed, wounded and missing. This shows how sharply the curve of casualties rises when one reverts from mobile to position warfare.'[23] Men alone, as the Italians had discovered, were not enough. The Aussies well dug in and supplied were not about to be easily ejected. Though they might be prone to flamboyance the Diggers were utterly formidable:

> When we got back to Tobruk we were told that our posts must be held at all costs; that even if tanks broke through we were to hang on and wait for the enemy infantry. We soon had a chance of testing out these tactics. On 13 April – after dark – enemy infantry got through our wire about 100 yards to the left of the post I was in ... They opened up on us but we were unable to challenge them by fire. So our patrol commander Lieutenant Mackle led a fighting patrol which drove them back at the bayonet. He took with him Corporal Edmondson and five others. They charged the enemy in the face of heavy machine gun fire and Edmondson was mortally wounded but he kept on and bayoneted two Germans and then saved Mr. Mackle's life by bayoneting two more who had Mr. Mackle at their mercy. Edmondson died but he was honoured with a VC.[24]

Nonetheless, the pendulum had swung again and Cyrenaica, so recently won, was now lost:

> So ended the first attempt to hold 'the gateway of Cyrenaica'. This astonishingly rapid reversal of fortunes, only a few weeks after the decisive victory over the Italians naturally led to much anxious enquiry. Yet the reasons are not hard to discern, for General Wavell's estimate of when the enemy would be fit to undertake any major enterprise

... seems to have been not unreasonable at the time. When it began to look like being too optimistic it was too late to do anything about it; the real disaster was that the sole British armoured brigade in Cyrenaica proved to be an armoured brigade in name only.[25]

The fierce fighting which raged before the Tobruk defences made a deep impression on those Germans who participated in their attacks. One young Panzer officer Leutnant, Joachim Schorm recorded his experiences in a series of vivid diary entries:

14 April 1941; at 0100 hours I am called and ordered to report to the Company Commander. Situation: MG Pioneers have worked a gap through the anti-tank defences; 5 Tank Regt, 8 MG, PAK, Flak-Artillery will cross the gap under cover of darkness and will overwhelm the positions. Stuka attack at 0645 hours; 0715 hours, storming of Tobruk. With least possible noise the 2nd Bn. Regt HQ Coy and 1st Bn move off with cars completely blacked out; bitterly cold. Of course the opponent recognises us by the noise, and as ill-luck would have it, a defective spotlight on one of the cars in front goes on and off ... Soon arty fire starts up on us, getting the range. The shells explode like fireworks. We travel 10km, every nerve on edge from time to time isolated groups of soldiers appear – the tank support men of 8 MG – and then suddenly we are in the gap. Already the tank is nose first in the first ditch. The motor whines; I catch a glimpse of the stars through the shutter, when for the second time the tank goes down, extricating itself backwards with a dull thud with engines grinding.[26]

The attack presses on, as light thins and defenders find the range:

Slowly, much too slowly, the column moves forward. We must, of course, regulate our speed by the marching troops. In this way the enemy has time to prepare resistance. In proportion, as the darkness lifts, the enemy strikes harder. Destructive fire starts up in front of us now -1 -2 -3 -10 -12 -16 and more. 5 batteries of 12cm calibre rain their hail upon us the 8 MG Coy presses forward to get at them. Our heavy tanks, it is true, fire for all they are worth, just as we do; but the enemy with his superior force and all of the tactical advantages of his own territory makes heavy gaps in our ranks.[27]

Every Axis move was greeted by the doughty defenders with fresh exertions:

On Easter Monday we got our chance as anti-tank gunners. About fifty German tanks broke through the outer perimeter defences and headed for our gun positions about three miles inside. In the half light of dawn we first engaged them with high explosive at about 2000 yards. But they came on firing their 75mm guns and machine guns. With their tracer bullets firing everywhere it looked like Blackpool illuminations ... When they'd got within about 700 yards of us we let them have it over open sights. In a twenty minute battle our troop fired about 100 rounds per gun, and that stopped them. We knocked out seven with our 25-pounders before they turned back.[28]

Wavell was not alone in having critics; success breeds jealousy in the same way as defeat brings recriminations. Rommel had few friends in OKW and plenty of enemies, Halder in particular. In his frequent references to General Rommel, Halder may have been influenced by the fact that Rommel was not a general who had made his way up the General Staff ladder; he had not even been chosen for his present post by the Army Command, but by Hitler himself. Halder noted savagely on 23 April:

Rommel has not sent in a single clear report, and I have a feeling that things are in a mess ... All day long he rushes about between his widely scattered units and stages reconnaissance raids on which he fritters away his strength ... and the piecemeal thrusts of weak armoured forces have been costly ... His motor vehicles are in poor condition and many of the tank engines need replacing ... Air transport cannot meet his senseless demands, primarily because of lack of fuel ... It is essential to have the situation cleared up without delay.[29]

While Halder fumed in jealous impotence Leutnant Schorm was enjoying the sharp end of those realities the general had alluded to:

Wireless; 0900 hrs anti-tank gun – 1,700 metres, tank. We are right in the middle of it with no prospect of getting out. From both flanks armour-piercing shells whiz by at 1,000 metres per sec ... Wireless; turn right. Retire. Now we come slap into the 1st Bn which is following us. Some of our tanks are already on fire. The crews call for doctors who alight to help in this Witches' Cauldron. English anti-tank units fall upon us with their machine guns firing into our midst; but we have no time. My driver, in the thick of it, says, 'The engines are no longer running properly, brakes not acting, transmission working only with great difficulty.' We bear off to the right; 600 metres off on the reverse slope, anti-tank guns. 900 metres distant, in the hollow behind is a tank. Behind that in the next dip, 1,200 metres away other tanks. How many? I see only the effect of the fire on the terraced-like dispositions of the enemy. Judging from their width and thickness there must be at least 12 guns. Above us Italian fighter planes come into the fray. Two of them crash in our midst. The optical instruments are spoilt with the dust. Nevertheless I register several unmistakable hits. A few anti-tank guns are silenced, some enemy tanks are burning. Just then we are hit, and the wireless smashed to bits. Now our communications are cut off. What is more our ammunition is giving out. I follow the battalion commander. Our attack is fading out. From every side the superior forces of the enemy shoot at us.[30]

Halder, like a prissy headmaster, had decided to send out Von Paulus, (future doomed commander of the Stalingrad garrison), then a member of the staff, to rein in this reckless prefect. Rommel could not comprehend why news of his successes was received with at best indifference if not downright disdain. Of course he did not know what was brewing: a conflict with Soviet Russia which would soon assume titanic proportions. He resented the constant snubs and bad-tempered efforts to keep him on a tight rein. As well as a constant soldier Rommel was a dutiful husband who habitually wrote to his beloved wife 'Dearest Lu' every day, as he did on 2 June:

It was 107 degrees here yesterday, and that's quite some heat. Tanks standing in the sun go up to as much as 160 degrees, which is too hot to touch … My affair with the OKW is under way. Either they've got confidence in me or they haven't. If not, then I'm asking them to draw their own conclusions. I'm very intrigued to know what will come of it; it's easy enough to bellyache when you aren't sweating it out here.[31]

For the soldiers of the Afrika Korps bloodied before Tobruk, there is no shame in their apparent failure. Schorm is rightly proud of his unit's performance:

We simply cannot understand how we ever got out again. It is the general opinion that it was the most severely fought battle of the whole war. But what can the English think of us. A weak battalion, only two companies strong, bursts through the complex defence system until it is just 2 kilometres from the town, shoots everything to bits, fights the enemy on all sides, and then gets away again. The day will go down in the record of the regiments and deserves a special mention.[32]

Allied Diversions

In East Africa the Duke of Aosta commanded perhaps 75,000 Italian troops well placed to invade British Somaliland which fell in August 1940. Britain had recognised the exiled Haile Selassie and offered aid. Despite the impossible odds and the relatively small Imperial casualties (around 250) Churchill felt the loss of British Somaliland keenly and chose to blame Wavell. The retreat was in fact skilful and British forces withdrawn to the safety of Aden but this did not placate the Prime Minister – 'A bloody butcher's bill is not the sign of a good tactician' (Italian losses had exceeded 2,000). Wavell had to detach forces to mount a counter-offensive in East Africa. Led by Lieutenant-General Alan Cunningham, they swiftly overran Italian Somaliland while British Somaliland was liberated by an amphibious operation mounted from Aden. On 5 May Haile Selassie again entered his capital of Addis Ababa and, after a further eleven days, Aosta conceded defeat. Some 230,000 Italian troops were captured and the campaign ranks as a significant Allied victory.

As early as March 1941, Wavell had been attempting to hive off Iraq and have the responsibility grafted onto Auchinleck's Indian command. Disturbances in May came at a critical moment for Middle East command with Greece lost, Rommel squeezing in the desert and the battle for Abyssinia raging. Auchinleck was completely in accord and the early operations in Iraq came under his aegis. Churchill, however, changed his perception and chose to view Iraq as part of Wavell's responsibilities, despite the latter's vociferous protests: 'I have consistently warned you [Chiefs of Staff] that no assistance could be given to Iraq from Palestine ... merely asking for further trouble ... My forces are stretched to the limit everywhere ...'[33] These protests were entirely justified and a less biased critic than Churchill might have taken heed but Wavell's credit balance was already slipping into deficit.

British reinforcements from Palestine and Transjordan were thrown into the fight which quickly developed into a rout but, no sooner had the dust settled in Iraq, than it was judged to be time for a reckoning in Syria. By 21 June Imperial forces had wrested control of Damascus but intense combat ensued in Lebanon before the anglophobe General Dentz sued for an armistice. Terms were finally agreed at Acre, of crusading fame, on 13 July. It is hard to see how any commander could have achieved more given the scale and urgency of demands but Churchill's distrust of his Middle East commander was not clouded by reason. As John Strawson rather acidly observed in likening Wavell to a fit successor to Marlborough: 'He was serving a man who, family connection aside, thought of himself as an actual one.'[34]

With the imminent arrival of 15th Panzer, Wavell recognised that his deficiency in armour would become even more telling. For once he and Churchill were on the same wavelength and the Prime Minister took the courageous decision to strip home defence of resources and send these, via the dangerous waters of the Mediterranean, to Alexandria. Operation 'Tiger' was thus an enormous gamble and also an unqualified success. Only one transport and its precious cargo were lost, the rest berthed on 12 May. Wavell would thus gain 238 new tanks and 43 Hurricane fighters. Churchill was inordinately proud of his 'Tiger Cubs' and hoped for great things to follow.

Meanwhile in beleaguered Tobruk the improvised 'Bush artillery' had been doing good service:

No better example of the Tobruk garrison's disregard for convention and readiness to meet any contingency could be provided than by the Bush artillery – odd batteries of captured Italian field pieces, mostly 75mm and 79mm calibre, manned by engineers and infantry, and used with great effect by these amateur gunners for the purpose of harassing the enemy … Lacking sights, the guns were aligned by looking along the barrel, judgement by trial and error was established and a telegraph pole served as an OP. In less than a month the Bush artillery accounted for at least twenty-five enemy MT. Several times it silenced enemy MG fire and assisted fighting patrols returning to the lines …[35]

The war might be fought without hate but it was sometimes devoid of compassion, replaced by graveyard humour:

One poor Jerry was trapped on the wire; wounded, bent double, making a hell of a noise. There was one Aussie, dancing around him with his rifle and bayonet, shouting to his cobbers: 'What shall I do, with the bastard?' Silence from the trenches, then a quiet call: 'Stick it up his arse and shut up and get back here, you flaming galah.' This was done.[36]

While politicians and generals pondered strategy, the troops in the desert struggled to adapt to their harsh and alien environment:

The war in Africa is quite different from the war in Europe. That is to say, it is absolutely individual. Here there are not the masses of men and material. Nobody and nothing can be concealed, whether in battle between opposing land forces, or between those of the air, or between both, it is the same sort of fight – face to face, each side thrusts and counter thrusts. If the struggle was not so brutal, so entirely without rules, one would be inclined to think of the romantic idea of a Knights' Tourney.[37]

Von Paulus had reached North Africa on 27 April. While he reluctantly acquiesced to another, and equally unsuccessful, attempt on Tobruk, he reported, undoubtedly as Halder would have wished, that the army was grossly over-extended and should confine its role to the defensive. Von Paulus, unlike Rommel, was privy to Barbarossa. Ultra intercepts picked up on the cable traffic, yielding intelligence that appeared to favour an early counter-offensive. 'The 'Tiger' convoy would soon be arriving, but without waiting for it General Wavell decided to strike a rapid blow in the Sollum area, and for this purpose allotted all the available armour, such as it was to the Western Desert Force.[38]

'Brevity' & 'Battleaxe'

Brigadier Gott was entrusted with undertaking Operation 'Brevity': a limited offensive aimed at driving the Axis from Sollum and Capuzzo, wreaking as much havoc as possible and driving forwards towards Tobruk, as far as supply and prudence would permit. Any successes would form the curtain-raiser to a far more substantive blow, Operation 'Battleaxe', which Wavell was now planning. 'Strafer' Gott began well with Halfaya falling but Axis opposition stiffened and few other gains were achieved; those that were, including Halfaya, swiftly fell to counter-attacks. 'Brevity' was a failure. Rommel was not caught unawares:

Intercepted signals had warned the Germans to expect an attack, which, when it came, caused some apprehension for it was thought to be the beginning of an attempt to relieve Tobruk and there was not enough transport to send forward strong reserves to deal with it.[39]

General Sir Noel Beresford-Peirse was to have command of 'Battleaxe' with 4th Indian Division (Messervy), now returned from service in East Africa and 7th Armoured Division, (Creagh). Messervy, with 4th Armoured Brigade in support, was to attack toward the Bardia,

Sollum, Halfaya (where the Axis were led by a militant cleric Major the Reverend Wilhelm Bach) and Capuzzo area while his open flank was covered by 4th and 7th Armoured Brigades. The intention was that the British armour would draw the Axis out into a decisive engagement. The date for the offensive to open was fixed for 15 June. Unlike his opponent, Beresford-Peirse maintained his HQ at Sidi Barrani some sixty miles from the action. Rommel was ready; he had some 200 tanks fit for service. He would not be taken by surprise.

In the desert, junior officers of both sides struggled to maintain equipment and supply. Leutnant Schorm was no exception:

> Now I have the strongest company in the regiment: 4 Mark II tanks, 4 Mark III. Gradually, however, the job of Company Commander is becoming difficult, I have absolutely no support of any description; everything is in the desert. Where are the tanks, where are the motorcycle sections of HQ's Combat Group, where the 1st and 2nd baggage convoys, where the Company office? And I have no motor car and no motorcycles – and then the reports, and the paper-war which begins as soon as the last shot has been fired.[40]

No doubt many Allied officers felt exactly the same emotions and frustration!

The objectives of 'Battleaxe' were threefold:

1. A successful advance against the enemy in the Sollum–Capuzzo area.
2. An advance towards Tobruk, coordinated with sorties by the garrison.
3. Exploitation of gains as opportunities arose.

Thus, Churchill's cherished 'Tiger Cubs' were blooded. 4th Indian Division could make little initial headway and, well dug-in, the dreaded 88mm flak guns took a fearful toll of both I tanks and cruisers. The Matilda, proof against much Axis ordnance, was no match – painfully slow and like all British tanks, fatally under-gunned: 'The means and methods that had done so well against the Italians were not good enough against the Germans.'[41] Having blunted the British attacks on 15 June, Rommel struck back the following day. 15th Panzer was stalled in the north but 5th Light Division was able to effect a minor breakthrough and push on towards Sidi Suleiman. Rommel, master tactician, was quick to see the potential, '... the turning point of the battle'.[42] He

ordered 15th Panzer to divert its main effort along the northern flank
of the break-in. He also judged that Beresford-Peirse would launch his
next thrust towards Capuzzo and resolved to strike first. Again, he was
successful and an intercepted message from Creagh to HQ, requesting
Beresford-Peirse to come forward, indicated the British were wavering.

For Paul Erich Schlafer, a former classmate of Hans Schilling's was
serving as a gunner Pz. Artl. Regt 33 in 15 Panzer. Now he was to
undergo his baptism of fire:

> My unit had passed Tobruk without any fighting and had taken up position near Fort
> Capuzzo. I joined my unit shortly before the Sollum battle of June 1941. at first I had
> the job in my gun crew of carrying the ammunition because I was still unfamiliar with
> the gun. During the battle though, I advanced from K5 to K2, the one who actually
> loads the howitzer, for the simple reason everyone else was lying flat on the ground and
> nobody was loading the howitzer. So I did it and it worked fine from the first time ...
> this is what I remember of my first battle. I was on guard duty during the night when the
> coloured signal flares from the attack went up. Our battery had six guns, two captured
> British 25 pounders and the usual four light German howitzers. Around 1,000 hours,
> the British tanks advanced in front of us, but we managed to stop them and force them
> back. The British tanks then started coming at us from one side and from the rear and I
> have forgotten how many we shot up in all – my friend H. Kollenberger got two with his
> British gun and my howitzer also got two. The tanks kept coming and when they were
> only 50 metres in front of us we quickly got our things together and escaped south, the
> only side left open to us. Our first battery had been overrun and suffered heavy losses.
> Oberleutnant Wild, the leader of this battery, had lost a leg. I saw him stand up to give
> orders but a British tank rolled right over him ...[43]

Wavell had earlier reported to London in cautiously optimistic terms;
the Guards had taken Capuzzo on the 15th: 'There is no reason to be
dissatisfied with the progress made.'[44] By dawn on the 17th, however,
the two arms of Rommel's pincer were approaching convergence. Creagh had
warned, in his communication, that 7th Armoured's tanks were seriously
depleted and British forces, still in the Capuzzo–Halfaya area, were at risk
of encirclement. Such a clear loss of confidence acted as a further spur to
Rommel. Wavell himself had arrived from Cairo and was with Beresford-
Peirse when the message came in. Both now dashed to 7th Armoured HQ
but the retreat was already underway. Messervy, after urgent communication
with Creagh, had agreed with his pessimistic assessment and ordered a

withdrawal. Wavell could do nothing other than concede and simply add that as many damaged vehicles should be got away as possible. After all the effort and optimism of Operation 'Tiger' the precious resources had mostly been expended to no avail. It was a bitter moment.

For German soldiers such as Erich Schlafer the deliverance came unexpectedly:

> We were all completely surprised when we were told we had won the battle ... Whenever Rommel flew over our unit we always cheered and shouted 'Erwin'. Rommel could not hear this of course – otherwise we would not have dared to do it. Though Rommel was loved by all his troops, he kept us under very strict discipline; we would have been disillusioned if this had not been the case.[45]

British losses had not been catastrophic: 122 killed, 588 wounded, 259 missing; 36 planes and four guns were lost. In terms of materiel, however, 64 Matildas and 27 Cruisers had been destroyed or abandoned on the field. In contrast, German losses, in terms of tanks, were only a fraction, perhaps a dozen in all.

Wavell did not hesitate to take the blame upon himself knowing with full certainty what the consequences must be:

> Fear this failure must add much to your anxieties. I was over-optimistic and should have advised you that 7th Armoured Division required more training before going into battle ... I was impressed by the apparent need for immediate action.

Churchill's reply cannot have come as any surprise:

> I have come to the conclusion that public interest will best be served by appointment of General Auchinleck to relieve you in command of Armies of Middle East.[46]

Wavell was to take over the Auk's command in India, his role in the Desert War at an end. Rommel, who was always generous in his assessment of Wavell, ironically far more so than Churchill, was established as a desert commander of genius. He was perceived as possessing the 'Rommel touch' (*fingerspitzengefuhl*). His practice of restless leadership front the front contributed to this as did a team of excellent wireless intercept operators. The Axis 'star' was Captain Seebohm, whose loss in action in July 1942 constituted a substantive blow.

Battered Tobruk had been attacked again and again. Leutnant Schorm was again in the thick of the fight:

We intend to take Tobruk; my 4th attack on the town. Up at 0330 hrs; leave at 0430 hrs. We lose touch in the darkness and dust – and join up again. We file through the gap where so many of our comrades have already fallen. Then we deploy at once – 6th Coy on the left 5th Coy on the right; behind HQ, 8th and 7th Coys. The regiment is now Hohmsnn's Mobile Bn, and consists of 5 (1 and 2), 6 (5 and 6), 7 (the remainder), 8 (4 and eight) Companies, altogether 80 tanks … The English arty fires on us at once. We attack. No German patrol goes out in front to reconnoitre; tier on tier of guns boom out from the triangular fortification in front of us. The two light troops of the Coy and my left section are to make a flanking movement. I attack. Wireless message: Commander of 6th Coy hit on track. Then things happen suddenly … a frightful crash in front and to the right. Arty shell hit? No? It must be a mine. Immediately send wireless massage: 'Commander Schorm on a mine,' try to turn round in your own tracks. 5 metres back. New detonation – mine underneath to the left. On reversing, went on a mine again. Now mounting tank 623. Back through the artillery fire for 100 metres …'[47]

The legend of the 'Desert Fox' was set to grow.

What did I see in the desert today –
Anything new in the 'Blue'?
I found a crevice in the rocks
Where a single violet grew,
As fresh as in the woods and lanes of home –
The green fields once we knew.
And I saw the Faith in the eyes of men,
And I knew their hearts were true.

L. Challoner [48]

4

'Crusader':
August 1941 – January 1942

Hoist our Banner highly
Our cause shall not be lost,
For we were the proud Eighth Army
Our emblem was the cross
Crusader knights of freedom,
Our country is our pride;
We won't forget those fallen
Who fell there by our side.
So hoist our banner highly,
Our cause shall not be lost;
For we were the proud Eighth Army
Our emblem was the cross.

'An Eighth Army Hymn' by Trooper T. Smith, 1st Holding Battalion RAC (to the tune of 'Onward Christian Soldiers')

The Auk

Auchinleck had made an impressive Commander in Chief in India and Churchill, as ever, had great expectations. The 8th Army, as Western Desert Force was now to be designated, would be led by General Alan Cunningham who had done such notable service in East Africa. Despite the bruising battles already fought, tough Afrika Korps veterans like Leutnant Schorm were ready for more:

At noon, sandstorm began. In the chief's tent there's a good deal of grumbling. What is there for a soldier to do when there is no fighting? And nothing to eat; this morning the bit of cheese wasn't even enough to go round for breakfast. The men want to attack, want to get into Tobruk. There, there's loot to be had; replacements from Germany don't arrive.[1]

The general immediately found himself constantly being badgered by Churchill to launch an offensive. Winston had learnt nothing from past failures. His subsequent exhortation to victory, on the eve of 'Crusader', was stirring stuff:

> For the first time British and Empire troops will meet the Germans with ample equipment in modern weapons of all kinds. The battle itself will affect the whole course of the war. Now is the time to strike the hardest blow yet struck for final victory, home and freedom; the Desert Army may add a page to history which will rank with Blenheim and with Waterloo. The eyes of all nations are upon you ... May God uphold the right![2]

Knowing he would be under considerable pressure, Auchinleck was determined not to give way and court further disaster. In this, he had the support of the CIGS, Sir John Dill who had written privately to him on 26 June:

> The fault was not Wavell's except in so far as he did not resist the pressure from Whitehall with sufficient vigour ... You should make it quite clear what risks are involved if a course of action is forced upon you which, from the military point of view, is undesirable ...[3]

In July the President of the Board of Trade, Oliver Lyttelton, appointed as the War Cabinet's 'man on the spot' in Cairo, took up office and thereby relieved the C in C of a significant burden. He and Auchinleck established an early and cordial relationship. Despite continual badgering, the C in C refused to countenance any attack prior to 1 November. He would not commit till he felt he enjoyed an overall material supremacy of at least two to one. Though the Prime Minister might rant, even summoning Auchinleck back to the UK for a further browbeating, he would not be moved. As Churchill later wrote:

> He certainly shook my military advisers with all the detailed arguments he produced. I was myself unconvinced. But General Auchinleck's unquestioned

abilities, his powers of exposition, his high, dignified and commanding personality, gave me the feeling that he might after all be right, and that even if wrong he was still the best man.[4]

It was now largely a race for adequate re-supply. With so many ships lost, Rommel's position was distinctly inferior as General Bayerlein confided: '... by the end of September, only a third of the troops and a seventh of the supplies which we needed had arrived'.[5] Rommel, as before, remained obsessed with the reduction of the Tobruk garrison where four Italian divisions, stiffened by three German battalions, were bogged down. Auchinleck was steadily building his strength with both armies looking at mid-November as the start date for further offensive action. Throughout September and October the British build-up continued. These new arrivals found themselves heading into a barren and forbidding terrain:

In some areas sandstorms are blowing and the desert is obscured in pallid, sunlit wooliness. We close the wooden compartment shutters, but the driving dust seeps through, and the atmosphere is like a fog ... The desert, omnipresent, so saturates consciousness that it makes the mind as sterile as itself. It's only now you realise how much you normally live through the senses. Here there's nothing for them ...[6]

'Crusader'

There were high hopes for 'Crusader' yet nobody need be deluded by the difficulty of the task: 'We have attacked in the Desert. Ironic to be fighting for territory we captured last year; I hate to think of so many friends struggling down there in the dust.'[7] Even when matters were relatively calm there was constant bickering and patrolling. Leutnant Schorm and his comrades faced the predatory attentions of the ever-active British armoured cars:

We set off again at 0230 hrs. Already as dawn comes, we see little points on the horizon: in front of us to the right, to the left and behind us, which amazingly never get any nearer. These are English armoured cars which are watching our movements. They are afraid of our own armoured cars, but not of our much slower tanks so long as they keep out of range of their guns ... Nevertheless, from time to time they pop out as quick as lightning from behind a rise in the ground, fire off a cone of MG bullets into the column, and are off again.[8]

30 Corps would attack in the north past Fort Maddalena (where the General's HQ would locate), push on towards Sidi Rezegh, seeking to pull the Axis armour into a decisive encounter; then the beleaguered garrison in Tobruk would mount a sally to link up. Meanwhile 13 Corps would advance to the south of Sidi Omar and deal with Axis forces in the frontier zone. The experience of desert warfare would show that success turned upon two key tactical elements: all-arms integration within formations and the need to concentrate armoured forces. Singleness of aim should drive the delivery of force. The 8th Army commander's plan, and he had no real experience of handling large armoured formations, had compromised the all-arms role to satisfy concentration of armour. Cunningham, whose HQ was some eighty miles to the rear of the main action, was a general who believed that once the plan was translated into action he must depend upon his subordinates to harvest the fruits. Rommel, of course, was very much the opposite. On 16–17 November, as formations of 8th Army advanced to their start lines, something like 100,000 men, 600 tanks and some 5,000 support vehicles were on the move. Howard Kippenburger, then a battalion commander, recalled:

> This great approach march will always be remembered by those who took part in it, though the details are vague in memory. The whole Eight Army, Seventh Armoured Division, First South African Division, and the Second New Zealand and Fourth Indian Divisions moved westwards in an enormous column, the armour leading. The army moved south of Sidi Barrani, past the desolate Italian camps of the previous year, along the plateau south of the great escarpment, through the frontier wire into Libya ...[9]

Ahead of the main thrust, on the night on 13/14 November a daring, if ill-starred, raid had been launched by 11th Commando under Lieutenant-Colonel Keyes, assisted by the experienced Colonel Laycock. Among the force objectives was an assault on Rommel's HQ which, in bald terms, equalled an assassination attempt. The raid failed and few survivors made it back to Allied lines. Countess Ranfurly recorded the news on 21 November: 'Bob Laycock's Commandos have raided Rommel's headquarters and it is rumoured that Geoffrey Keyes was killed and Bob is missing; by ill luck Rommel was away and so escaped capture or worse.'[10]

'Crusader' burst across the frontier on 18 November and sped forwards in a kind of dummy war; opposition was minimal and no immediate counter-punch developed. Rommel was still fixated on the impudent garrison of Tobruk and dismissed the offensive as a probing raid. He himself had earlier instigated just such a reconnaissance in force, 'Midsummer Night's Dream' to glean what he might of Auchinleck's intentions. By evening, 7th Armoured Brigade had reached Gabr Saleh, thrusting virtually unopposed. The Fox had been humbugged but, ironically, his very inertia had robbed Cunningham of the decisive clash of armour his plan demanded. 'The morning's reports strengthened General Cruewell's view that a British offensive was developing. Rommel, however, would have none of it ...'[11]

Disconcerted, Cunningham proposed, on the second day, to split his armoured forces and seek out the foe. By now the Fox was alert and began to concentrate his own armour for a riposte. Gott, at this point commanding 7th Armoured Division, expressed the view that the moment was now ripe for a break-out from Tobruk. This was contrary to the previous planned assertion that the Panzers must first be humbled. Nonetheless, Cunningham agreed and the move was planned for morning on 21 November.

Meanwhile, armoured units were colliding piecemeal in the tanker's equivalent of a 'soldier's battle'. Not the precise, staff-college business of ordered formations but a swirling, dust shrouded, grinding melee. Captain Sean Fielding vividly recalled:

Round and about are many Italian tanks and some of ours ... All very badly shot up and some with their dead still in them. The oddest details remain in one's mind. The commander of one Wop tank, lying dead beside his machine, had his fingers crossed; and he had absurdly small feet cased in new boots ...[12]

Armoured units, like men o'war, clashed in the openness of the desert, a merciless and unforgiving ocean of rock and sand. Tanker Bob Sykes serving like Robert Crisp in a Stuart or 'Honey':

I cannot describe the confusion of this all-out tank battle; we were here, there and everywhere. I kept switching from tank to tank – out for a breather and some replenishments and back in again. I do not know who was keeping the score but we were losing a great deal of equipment and men. With our light tanks we were weaving in and out of the battle zone, right in the thick of it. We had developed a tactic of going at the back of the German tank where it was only lightly armoured, and piling into it with some pretty disastrous effects to the engine; the noise, the heat and the dust were unbearable.[13]

Despite the ferocity of these initial exchanges, the main armoured forces of both sides had yet to engage. Cunningham, nonetheless, appears to have considered that a major engagement had indeed occurred and was disposed to believe over-optimistic assessments of enemy losses. Not only were these wildly exaggerated but DAK was still far more accomplished at retrieving damaged machines from the field and restoring them to battle-worthy. Reassured, Cunningham gave the order for the Tobruk break-out, codenamed 'Pop'. This threw into sharp relief the need to hold the tactically significant ridge at Sidi Rezegh which lay between Gabr Saleh and the town. This otherwise unremarkable feature would now become a boiling cauldron. More and more Axis armour was fed in as the battle for the ridge intensified, drawing in much of 8th Army's own tanks. The fighting was close and frightful; 7th Hussars were decimated while Jock Campbell performed prodigies of valour which earned him his well-merited VC. As tanks surged around the disputed higher ground that ring of Axis forces besieging the port remained unbroken:

> The sortie from Tobruk was opposed partly by Germans, and not entirely by Italians as had been expected. The enemy were well dug in behind wire and mines. They resisted stubbornly and brought down intense artillery and machine-gun fire ...[14]

Despite the fact that by evening on the 21st the break-out had been contained, Cunningham remained buoyant and Auchinleck was sending confident cables to London:

> It is authoritatively stated that the Libyan battle, which was at its height this afternoon, is going extremely well. The proportion of Axis tank casualties to British is authoritatively put at three to one. General Rommel, the German commander, is trying to break through, but his situation is becoming more unfavourable ...[15]

Though Rommel had been obliged to divide his available forces, he was far from defeated. Even as Churchill was drafting a victory address the Fox struck back on the 22nd, sending his Panzers in a flanking arc to strike at Sidi Rezegh from the west. This manoeuvre netted tactical gains and various support units were overrun. Throughout the next day fighting raged unabated, a rough and savage collision of armoured leviathans, wheeling and blazing. Fritz Bayerlein described the action from an Axis perspective:

Guns of all kinds and sizes laid a curtain of fire in front of the attacking tanks and there seemed almost no hope of making any progress in the face of this fire-spewing barrier. Tank after tank split open in the hail of shells. Our entire artillery had to be thrown in to silence the enemy guns one by one. However, by the late afternoon we had managed to punch a few holes in the front. The tank attack moved forward again and tank duels of tremendous intensity developed deep in the battlefield. In fluctuating fighting, tank against tank, tank against gun or anti-tank nest, sometimes in frontal, sometimes in flanking assault, using every trick of mobile warfare and tank tactics, the enemy was finally forced back into a confined area.[16]

Sidi Rezegh

Tanks were shot to pieces, others simply broke down, both sides suffered loss; wrecks littered the scarred waste like primeval skeletons. The New Zealanders suffered grievous loss, though less than the South Africans. Jock Campbell was still on hand to rally, exhort and lead but Allies losses were significant, there was no victory in sight.

The fighting about Tobruk and Sidi Rezegh which began on 21st November, and lasted with few pauses for three days, was the fiercest yet seen in the desert. Round Sidi Rezegh airfield in particular the action was unbelievably confused, and the rapid changes in the situation, the smoke and the dust, the sudden appearances of tanks first from one direction and then from another, made great demands of the junior leaders; they certainly did not fail ...[17]

One Allied witness likened the great swirling melee to:

... a naval battle, something of a medieval cavalry charge, but all speeded up madly as you might speed up a cinema film ... Inside that frantic jumble tanks were duelling with tanks in running, almost hand to hand fights, firing nearly point blank, twisting, dodging, sprinting with screaming treads and whining engines that rose to a shriek as they changed gear. As each new tank loomed up ahead gunners were swinging the muzzles of their guns automatically, eyes strained behind their goggles, fighting through the smoke and dust to discriminate friend from foe ...[18]

Robert Crisp commanded a light tank, the US Stuart, referred to by the British as 'Honeys'; light, fast and very agile, these whippets of the desert did good service but were generally out-gunned by Panzer Mark III and IV. Crisp, who was later to write up his experiences in a justly famous account, took part in the battle for Sidi Rezegh:

As my Honey edged up to the final crest I was immediately aware of the dense throng of traffic in front of me. The Trigh was black and broad and moving with packed trucks and lorries. Over it hung a thick, drifting fog of dust so that only the nearest stream of vehicles was clearly discernable. There was not a panzer in sight. The tail of the enemy column was just on our right front, and it looked as though we could not have timed it better. The Germans gave no sign of having seen us, or of being aware of our tanks poised for the strike within a thousand yards of them. They moved slowly westwards wondering, no doubt, what the devil Rommel thought he was playing at with these mad rushes up and down the desert, and beefing like hell about the dust.[19]

Like hawks poised to swoop the light tanks made sure of their quarry:

I looked approvingly to right and left, where the rest of the squadron were lined up following the curve of the contour. From each turret top poked the head and shoulders of the commander, eyes glued to binoculars trained on that enemy mass. It must have been quite a sight to somebody only a week out from base camp in England ... The order went through all the intercoms, from commander to crew: 'Driver, advance. Speed up. Gunner, load both guns.' The Honeys positively leapt over the top of the ridge and plunged down the steady incline to the Trigh. I knew my driver, who was getting used to this sort of thing, would have his foot hard down on the accelerator, straining his eyes through the narrow slit before him to the stationary and bewildered; many lying on their sides or backs with wheels poking grotesquely upwards. Dark figures of men darted wildly about. Even as I watched a great lorry went plunging down the escarpment out of control; it struck some outcrop and leapt high in the air, somersaulting to the bottom in a fantastic avalanche of earth, rock and scrub and odd shaped bundles of men integrated with jagged pieces of wood and metal. The concentration of transport in the wadi below was a wonderful target. I said quickly into the mouthpiece: 'Both guns, men and vehicles; fire with everything you've got.'[20]

The fight was not destined to be as one-sided as the initial clash suggested:

> Suddenly there was a fearful bang, and simultaneously I was drenched from head to foot in an astonishing cascade of cold water. For a moment or two I was physically and mentally paralysed. I just could not believe anything like that could happen. Then realisation came swiftly and terribly ... the water tins on the back of the tank had been hit. It could mean only one thing. As I looked backwards I was already giving the order to the gunner to traverse the turret as fast as he bloody well could. In one comprehensive flash I saw it all, and the fear leapt up in me. Not fifty yards away a 50-mm anti-tank gun pointed straight at the Honey, pointed straight between my eyes ...[21]

Axis gunners were already taking ample revenge for the ravishing of their convoy with numbers of the light tanks already knocked out:

> It took less than a second for the whole scene and its awful meaning to register on my mind. I could see the German gunners slamming the next shell into the breech as the turret whirled. I yelled 'On, Machine Gun; fire'. In the same moment I saw the puff of smoke from the anti-tank gun and felt and heard the strike on the armour plating. Quickly I looked down into the turret. A foot or two below me the gunner was staring at his hand, over which a dark red stain was slowly spreading. Then he gave a scream and fell grovelling to the floor. In the top right corner of the turret a jagged hole gaped, and through it, like some macabre peepshow, I could see the gun being reloaded. I knew that in another few seconds I would be dead, but something well beyond reason or sanity impelled my muscles and actions.[22]

Crisp hammered away with the MG till the over-heated weapon jammed. The only chance was to get the damaged tank over the lip of the rise and out of the gunner's sights. His driver had been half-throttled by twisted earphone leads but somehow the vehicle staggered forward and ground over the rim:

> In the turret we were hurled about like corks, and then the bouncing stopped and we rode smoothly down the slope. We were out of sight of the guns on the escarpment and, with a great rush of disbelief; I knew we were going to get away with it.[23]

As they pelted downhill a trio of Axis motorcyclists wisely raised their hands but the tank careered on, leaving their would-be prisoners in the same petrified state of capitulation:

> So much had happened in a few minutes, or a few hours it might have been, and I had looked so closely into the valley of the shadow, that I found it difficult to return to reality. I just could not fully absorb our situation.

Having survived this encounter Crisp nursed his battered tank back up the slope to return to the fight. What he saw there horrified him:

> Not much more than 500 yards away, like a projection on a cinema screen, lay the battlefield. My eyes lifted to the tall black columns, leaning slightly with the wind, and followed them down to the Honeys gasping smoke. Four of my tanks were blazing infernos; three others just sat there, sad and abandoned; a line of anti-tank guns with their crews still manning them expectantly lined the edge of the drop.

Men were dead or captured, being rounded up by Axis infantry and gunners. Crisp attempted to send a signal to any survivors hoping for escape but the response was a stream of barking MG fire.

> I dropped back into the turret. I said wearily over the intercom: 'OK Whaley. There's nothing we can do, let's go back.'[24]

A glance at his watch informed Crisp that the whole action had lasted seventeen minutes.

James Fraser, serving with 8 RTR and destined to win the MM, was part of a Valentine tank crew in this battle:

> We were doing an attack on the Sidi Rezegh aerodrome. We were equipped with Valentine tanks with a three man crew, of which I was the driver, plus an officer named Pete Kitto and the gunner, a lad from Skipton. We were armed with two-pounder guns but they were useless against the German tanks. We'd come under heavy fire and my tank was engaged on the side but it must have been a glancing blow – it didn't do any damage. I swung around and an armour piercing shell went through the back of the tank, right into the engine, and stopped it. Fortunately the engine was diesel and there was no fire, unlike a Grant tank which, with its high-octane petrol, was like a mobile crematorium – as soon as it was hit it would just go up and explode like a tin of bully beef.[25]

With the vehicle damaged it was a matter of whether bailing out under enemy guns or staying put was the lesser evil. They sat it out in the hulk while British tanks flamed through the darkness. Come morning the tank commander rather unwisely opted to stand atop the turret for better observation – 'an anti-tank rifle fired and chipped half his knee away'. With their officer wounded, Sykes assumed command and they laboured away on foot, carrying the casualty. Though chased by the rattle of small arms, they made good their escape and were eventually picked up by South African armoured cars: 'I was transferred back to my own unit and picked up another tank.'

Rommel planned a counterstroke of breathtaking audacity, one which sent shudders through his more cautious subordinates. He had resolved to draw off some of his forces from the furnace of Sidi Rezegh and strike towards Egypt. This was at the very moment Cunningham was suffering something of a personal crisis. On the 23rd he had broached the possibility of breaking off the action and retreating. This was not something the 'Auk' was prepared to countenance. By next day the C in C had decided to remove his 8th Army commander and appoint Ritchie in his stead. Now Rommel was driving his spearhead eastwards. Under his personal command he led the remnants of 15th Panzer and Ariete. The blow threatened to sever 30 Corps' line of retreat and swept through rear echelons like the grim reaper. Cruewell, his reservations dismissed, was ordered to send 21st Panzer to drive 13 Corps back onto the web of frontier minefields. For both sides this was to be the crisis.

> In his memoir of the desert war ... Douglas used what seemed to be the perfect literal metaphor of protection, the belly of a Crusader tank ... That was his home ... the limited apprehension of the world that a moving tank allows. He likens the view to that rendered by 'a camera obscura or a silent film ... Men shout, vehicles move, aeroplanes fly over; and all soundlessly, the noise of the tank being continuous perhaps for hours on end, the effect is of silence ... an illimitably strange land, quite unrelated to real life. The illusion is breached when the crew halt beside a burnt out shell and the scorched remains of its occupants'.[26]

A Gambit for the Fox

In typically more objective style the Official History considers the soundness of such tactics:

Whether this [Rommel's gambit] was a good decision is an interesting point. There can be no doubt that the moment had come to exploit the success gained around Sidi Rezegh; the question was how to do it. Cruewell on the other hand, saw a chance of wiping out the British armoured force altogether ... But when Cruewell made his report on the morning of 24th November it must have seemed to Rommel that although the British armour could not be written off it could be disregarded for the time being.[27]

Auchinleck, despite the seriousness of the situation, did not lose his nerve and Rommel's sweeping stroke soon ran into difficulties. Ariete could not get past the South Africans while 21st Panzer could make no headway against 4th Indian Division. Freyberg and the New Zealanders were fighting hard for Tobruk though, as the New Zealand Official History confirms, their casualties were high:

There was an enormous number of dead and wounded all over the battlefield. A significant feature was the sight of many men who had been hit by solid shot of anti-tank guns, fired at point blank range. These projectiles had torn large portions of flesh from the bodies of their unfortunate victims and it would be hard to imagine a more unpleasant sight or a more heavily contested battlefield.[28]

During the 'Crusader' fighting Desert Air Force was flying effective sorties against Axis ground forces, denying Rommel the comfort of 'flying artillery' which had shielded and aided previous operations. The DAK diary for 25 November reflects a mounting frustration: 'Continuous heavy raids in the Sidi Omar area. Heavy losses among our troops; where are the German fighters?'[28] Within 8th Army, news of Cunningham's replacement produced no outpourings of grief. Robert Crisp recorded:

General Cunningham had been relieved of the command of the Eighth Army and had been replaced by General Ritchie. This was a shock to all of us, but not really a surprise. Even right down at the bottom of the ladder, it was impossible not to be aware of the absence of firm direction and purpose from above. Everybody welcomed the change as the beginning of an era of greater decisiveness; nobody had ever heard of Ritchie.[29]

On 27 November, union with 70th Division was effected, the heroic garrison finally relieved. British armoured forces at Sidi Rezegh, despite their fearful pounding, were reorganising and still very much in the fight. Rommel's units by contrast were equally battered but now dispersed and vulnerable. At DAK Headquarters Colonel Westphal had already assumed responsibility for the recall of 21st Panzer. Rommel, now out of touch, on flying back that evening tacitly approved and began drawing back 15th Panzer as well.

> So ended General Rommel's spectacular stroke; without compelling the British to alter their plans it had caused some temporary embarrassment and local confusion. It failed completely in its purpose of relieving the frontier troops. The Germans lost at least thirty of their hundred tanks, while the British armour was given a chance to refit – a chance of which good use was made.[30]

His priority now was to try and re-establish the ring around Tobruk. From 28 November, there was more savage combat around El Duda, Belhammed and Sidi Rezegh. Ground was taken, lost and retaken; both sides sustained further, heavy losses. As November drew to a close German armour was battering the remnant of the New Zealanders, unsupported by Allied tanks. Freyberg was pushed back, his division's casualties dreadful; Tobruk was again encircled. The battle was by now one of attrition, a fight in which the Allies were better placed but Rommel was not yet ready to withdraw. On 2 December he threw his battered formations back into the fight for a further five days of murderous intensity. Robert Crisp recalled the numbing drain of constant battle:

> I can truthfully say that none of us had more than the vaguest idea where we were from day to day and hour to hour, or what was happening either to our own forces or the enemy's ... There was no such thing as advance and retreat. We roared off to areas of threat or engagement depending on the urgency of the information. We chased mirages and were chased by mirages. Every few hours a landmark of a name would punch our memories, with an elusive familiarity, and we would recall a forgotten early incident or a battle fought there days before that was now part of a past so near in time but so distant in event.[31]

In the relative comfort and security of the Delta, unheard of places such as Sidi Rezegh seemed very distant and the actions there confusing in the extreme:

A big tank battle is raging in the Desert near Sidi Rezegh. I think the Sherwood Rangers may be involved. Perhaps, after all, I am lucky that Dan is a prisoner and not in the midst of this turmoil ... I am afraid we are not yet as well armed as the Germans – their Mark 3 and 4 guns are excellent and they have the awful 88mm gun.[32]

The end of November as a crucial time: 'Crusader' was a long way from being over, but an important stage had been reached: 'The British were able to introduce fresh troops and the enemy was not.'[33]

This was now a soldier's battle, a grinding, bloody, slogging match, men against men, tank against tank, guns against tanks. M. E. Parker was serving as a junior officer in an anti-tank battery of 65th (Norfolk Yeomanry) Artillery:

Our objective was Sidi Omar which is where the International Wire takes a turn southwards. We were supported by 42 RTR in Matildas, most of which were written off by German 88s in the initial assault. The 88s were in turn shot up by a 25-pounder which was wheeled up and which took them on over open sights. It took three days to capture Sidi Omar: we held one half and the Italians, plus German gunners, the other ... It was decided to concentrate a 'stonk' on the remaining portion. The barrage was by no means small and when it was over a considerable number of Italians had had enough and surrendered. The following day after a repeat performance – before the final assault – an Italian came in an aplogised for being late in surrendering; he explained that he had been asleep.[34]

By 7 December the pace of attrition had forced Rommel to recognise the need for a withdrawal. Both sides continued to incur casualties but the Allies could replenish at a far faster rate. Consequently, Rommel proposed to retire upon a fixed, defensive line running south from Gazala. The British, scenting victory, swooped after, hard upon the heels of the retreating Axis. By the 16th a further retirement became expedient and by 22 December, as 1941 drew to a close, the Axis forces had fallen back as far as Beda Fomm and Antelat. Further withdrawals, firstly to Agedabia and finally El Agheila followed and, though constantly harassed, the rearguard provided an effective screen. By now both sides were equally exhausted.

'Crusader' was a British victory, in that Tobruk was relieved, the enemy was driven from Cyrenaica with heavy losses, and all the Axis troops holding positions on the

Egyptian frontier were destroyed or captured. This all took longer than expected, however, and in doing it the British exhausted themselves.[35]

Winter quarters in the Western Desert were generally disagreeable:

Flies produced more casualties than the Germans. It is impossible to describe, without suspicion of exaggeration, how thickly they used to surround us. Most of us ate a meal with a handkerchief or piece of paper in one hand and our food in the other. While we tried to get the food to our mouths, free from flies, we waved the other hand about wildly; even so we ate many hundreds of flies. They settled on food like a cloud and no amount of waving about disturbed them. They could clean jam and butter from a slice of bread much quicker than we could eat it ... it can be realised how serious the menace of flies was considered when I say that, even in remote parts of the Desert, one came across notices saying 'Kill that fly, or he will kill you'.[36]

The pendulum had indeed swung but this placed fresh difficulties in the path of the British. As a direct result of this strategic shift, 8th Army was that much further away from its supply base and its communications were that much more attenuated. Conversely, the army which had retreated was so much closer to its base, thus supply and replenishment was that much easier. Technically, 8th Army had won the day and 'Crusader' ranks as a British victory. It was dearly bought. Allied losses in killed, wounded and missing were in the region of 18,000, while the Axis lost 20,000. Both lost heavily in tanks and guns.

Thus the British had succeeded in their object of clearing Cyrenaica of the enemy, though not by means of a rapid stroke, as had been planned, but only after a long and costly struggle which consumed so many of their resources that by the time they reached the western end of Cyrenaica their blow was spent.[37]

Though the Desert Air Force had been in the ascendant throughout, ground to air cooperation was by no means yet perfected: 'British superiority in the air made the failure to make full use of the day-bombers all the more disappointing.'[38] Similarly DAK did not enjoy close support and cooperation from the Luftwaffe:

... contrary to an impression widely held at the time, the enemy did not have a highly organised and efficient system of army/air cooperation; the British had at least laid the foundations of a system and were bent on making it work although they had not yet overcome all of the difficulties.[39]

Cyrenaica was indeed re-taken but, in the Far East, there had been serious reverses: both *Prince of Wales* and *Repulse* had been lost to Japanese air attack. The Russians had been defeated in a series of epic *Kesselschlact* or 'cauldron' battles and the Germans were at the gates of Moscow. Malta was under tremendous pressure and Rommel's prospects of adequate re-supply that much brighter. The Desert Fox was again restive and not intending to sit on the defensive. On 17 January he confided in his daily letter home:

The situation is developing to our advantage ... and I'm full of plans that I daren't say anything about round here. They'd think me crazy. But I'm not; I simply see a bit further than they do. But you know me.[40]

5
'Msus Stakes' & 'Gazala Gallop': January – June 1942

In those moments in between of what is
And what was meant to be.
There in silence you will find me.
A faceless face, an unknown name.
The unknown soldier, my simple grave.
There friends and family came not visiting.
There my widow could not weep for me.

In life I was not alone.
In life, I was not unknown.
I had a wife, a son, a home.

'The Unknown Soldier' by Samantha Kelly

On the surface, it appeared that the 'Crusader' battles had resulted in a significant victory for 8th Army but this was largely illusory and the thinning of British dispositions left the gains in Cyrenaica, so dearly won, again at hazard:

> To supply the 13th Corps and its attached troops ... required some 1,400 tons [of supplies] a day. The average daily amounts received at Tobruk by sea and by lorry convoys ... together came to 1,150 tons ... there was thus a shortfall of some 250 tons on daily needs alone ... The fact is the administrative resources of 8th Army were now stretched to the limit.[1]

Rommel Attacks
Rommel had also noted these deficiencies and a subtle shift in the

balance of resources provided him with an opportunity, one which he, as arch-opportunist, was not about to ignore: 'At a staff conference held on 12 January his senior intelligence officer, Major F. W. von Mellenthin, predicted that for the next fortnight the Axis forces would be slightly stronger than the British immediately opposed to them.'[2] On 21 January, the Desert Fox threw two strong columns into an attack, one advancing along the coast road, the other swinging in a flanking arc, north of Wadi el Faregh. Caught off-guard and dispersed, British units began to fall back. General Ritchie was, at this time, far to the rear in Cairo and disposed to regard these moves as nothing more than a raid or reconnaissance in force. He and Auchinleck did not detect the tremors of disquiet that commanders on the ground were experiencing. Early cables suggested the situation might be ripe for a strong riposte.

It has been said of military matters that 'too often the capacity to advance is identified with the desirability of advancing'.[3] Never was this truer than in the Desert War and the reality was that Rommel had seized and was maintaining the initiative. DAK had also perfected its offensive tactics as Panzer officer Heinz Schmidt recorded:

> With our twelve anti-tank guns we leap-frogged from one vantage point to another, while our panzers, stationary and hull-down, if possible, provided protective fire. Then we would establish ourselves to give them protective fire while they swept on again …[4]

Lieutenant D. F. Parry, commanding the maintenance section of an anti-aircraft battery based in Benghazi, was one who realised matters were turning grave, despite more cautious official communiqués:

> It took over twenty-four hours for the news of the disaster in the south to filter through to Benghazi and as always the news was played down: 'There has been a slight penetration of our lines at Sirte but necessary measures are being taken to restore the situation.' This was followed by: 'It has been found necessary to form defensive positions to the east of Sirte; however, the situation is stabilising and Benghazi is not in any danger.' Some days later: 'As a precautionary measure steps will be taken to evacuate Benghazi', followed by 'Your workshop will leave Benghazi and proceed to Tobruk'.[5]

By 24 January the 'Auk' was sending signals in an altogether more sober tone. Rommel was still advancing, his own supply difficulties notwithstanding. When one officer had the nerve to point out fuel stocks were critical he received the curt advice: 'Well go and get it [fuel] from the British'. Within a day there were plans to evacuate Benghazi, producing a rather plaintive cry from Whitehall: '... why should they all be off so quickly?' Both Ritchie and Auchinleck flew to the front but the local commanders, their instincts more finely tuned, were preparing for withdrawal. 4th Indian Division was pulling out from Benghazi as 1st Armoured prepared to regroup near Mechili.

Swift as a terrier Rommel, alerted by wireless intercepts, planned a double-headed thrust. One pincer swept along the coast road while the second, the Fox in the lead, pushed over higher ground to sweep around and come upon the port from the south-east. A dummy lunge toward Mechili was intended to fool Ritchie and succeeded. He dispatched his armour leaving Benghazi exposed. General Tuker, commanding 4th Indian Division, whose appreciation of the unfolding tactical situation jibed with that of his superiors, lamented:

> We rang Army – and learnt to our consternation that the whole of the eastern flank had gone off on a wild goose chase after a phantom force of enemy armour falsely reported to be moving on Mechili ... Dispersion, dispersion, dispersion.[6]

Von Mellenthin, commenting on the effectiveness of the panzer tactics and the speed of the British withdrawals, observed scathingly: 'The pursuit attained a speed of fifteen miles an hour and the British fled madly over the desert in one of the most extraordinary routs of the war.[7] If Ritchie was groping in the fog of war thrown up by his brilliant opponent, Rommel himself faced other enemies much nearer home. General Bastico had become alarmed because the limited spoiling attack, to which he had agreed, was turning into a full-blown offensive of which he strongly disapproved. He signalled his fears to Comando Supremo and asked that General Rommel should be made to take a more realistic view. This brought Cavallero to Rommel's headquarters on 23 January, accompanied by Field Marshal Kesselring and bearing a directive from Mussolini. In this it was stated that there was 'no immediate prospect of sending supplies and reinforcements to Africa in the face of present British naval and air opposition'.[8]

Rommel was instructed to halt further attacks and establish a defensive position. Despite the weight of the delegation ranged against him he demurred and reminded his superiors that only the Führer himself could apply restraint. Kesselring, who was inclined to back Cavallero and no particular admirer of Rommel, could not move the General and the party were sent packing, 'Smiling' Albert now 'growling' in frustration. Meanwhile, and without armour, Tuker could not maintain a viable defence and quite rightly withdrew. 7th Indian Brigade was garrisoning the port while the remainder of the division was holding a line east of Barce. These troops encountered the sweeping arm of Rommel's flanking move in a series of sharp encounters and escaped the net only with difficulty.

'Msus Stakes'

Sergeant Grey DCM MM of the Cameron Highlanders found himself in the thick of the confused fighting and at one point made prisoner. His captors, including a German and an Italian officer, expected him to lead them to his comrades:

> There seemed no alternative, so I pointed to my left … I started off up the hill, with the officers on either side and, stumbling in the dark, managed to bring my platoon well on to my flank. Then I aimed for their position, which I could just distinguish in the dark. I heard a Jock say, 'Here the b******s come.' Then the Italian said: 'Shout to them to surrender!' So I shouted: 'McGeough, McGeough!' (I knew he was a good shot), got within ten yards of them, shouted 'Shoot!' and fell flat. The boys shot and got the German in the head and the Italian in the stomach.[9]

On 29 January Rommel rode triumphantly into Benghazi while the 8th Army scattered back to a defensive position astride the line from Gazala in the north to Bir Hacheim, '… back in fact to the very place where, only seven weeks before, General Rommel had broken away because he judged the tactical balance to be against him'.[10] Early in February, Godwin-Austen, commanding 13 Corps asked to be relieved. He considered Ritchie's intermeddling in his decisions had eroded his position to an intolerable degree. This may have left a bitter taste as the corps commander had likely had his finger more firmly on the pulse than his superior.

This need not imply that all was entirely well 'on the other side of the wire':

The [Axis] chain of command creaked from time to time, but the firm hand of General Rommel made up for its many weaknesses. He was not the commander in chief, it is true, but he was emphatically the man whose views mattered, for he did what he felt to be militarily right in spite of the frequent protests of his superior, General Bastico. And then, having made up his own mind on the policy, he had a habit of becoming a tactical leader, and by taking command personally at the most important spot, ensuring that his ideas were carried out.[11]

Rommel's own post-mortem on the fighting up till early February, forming a portion of his official report, while allowing for some artful editing, contains a very fair assessment of British shortcomings:

The assembly of all the forces for the autumn offensive was cleverly concealed (wireless deception was also used) and was favoured by the weather. The attack therefore came as a complete surprise, but although the British command showed skill and prudence in preparing the offensive they were less successful when it came to carrying it out. Disregarding the fundamental principle of employing all available forces at the most critical point ... Never anywhere at any time during the fighting in Libya did the British High Command concentrate all its available forces at the decisive point ... British troops fought well on the whole though they never attained the same impetus as the Germans when attacking ... The military result was that the British 8th Army was so severely beaten that it was incapable of further large-scale operations for months afterwards.[12]

Despite being penned by the enemy this was by no means an overly harsh assessment. Throughout the 'Msus Stakes' the 8th Army had been hamstrung by inaccurate intelligence, uncertainties of supply, inadequate training and a total lack of flexibility. The retreat resulted in the loss of 1,400 men, 70 tanks and 40 guns.[13] General Sir Alan Brooke, now CIGS confided to his journal: 'It was his [Churchill's] darkest hour ... The weight of his burden would have crushed any other man.'[14] By late February Brooke was warning that Malta's position was extremely precarious and the outcome doubtful, 'unless we could recapture Benghazi before May at the very latest'.[15] On 29 January, Auchinleck had sent a cautious if not disingenuous cable: 'It must be admitted that the enemy has exceeded beyond his expectations and mine and that his tactics have been skilful and bold.'[16] His next communication, a bare twenty-four hours later, sounded a rather more dolorous note:

I am reluctantly compelled to [the] conclusion that to meet German armoured forces with any reasonable hope of decisive success our armoured forces, as at present equipped, and led must have at least two to one superiority.[17]

Rommel consistently displayed the remarkable ability to convert limited tactical successes into major gains. His policy of leading from the front, though fraught with risks, had so far paid handsome dividends. Even though 8th Army command might be depressing the War Cabinet with what appeared to be excessive caution, Auchinleck and Ritchie were if anything understating British weaknesses. The policy of senior officers to lead from a distance placed a greater burden on corps and divisional commanders. When the latter painted a sombre picture of the true state of their units, these assessments, though valid, were hardly ever greeted with rapture. Messervy, when reporting his tanks to be in far worse state than Ritchie was wont to assume, felt his observations considered 'subversive'.[18] Tuker was no less outspoken:

You will notice also that the principle of security was neglected, for nowhere west of Tobruk was there a firm base on which 13 Corps could fall back, or behind which it could be ready for a counter-offensive.[19]

On 26 February, the Prime Minister sent a peevish telegram to the C in C Middle East:

According to our figures, you have substantial superiority in the air, in armour and in other forces ... The supply of Malta is causing us increasing anxiety ... Pray let me hear from you.[20]

To afford the island fortress much needed relief, Whitehall needed an offensive in mid-March or early April at the latest. Auchinleck would not agree a date before the middle part of May. Lyttelton had meanwhile retuned to England to become Minister of Production; his successor as Minister of State in Cairo was the Australian Richard Casey. A part of Auchinleck's difficulties was the mechanical inferiority of his tanks. Simply to have more machines than your opponent was of no consequence if those you had were unreliable. British tanks, particularly the Crusader, were markedly outclassed by German models and mechanically unsound to boot. Lyttelton was acutely aware of these shortcomings:

On top of this mechanical failure must be reckoned the superior gun position of the German tanks ... the Germans had developed a better form of tactic in the employment of their armoured formations; their tanks moved slowly from position to position waiting till they had discovered the location of our artillery and anti-tank weapons ... They kept out of range of the latter and suffered little damage from the former.[21]

Churchill, though he railed at the bad designs, continued to press Auchinleck for an early offensive and the 'Auk', to his credit, remained obdurate. A snappish exchange of cables ensued:

We consider [3 March] that an attempt to drive the Germans out of Cyrenaica in the next few weeks is not only imperative for the safety of Malta on which so much depends, but holds out the only hope of fighting a battle while the enemy is still comparatively weak ...[22]

We are agreed [8 March] that in spite of the risks you mention you would be right to attack the enemy and fight a major battle.[23]

When the Auk refused to bend and refused to hazard Egypt to succour Malta, he was summarily ordered home. He demurred, leaving Churchill with the choice of either 'backing him or sacking him'. Brooke and other wise counsels prevailed against the latter course and Auchinleck won his breathing space. Clement Attlee had been nominated to chair an enquiry into the mechanical defects of the British tanks which found the C in C's concerns fully justified. The Prime Minister's personal emissaries, Sir Stafford Cripps and General Sir Archibald Nye, vice-CIGS, were minded to side with Auchinleck. Their representations earned a sarcastic reply:

I have heard from the Lord Privy Seal [Cripps]. I do not wonder everything was so pleasant, considering you seem to have accepted everything they said, and all we have got to accept is the probable loss of Malta and the army standing idle, while the Russians are resisting the German counter-stroke desperately, and while the enemy is reinforcing himself in Libya faster than are we.[24]

'Gazala Gallop'

Auchinleck quickly found that he could not hope to meet his own deadline of mid-May; mid-June looked possible but a delay till August could not be fully discounted. Rommel, disobligingly, intended his own imminent assault to be directed in the south swinging on the pivot of Bir Hacheim, which he expected to overcome without undue difficulty. The attacks in the centre and north would, in the case of the former, be secondary and, in the latter instance, a mere feint. The Fox himself would lead the main armoured thrust in the south which would, having dealt with the Free French at Bir Hacheim, sweep around behind 8th Army and begin rolling up the line. Italian armour would attempt to batter through British minefields in the centre while Cruewell would command joint infantry forces in the north. Ritchie's deployments were piecemeal and ill-considered. In the north 13 Corps was spread in a series of defensive 'boxes' with 30 Corps to the south disposed by brigades together with the bulk of available armour. Auchinleck, in all fairness, was not unaware of the current failures in British tactical doctrine:

The experience of the winter fighting had taught General Auchinleck to decide upon two important changes in the organisation of the army. It was not only the enemy who had noticed that the British armour, artillery and infantry had often been unsuccessful in concerting their action on the battlefield. General Auchinleck accordingly made up his mind 'to associate the three arms more closely at all times and in all places'. He thought that the British type of armoured division would be better balanced if it had less armour and more infantry – like a German Panzer Division. In future, therefore, an armoured division would consist basically of one armoured brigade group and one motor brigade group. The former would contain three tank regiments, one motor battalion, and a regiment of field and anti-tank guns, and the latter three motor battalions and a similar artillery regiment. In addition, both types of brigade group would include light anti-aircraft artillery, engineers, and administrative units. The Army tank brigades, each of three regiments of 'I' tanks, would not form part of a division, but would continue to be allotted as the situation demanded.[25]

Rommel's offensive and the Battle of Gazala, dubbed 'the Gazala Gallop' by 8th Army, can be divided into four phases:
1. Rommel launches his flank attack, 26–29 May, attempting to overrun British defences from behind.
2. Fighting in the 'Cauldron' – Rommel tries to re-supply and consolidate his forces.

3. The reduction of Bir Hacheim, and the pounding of British armour 11–13 June, followed by withdrawal from the Gazala line.

4. Storming of Tobruk.

In the fighting 100,000 Allied troops, 849 tanks and 604 planes would face some 90,000 Axis with 561 tanks, (228 of which were of the inferior Italian sort) and 504 aircraft.

At this time John Hackett, of Arnhem renown, was serving as a major in 8th King's Royal Irish Hussars and like Robert Crisp he was in a Honey. On 27 May his mission was to check out the intended Axis thrust south of the Free French redoubt:

> I got C squadron on the move very quickly – they were a very handy lot. We went up a slope in this typically undulating desert country, and as I reached the top of this rise the commanding officer said to me over the radio: 'Report when you first see them.' I came over the top and there in front of me was the whole bloody German army, as far as I could see, coming my way.
>
> Hackett, having affixed his dashing black pennant to signal the attack, rather than relying on the unreliable net, drew the weight of Axis fire against his own vehicle which was soon disabled, about three minutes after putting up the black flag.[26]

Bir Hacheim, the pivot upon which the Axis southerly attack was to turn, proved a far tougher nut than Rommel had anticipated. His two more northerly assaults both failed to break in, stalled against minefields and determined resistance. The new Grant tanks and heavier punch of the 6-pounder AT guns made their presence felt. Failure to eliminate Bir Hacheim spoilt the smooth execution of his plan, supply lines were attenuated, vulnerable to marauding columns of light armour and armoured cars.

Despite the Axis' potentially exposed position, Ritchie failed to concentrate his armour, an error which amazed his more nimble opponent:

> Ritchie had thrown his armour into the battle piecemeal and had thus given us the chance engaging them on each separate occasion with just about enough of our own tanks; this dispersal of the British armoured brigades was incomprehensible.[27]

Many of the Allied tank officers had approached this battle with far greater confidence than before, believing the improved firepower of their Grants would even the odds. Colonel G. P. B. Roberts, leading

3rd RTR described the fighting which subsequently took place south of El Adem:

> There they are – more than a hundred. Yes, twenty in the first line, and there are six, no eight lines, and more behind that in the distance; a whole ruddy Panzer Division is quite obviously in front of us. Damn it. This was not the plan at all – where the hell is the rest of the Brigade?[28] Despite the odds the 75mm gun did good service in the melee; '75 gunner, enemy tank straight ahead receiving no attention – engage ... Good shot that got him – same again.[29]

Thrown in piecemeal fashion, 2nd and 22nd Armoured Brigades, despite gallant and costly efforts, were insufficient to stem the onslaught. DAK was now within an area known as the 'Knightsbridge' Box. South Notts Hussars were providing the eyes and guns for 22nd Armoured and a brace of armoured cars, one commanded by Captain Garry Birkin the CO and the other by his brother Ivor. Sergeant Harold Harper was in the patrol:

> We had only done six or seven hundred yards when we heard a garbled message from the commander's radio which immediately told us something was wrong. Captain Birkin jumped out and dashed across to the armoured car and I followed him. I've never seen anything quite like it in my life. Major Birkin lay flat on the floor, obviously dead. I went to the back and opened up the doors of the armoured car. Apparently an armour piercing shell had gone clear through the middle of the battery commander as he was standing in the turret and then chopped off the heads of the two radio operators. All you could see was the two lads, hands still holding their mouthpieces – although their heads had rolled off onto the floor; the third radio operator, who had sent the message, jumped down from the armoured car and raced off.[30]

Harper had to take charge as the younger brother was traumatised by the ghastly death of the elder. In the confusion the surviving car collided with a Grant tank belonging to Royal Gloucester Hussars. The armoured car burst into flames and even worse, in their mad career, they found they had run over the surviving member of the other crew and fractured his leg:

> We then jumped on the back of a passing tank of the CLY and lay flat on it. The tank commander had no idea we were there and kept firing. We had to keep dodging as best

we could when the turret and barrel kept swinging round. One of the chaps fell off and we thought he'd been crushed to death, though I found out later that he lived. Most of us received wounds of some sort from the German shelling. I'd crushed my ribs as we collided with the Grant tank and later I got some shrapnel in my left knee.[31]

On 30 May 150th Brigade, left horribly exposed, was overrun:

Help did not arrive. At first light on 1st June the enemy attacked from all sides, and platoon by platoon the brigade was overrun and captured. The last sub-unit to go down was believed to be the platoon of the 5th Green Howards commanded by Captain Bert Dennis.[32]

It was not till 1–2 June that Ritchie decided to storm the Cauldron. As the Official History tersely records: '… British operations on the night of 1st/2nd June were a fiasco'.[33] The subsequent attack put in before dawn on the 5th – Operation 'Aberdeen' – was a tragedy. 7th Armoured and 5th Indian Division stormed their objectives only to find they had missed the enemy and landed a blow in the air: '… evil consequences were to follow quickly'.[34]

Exposed to relentless counter-attacks, several regiments and their supporting guns were decimated. Major A. H. G. Dobson of RE describes the fate of 150th Brigade:

All the guns had been lost or were out of ammunition. It was just the foot soldier sitting in a hole in the ground with a Bren gun and he hadn't really much hope by that stage. I remember the sapper commander on the phone saying 'I can see the tanks coming now,' and by the time they were 50 yards away he said, 'I don't think I shall be telephoning much more.' That was the end of his particular unit, and this went on all the way round.[35]

When the minefield barrier was finally breached and Axis support came through, Bir Hacheim was further isolated, pressure ratcheted to an irresistible level. On 9 June, the survivors, battered but unbowed, fought their way clear of the trap. Of the 3,600 who had begun the fight 2,700 escaped:

The defence of Bir Hacheim had achieved several purposes. At the outset it had made longer and more difficult the enemy's temporary supply route; it had caused him many casualties; and it gave the British a chance to recover from their defeat in the Cauldron.[36]

Driver Robert Crawford described how vulnerable supply columns of both sides were to the attentions of marauding armour:

> He [a survivor] described how they were moving up towards Bir Hacheim when they ran into the tank ambush. The tanks closed in from all sides, blazing away with their guns. The Bren guns of the supply column hardly had a chance to answer before the gunners were mown down. Then carnage was let loose as the tanks drove straight over the column, smashing lorries onto their sides in all directions; within a few minutes the column was a mass of blazing wreckage with bodies strewn everywhere ...[37]

With this obstacle removed, Axis forces were freed for a further thrust, this time toward El Adem, with a demonstration to distract the British in 'Knightsbridge'. By dark on 11 June, Rommel had attained El Adem having, once again, wrong-footed his opponents. Next day he moved in an attempt to surround the remnants of 2nd and 4th Armoured Brigades. There was now a very real risk the largely static infantry formations to the north could be surrounded and heavy clashes occurred in the vicinity of Rigel Ridge. Here the Scots Guards fought tenaciously, earning high praise from Rommel. Nonetheless, relentless pressure and mounting losses forced the British from the higher ground; 22nd Armoured lost some two thirds of its tanks.

As the Axis held the field, they were able to recover many of their damaged vehicles with customary efficiency, 8th Army could not and those left damaged were effectively written off. Despite this, British units were improving their overall rates of recovery and repair: 'Ever since the opening of the battle the British had striven hard to get damaged tanks into action again quickly.'[38] Many damaged vehicles were recovered and innumerable 'roadside repairs' successfully carried out. Casualties among experienced crews were nonetheless heavy, the tankers 'only too well aware of the shortcomings of their own tanks'.[39] The Crusader had an evil propensity for bursting into flames, immolating its crew. The lighter Stuarts, though agile, were only really suited to a reconnaissance role while the Grant which had achieved successes was hamstrung by its inability to take an effective hull-down position, limited traverse and a lack of effective AP shells. The 2-

pounder anti-tank gun, without AP and ballistic capped ammunition, was useless against the up-armoured panzers.

Lieutenant Parry recounted the contents of a radio conversation he inadvertently logged onto between 30 Corps HQ – well to the rear – and an officer rather nearer the front. In this the officer repeatedly advised large German formations were looming only to be constantly assured no such units could possibly be in his sector:

> Officer: Through the haze I can now identify tanks, difficult to identify but possibly German Mark IVs.
>
> 30 Corps: We repeat, there are no, repeat no, forces in your vicinity.
>
> Officer: I am counting Mark IVs – one, two, three, four, five, six, seven – there is no doubt, repeat no doubt, that this is a large German force. Mark IVs number over thirty, and there are also Mark IIIs and a large number of motorised infantry. This could be, I repeat, this could be the Afrika Korps moving at a speed of approximately 30 miles per hour towards El Adem.
>
> 30 Corps: [with an air of resignation] There are no forces in your area ...[40]

Very shortly afterward the transmission broke off – a most telling silence.

The End for Tobruk

By 14 June, Ritchie was seeking permission to draw off, fall back to the frontier and save his forces from encirclement. Auchinleck was not yet ready to throw in the towel, insisting that further counter-attacks be launched to deny the approaches to Tobruk. As C in C he had to answer to the Prime Minister who was already querying his intentions: 'Presume there is no question in any case of giving up Tobruk?'[41] Rommel felt a surge of confidence which he transmitted in his daily correspondence to his wife on 15 June: '... the battle has been won and the enemy is breaking up ...'[42] As early as January 1942, the joint Middle East commanders, Auchinleck, Cunningham and Tedder had agreed that Tobruk, if isolated, should not once again be defended. By 17 June, Rommel had secured Gambut airfield and beaten off the remnant of British armour. Tobruk was again invested. Two days later there was still some ill-founded optimism that the perimeter could be held on the basis or in the pious hope that Axis forces would settle down for a lengthy siege. The situation now within the ring was very different from before. Previously strong defences had been denuded and pillaged to meet the exigencies of the now-defunct Gazala Line and the garrison was badly placed to resist a sustained attack.

Rommel, scenting this weakness, unleashed the Luftwaffe who began blasting the fortress on 20 June as the precursor to a determined attack from the south-east. By 07.45 hrs the anti-tank ditch, equivalent to the medieval moat, had been breached and the perimeter was collapsing. There had been talk of a breakout should this occur but, in reality, no escape route was viable. Auchinleck's report to London, late on the 20th, sounded a note of impending catastrophe:

> Enemy attacked south-east face of Tobruk perimeter early morning after air bombardment and penetrated defences. By evening all our tanks reported knocked out and half our guns lost ... Major-General Klopper commanding troops in Tobruk last night asked authority to fight his way out feeling apparently could not repeat not hold out. Ritchie agreed ... Do not repeat not know how he proposes to do this and consider chances of success doubtful.[43]

Bernard Martin, a signaller serving with 67 Medium Regiment RA, was one of those immured within the doomed garrison:

> We were stuka'd and bombed continually for two or three days prior to the fall of Tobruk. I had very mixed feelings at the time; it came as a relief because of the incessant bombing and shelling but I also think we could have held out longer, like our predecessors did a year previously, however, I don't think certain people or sections of the army did enough to defend Tobruk.[44]

More fortunate was Captain Owen Bird, an MO serving with one of the South African battalions who, like many others, was determined to escape the net:

> We set off in my desert buggy and had to pass through a patrol gap on the minefield where the sappers had hastily lifted the mines. We got through safely but the ambulance just behind us was blown up. Fortunately nobody was hurt but the ambulance lay across the track and was causing congestion for the vehicles behind, which soon brought down heavy shell fire. We tried dragging the ambulance out of the way but it was firmly in the hole made by the mine blast; all we could do was gingerly lift the mines to the side and make a new track.[45]

With the erstwhile passengers in the wrecked ambulance clinging to the sides, his own overloaded truck managed, after a hair-raising ride, to slip the Axis hounds and reach safety.

Tobruk fell; it was a disastrous defeat. The debacles in Greece and Crete combined had not witnessed such fearful loss. Churchill was in the United States, within the sanctum of the Oval Office, when the dread tidings arrived. Casey had already cabled a warning to Washington but this was a terrible blow, first Singapore and now Tobruk. It is unquestionably true that a lesser man than Churchill would have been broken. There is perhaps no more telling testimony to the Prime Minister's indomitable genius that he emerged still doggedly defiant even from this latest blow. The objective analysis provided by the US military attaché in Cairo, Colonel Bonner L. Fellers, and reported on 20 June, was scarcely complimentary:

> With numerically superior forces, with tanks, planes, artillery, means of transport and reserves of every kind, the British army has twice failed to defeat the Axis forces in Libya. Under the present command and with the measures taken in a hit or miss fashion the granting of 'lend-lease' alone cannot ensure a victory. The Eighth Army has failed to maintain the morale of its troops; its tactical conceptions were always wrong, it neglected completely cooperation between the various arms; its reactions to the lightning changes of the battlefield were always slow.[46]

At the time it would have required a particular shade of optimism to disagree.

6
Mersa Matruh & First El Alamein: June – August 1942

Did you ever see a man bleed in sand? I
Asked him, did you ever see a soldier, a khaki
Hero with his life blood blotting entirely and quickly
Into the khaki sand? Did you ever see a man drown in
Quicksand
Or, let alone a man, a tree or a bedstead?

Patrick Anderson

Excellent as our tactical achievements were in all theatres of war, there was not that solid strategic foundation which would have directed our tactical skill into the right channels.

Rommel, *Krieg ohne Hass* ['War without Hate']

The Auk Takes Personal Command
It might be that 8th Army had taken a fearful pounding, losing heavily in men, vehicles and materiel but morale, if battered, had not collapsed. Dr Theodore Stephanides, Great War veteran and bosom friend of the Durrells, Lawrence and Gerald and a seasoned observer noted:

What impressed me most was the discipline and order which prevailed everywhere. It was almost impossible to believe that this was a hurried and unexpected retreat. Everybody seemed cheerful and in spite of the numbers and speed of the traffic, I did not see a single collision; Military Police were posted at various points to direct and regulate the traffic and everything proceeded as smoothly as clockwork, rather like a crowd leaving a popular race meeting.[1]

On 25 June 1942 General Auchinleck, accompanied by Dorman-Smith, arrived at Ritchie's 8th Army HQ. It was not a social call. The army commander was curtly relieved of his post and Auchinleck, as C in C, assumed direct tactical control of 8th Army. Dorman-Smith – 'Chink' – was to act as an unofficial chief of staff. On the flight from Cairo the two had discussed the current dire position, concluding that the only course open was for a further tactical withdrawal to the El Alamein line 150 miles east of Mersa Matruh, where the army was attempting a stand. Ritchie was apparently stunned at the suddenness of his taking off, yet it was evident he was hopelessly out of his depth:

> General Ritchie had become accustomed to consult the Commander-in-Chief, not because he had not the strength of character to make decisions for himself, but possibly because he continued to think more as a staff officer than as a commander.[2]

In the bitter wake of the catastrophe at Tobruk, Roosevelt had made the generous and important gesture of offering 300 new Sherman tanks with a further 100 105mm self-propelled guns. General Marshall had further proposed sending the US 1st Armoured Division. Such relief was welcome but for Churchill, the bile of humiliation and defeat still rising, this must have smacked of the same condescension shown by Hitler when he first sent succour to his defeated ally. Undeniably the situation of 8th Army was unfortunate:

> British troops in the Western Desert were now the equivalent of three and two thirds infantry divisions weak in artillery; three armoured regiments of which two were partly trained and one was composite; two motor brigades and some armoured car regiments. The New Zealand Division was beginning to arrive at Matruh; thus the force was not suitably composed for a campaign of manoeuvre.[3]

Despite the scale of the recent reverses, 8th Army HQ persisted in a degree of upbeat assessments whose optimistic tone rested on the belief that Rommel, for the moment, was spent and could not maintain his offensive. Given the British deficiency in mobile, armoured forces the policy was one which sought 'to delay the enemy at the frontier ... while withdrawing the main body of 8th Army to the Matruh defences'.[4] 'Chink' had given the assembled war correspondents a bracing and confident briefing on 21 June. If Rommel was not minded to agree then his nominal superiors at Comando Supremo most definitely were.

Colonel Fellers, who had been so scathing of the 8th Army's performance, was unwittingly providing the Axis with valuable information. He was that 'good source' referred to in Ultra decrypts as Italian Military Intelligence had cracked the US diplomatic cipher. Before he returned to the USA, toward the end of July, Fellers had provided them with key intelligence concerning losses in British armour: '… on 10 June there were only 133 tanks of all types in all the depots of the Middle East'.[5] After 25 July, the cipher was changed and this deadly leak sealed but significant damage had been done. In the circumstances, it is difficult to see what other course remained for Auchinleck, other than to take direct command. Ritchie was floundering and 8th Army left in a most parlous state. Brooke maintained his confidence in the 'Auk' and Churchill, who could be as magnanimous as he could be bullying, lent his hearty approval: 'I am so glad you have taken Command. Do not vex yourself with anything but the battle …'[6] 'Chink', whose views on his fellow officers tended to be unflattering, was made to 'writhe' when he learnt of Ritchie's dispositions for the defence of Matruh:

> Correctly both of 8th Army's Corps should have been deployed for battle, shoulder to shoulder, on the open desert south of the northern escarpment, with only a token force in the Matruh defended perimeter. No heed should have been taken of the now previously prepared defensive positions or incomplete minefields. Had this been done and the armour moved from the southern flank into centrally located Army reserve, Rommel's impetuous advance would have met a powerful force in place of a vacuum dividing two strong but uncoordinated wings.[7]

Mersa Matruh

Auchinleck was painfully aware of the political capital invested in the 'last ditch' position at Matruh. He had thus decided to make a stand there while allowing his army the necessary flexibility to fall back toward the El Alamein position, perhaps the worst of both worlds as it implied any withdrawal would literally be under the enemy guns. This obvious difficulty would be compounded by the fact the principal Corps positions were so far apart. Battle was joined on 27 June when 90th Light pushed past the ad hoc 'Leathercol' and 21st Panzer brushed aside 'Gleecol'. The gap between 13 and 20 Corps now yawned with the Littorio Division trailing the German armour and the remainder of Italian XX Corps behind 90th Light Division.

Harold Sell, an officer of 8 DLI which had suffered badly at Gazala, was still in the maelstrom at Mersa Matruh:

> We were all on the escarpment near Mersa Matruh. Enemy patrols were probing around, throwing grenades, with us shooting back at them. That night we were being shot at by German six-wheeled armoured cars. We had just been issued with new six-pounder guns. Nobody knew how to fire them but one of the gun crews decided to stalk an armoured car. They pulled the gun to where they could see the armoured car, opened the breech and focused on the car down the barrel. They quickly put in a round and fired. As it was only 100 yards away they blew it to smithereens.[8]

There was plenty of fight left in 8th Army.

'Pike' was the code for retreat and both were to converge on Minqar Omar which lay some thirty miles east. Gott had already acted but his disengagement soon ran into difficulties. In Matruh, General Holmes was completely out of touch and was even planning a counter-attack. This came to nothing and by 28 June his corps was isolated and encircled. Holmes then planned for breakout. Both 50th and 10th Indian divisions would begin to move after 21.00 hrs and hasten south for thirty miles before swinging eastwards into the vicinity of Fuka. British formations, thrown into brigade groups and moving in columns, endured a dangerous passage. Axis forces were already at Fuka where 21st Panzer had overrun the remnant of 29th Indian Brigade and a series of sharp, confused actions ensued. 10th Indian Division, in particular, suffered considerable casualties.

Prior to Rommel's offensive, supplies had been stockpiled for 'Acrobat' – the onward Allied rush into Tripolitania. Now, the hard-pressed rear echelon units of the RAOC and RASC struggled to salvage or destroy their precious stores in the confusion of defeat. Prodigies of deliverance were indeed effected but, such was the scale and extent of the build-up, that much still fell into Axis hands:

> The route was marked with great dumps of blazing stores. Everything that could not be removed was systematically destroyed. The night was lit by these beacons, until

parts of the road were like a red daylight, with thin, ghostly streams of men and towering shadows of lorries sidling past like phantoms of an inferno.[9]

If the Axis were doing well on the ground, their grasp of the skies was crumbling. Squadrons of Kesselring's planes were being fed into the endless mincer of the Eastern Front while sorties from Malta were exacting an increasing toll. For both sides, to be attacked from the air was a most disagreeable experience:

> During all these trips there were constant attacks by dive-bombers and messerschmitts. These were bad enough when the column was at rest, and you could hear or see them coming. But it was much worse when the first indication you had of an attack was when the lorry in front of you blew up or the bullets smacked through your own windscreen.[10]

The Luftwaffe threat was diminishing at a time when the Desert Air Force was coming into its own, soon to be reinforced by B-24 'Liberator' bombers. Though ground/air communications were still far from perfected, 'Mary' Coningham's squadrons did excellent service.

> For those who die in blood bruise and amazement,
> all pity fails – the anger, the distress,
> calmed or distorted, a dead face; appeasement.
> Remote in the elaborate cage of chess,
> a pencilling on maps, they cross no path;
> honour but find no anguish in that peace
> honour the failing majesty of death.
>
> Terence Tiller [11]

Choosing Ground

The ground south of Alamein is, for the most part featureless, till one reaches the rock-strewn hills that flank the waste of marsh and dune announcing the depression. Even these are no more than 700 feet above sea level but much nearer the sea are the twin eminences, rounded hillocks or 'tells' of which Tell el Eisa and Tell el Makh Khad would prove significant. The terrain is everywhere barren, loose, deepening sand alternating with unyielding rock which emerges in the narrow lateral ridges Miteirya, Ruweisat and Alam el Halfa. These insignificant features would assume considerable importance in the fighting to come and blood would be poured out in torrents to secure them. Once taken such features were heartbreakingly difficult to fortify, horribly exposed. In places the ground dipped into shallow depressions ('deirs'), natural saucers.

Lieutenant Brian (Barney) O'Kelly, serving in Intelligence, first heard of the El Alamein position:

> ... at the end of June [1942] an officer friend at GHQ had asked me if I'd ever heard of El Alamein. I had not. He told me it was the first feasible spot for halting the German advance that we would hold the enemy there and, with the new divisions, armour and material that were on their way we should counter-attack at the full moon late in October.[12]

'Chink' prepared a detailed assessment of the strategic imperatives at this time which, though it offered little guidance to the tactics to be employed in the forthcoming battle at Alamein, established 8th Army's key priorities. Supply was acknowledged to be critical; defence of the Red Sea ports would facilitate rebuilding the army's strength and thus its future mobility. At the same time, increased activity from Malta could damage the Axis. Dorman-Smith recognised that the Desert Air Force was becoming a force to be reckoned with and, for now, 'our only offensive weapon'.[13] Auchinleck's weakness was that he and Dorman-Smith were operating in a kind of vacuum. The army commanders could not readily divine his intent and the Auk did not issue any 'Backs to the Wall' oration and rallying cry. Put simplistically, the side which had the best tanks and in adequate numbers, together with commensurate strength in supporting arms would win. Heroic, if pointless, calls that 'every fit male be made to fight and die for victory'[14] meant nothing. The Italian collapse in the winter of 1940–41 showed that simply deploying large masses of infantry, 'bayonets on the ground' had no place in this most modern of modern wars. Given the circumstances, Auchinleck's reply to Winston's exhortations was the very model of patient diplomacy:

> As to using all my manpower, I hope I am doing this, but infantry cannot win battles in the desert as long as the enemy has superiority in armour, and nothing can be said

or done to change this fact. Guns and armour and just enough infantry to afford them and their supply organisation local protection is what is needed.[15]

Battered, ground down and in no small part bemused, 8th Army was still far from beaten. The Desert Rats were down but not out and their morale, despite such repeated pummellings, did not collapse. This resilience was a disappointment to Egyptian nationalists hoping for signs of cracking. The soldiers as ever found diversion in humour:

One of our sergeants had seen a letter in the *Daily Mirror* asking if someone would be kind enough to send a dartboard to the writers. The signature on the letter was 'Lonely Outpost', and was from a gun-site which the author said was no fewer than three miles from the nearest village and five miles from the nearest public house. Our sergeant collected 10s from us and sent the following letter to the *Daily Mirror* for onward transmission to the 'Lonely Outpost': 'Dear Lonely Outpost – Please find enclosed ten shillings with which to buy a dartboard for you at the "Lonely Outpost". We can appreciate how lonely you must be, three miles from the nearest village and five miles from the nearest pub. We are three hundred miles from the nearest town and five hundred miles from the nearest pub. [Signed] DESERT RATS.'[16]

As ever, the reflective view is provided by the Official History:

Ever since the fall of Tobruk Field Marshal Rommel had been striving to hustle the British and prevent them from forming a front behind which to absorb the land and air reinforcements they were likely to receive. General Auchinleck's object had been to keep the 8th Army in being. Although it had suffered severe losses in men and material and was much disorganised, it was bewildered rather than demoralised. Its framework still existed and the army was certainly capable of further efforts, as events were soon to show. But this did not alter the fact that it was now back in a 'last ditch' position. Rommel was certain to waste no time, no matter how exhausted his troops might be and no matter what they lacked – including the full support of their air force, which was still struggling to make its way forward. The task before the 8th Army and the Desert Air Force was clear; they must at all costs parry the blow that was surely coming.[17]

Battle is Joined

Rommel, on 30 June, was poised for the attack. His limited reconnaissance was soon to be found wanting for he had failed to appreciate the strength of the South Africans dug in around El Alamein. His plan was that both 90th Light and DAK would charge the gap north of Deir el Abyad. While the Light Division would seek to replicate its earlier success in interdicting the coast road and thus isolating the Alamein garrison, DAK would sprint south to swing around behind 13 Corps. As ever the Italian formations were given a subordinate role, one division assaulting Alamein from the west, another behind 90th Light and the remainder trailing the panzers.

Foul conditions delayed the progress of German armour and 90th Light bumped the Alamein defences and suffered under the intense weight of fire the South Africans brought down upon them. DAK found Deir el Shein unexpectedly held by 18th Infantry Brigade and a fierce battle erupted. Despite a very gallant stand, the survivors were forced to surrender by evening on 1 July. The loss of the brigade was yet another blow and an intervention by 1st Armoured Division was so long delayed as to be too late. 90th Light, having extricated itself from this initial contact, sought to resume its headlong dash but intense fire from South African positions descended like a deluge and stopped any advance dead in its tracks.

Hans Schmidt explains Afrika Korps' panzer tactics:

We had now developed a new method of attack. With our twelve anti-tank guns we leapfrogged from one vantage point to another, while our panzers stationary and hull down, if possible, provided protective fire. Then we would establish ourselves to give them protective fire while they swept on again. The tactics worked well, despite the liveliness of the fire, the enemy tanks were not able to hold up our advance. He steadily sustained losses and had to give ground constantly.[18]

Auchinleck had quickly appreciated that Allied outposts were exposed and moved to concentrate his forces. The Kiwis were given a more fluid role, their 6th Brigade pulled from Bab el Qattara with only a column remaining. The Indian Division was likewise to quit Qaret el Himeimat. As Rommel massed to attempt break-through at El Alamein, 30 Corps would hold the line while 13 Corps launched a blow towards Deir el Abyad. Both sides attacked during the afternoon of 2 July. In the north Pienaar's South Africans again resisted the Axis strike, aided by another scratch formation, 'Robcol', drawn from 10th Indian Division. 90th Light was again harassed by the incessant attentions of Desert Air

Force and could make no headway. To the south and west, just beyond Ruweisat Ridge, British and German armour were heavily embroiled. At the end of a hard day's fighting, neither side could claim victory, but the Axis offensive had not progressed.

H. Metcalfe was a veteran tanker at this time. His previous unit having been shot up in the earlier debacles, he served with 4th/8th Hussars, an amalgamation of survivors from both regiments:

> Warnings came of an enemy attack, so it was off to sleep fully dressed except for boots. Five days later, just before midnight, we were alerted [by] heavy gunfire, and we waited for the signal in the sky that would denote a major enemy attack. Red over white over green; it was a major attack; we moved out to battle positions. Through the radio a message: 'There will be no retreat. You die where you stand.' That last bit didn't sound very encouraging.[19]

During the hours of darkness air attacks continued till battle was rejoined on the morning of 3 July. There was yet more heavy fighting south of Ruweisat Ridge. In the south, Freyberg's New Zealanders scored a signal success when they overran the artillery component of Ariete Division, netting a fine haul of prisoners and captured guns. 5th New Zealand Brigade was in action against the Brescia division at El Mreir. By now the Axis formations were severely ground down. Rommel reported his own divisions could only muster 1,000 or 1,200 men apiece and incessant aerial bombardment was playing havoc with already overstretched supply lines. Skirmishing continued throughout 4 July but the main German effort was, for the moment, spent. It had been a failure.

> The early morning light revealed the enemy like a great black snake, its head getting on with the job of getting through the minefields. Now to the business of stopping him. The enemy was already suffering under the combined weight of fire from infantry, tanks and artillery, plus bombing. The enemy were through the minefields, the infantry came back under covering fire from tanks and artillery. The tanks and twenty-five-pounders alongside now took over. Slowly we retreated under the weight of the attack, but it was no walk over for the enemy. Guns and tanks worked together – first one, then the other, retired, exacting a heavy toll. The enemy was moving very slowly; he was in very bad shape.[20]

Auchinleck, sensing the enemy was severely weakened, began to think in terms of turning the stalemate into a rout, proposing to unleash 13 Corps towards the Axis rear but the British armour, probing forward, was held by a scratch gun line. Next he planned a concentrated advance towards Deir el Shein but again this made little headway. SAS and LRDG were active against enemy airfields, destroying some aircraft on the ground. Rommel was in fact preparing to draw off his armour and the exhausted 90th Light leaving Italians to hold the line while the Germans drew breath and replenished. In this at last, the Luftwaffe was able to lend support and the high pitched screaming of Stukas again filled the desert air. Auchinleck, for his part, had now decided his main blow should fall in the north and concentrated his forces accordingly. This neatly foiled an attempt by 21st Panzer to catch the New Zealand Division and the intended Axis blow fell on empty ground.

Von Mellenthin was critical of his commander's performance. He believed any hope of a breakthrough had gone by 1 July and that operations '... were hopelessly prejudiced ... Our one chance was to outmanoeuvre the enemy, but we had actually been drawn into a battle of attrition.' 1st Armoured Division was given an extra day to reorganise, and when the Afrika Korps advanced on 2 July it found the British armour strongly posted on Ruweisat Ridge and quite capable of beating off such attacks as Rommel could muster. The South African positions were strong, and 90th Light never had a chance of breaking through them. The Desert Air Force commanded the battlefield.

Echoes of the fighting rolled across the Middle East. Countess Ranfurly was, at this time (20 July) in Jerusalem:

> ... down between the Quatara Depression and the sea the two great armies face each other. The situation is still pretty dangerous but that we have held on as long as this makes us hopeful; each day we expect to hear that the battle has begun again.[21]

Auchinleck Takes the Offensive

Having rightly judged the foe to be exhausted, Auchinleck began a series of counter-strokes, the first of which involved 30 Corps in an attempt to seize the rocky knolls of Tel el Eisa and Tel el Makh Khad. Possession of these would facilitate further moves southwards toward Deir el Shein and raids westwards against Axis airfields; 13 Corps was to prevent any enemy reinforcement northwards and be ready to exploit opportunities. On 3 July, Morshead's 9th Australian Division had returned to the line and was now tasked with taking Tel el Eisa while the South Africans stormed Tel el Makh Khad. Both had armoured support and the attack at first light on 10 July was preceded by a 'hurricane bombardment'. Both formations made good progress, taking many Italians prisoner.

Maurice Trigger, aptly named, was serving in the 2/2nd MG Battalion:

> On the way through we were full of death and glory at the thought of going into action, having a wonderful time hanging on the back of the trucks. Then three trucks in front of us hit a landmine. I remember the yelling and screaming of the fellows after the explosion died down, like dogs yelping. Our death and glory attitude deflated like a bloody airship hit by a bullet; we were seeing what could happen and everyone was quite subdued after that.[22]

Von Mellenthin, in charge of HQ while Rommel was absent and located only a few miles up the coast, collected a makeshift battlegroup and held the line while the Desert Fox brought up more reinforcements from 15th Panzer. A late counter-attack made some progress but was seen off. The following day the Australians attacked again in a further attempt to secure the entirety of their objective. Fighting on the ground was matched by the fury of combat in the air, skies crossed with trails and bruised by the chatter of guns, Allied fighters duelling with Axis. For the next three days Rommel sought to recover lost ground and eliminate the newly formed salient but his attacks were repulsed and efforts to drive a wedge between the hills and the Alamein box were equally abortive. The initiative now lay with 8th Army.

Major Charles Finlay on the staff of 26th Brigade watched the Axis counter-attacks develop:

> At one stage on 12 July they sent the whole of the 90th Light Division into the attack. Brigadier Ramsay, the Commander Royal Artillery of the 9th Division, was given the artillery of the two divisions south of him to go to work on the Germans. They really tore into them. I think they lost twenty-two tanks in that afternoon. The Germans always used to attack then, out of the setting sun; it was very hard to see them in the desert. The German tanks had to keep going to avoid the shellfire, whereas the infantry in the personnel carriers were being blown to pieces. The infantry became

1. Battalion HQ in an old Roman tomb. Bunks are rigged in the coffin niches.

2. An armoured car passes through the 400-mile-long barrier of Italian wire which was the first obstacle to British patrols.

Above: 3. Hurricanes throw dust-clouds behind them as they take off from the desert.

Below: 4. Blenheim bombers, escorted by their own winged shadows, leave to harass the enemy.

5. British troops ready for the final assault on Bardia.

6. A British howitzer opens the attack at Bardia.

7. British troops attack at Bardia.

Above left: 8. Gun and gun crew rest in the desert, sheltered from dust and cold.
Above right: 9. A machine-gun crew in action before Derna, part of the fight of Beda Fomm.

10. The British long-range patrols spent weeks at a stretch in a wilderness almost empty of life.

11. The British long-range patrols consisted of small but extremely mobile motor columns, capable of travelling, entirely self-contained, with no help for casualties to men or machines, for 2,000 miles or more.

12. The radio operator links the heart of the desert with GHQ and the outside world.

13. The patrols travel by the sun and stars over vast areas of unmapped territory.

14. Australian troops.

15. New Zealand troops.

16. Free French soldier.

17. Casualty of war.

18. Firepower – the formidable
British 25-pounder in action.

19. The formidable Mark IV Special with a long 75 mm gun.

20. The end for one Mark III Panzer.

21. Australians move up purposefully.

22. Crusader tanks, unreliable, under-gunned and under-armoured.

23. A break in the business of war.

24. The tank kills.

25. The enemy – beaten but not cowed.

26. The 'Auk'.

27. Field Marshal Montgomery.

28. The Desert Fox.

29. 'Balaklavering'.

30. Carriers – often the unsung heroes and universal workhorse.

31. Battered survivor.

Above: 32. Ready for the Luftwaffe.
Right: 33. Wavell, the architect of 'Compass'.

34. On patrol.

35. Several 'acres' of Italian POWs.

36. The ubiquitous Willys Jeep in action.

37. Mobility and speed. British armoured cars in action.

38. Mortar team in action.

39. Kiwis prepare.

separated from their tanks and when they arrived at their objectives there was no infantry support; this set the Germans back on their heels pretty solidly.[23]

Another Aussie machine-gunner, Corporal Victor Knight won the DCM for his gallantry in seeing the Axis attackers off:

> They put in another attack with tanks, after blasting us with shells and bombs and Stukas which really bashed up our side of the hill. I brought the lads up and started to fire at them. Then one of my boys, Jimmy Nimmo – who'd been over the hill to pick up ammunition – said, 'Hey Vic, they're coming in from the other side.' So I scrambled up the hill and saw tanks and infantry coming in at the rear. I grabbed the blokes and took the guns over the other side – there was no cover – and began firing at the advancing Germans for about three hours. We had to urinate on the barrels to keep them cool enough to keep firing. We had oil available and we simply poured it from a four gallon drum into the working parts, keeping the guns firing all the time.[24]

The fight continued to rage as the Axis worked their way closer to the extent that Corporal Knight was anticipating recourse to the bayonet. By the end of this hard fought action, with the Germans seen off, he reckoned their casualties at some 600.

Having got the Axis off-balance, Auchinleck decided to maintain pressure by striking southwards against the long, lateral finger of Ruweisat Ridge. This otherwise unprepossessing feature would witness hard fighting through 14–15 July, and again on the 21st. The task of securing the western flank of the ridge was given to 13 Corps while 30 Corps was to take the eastern extremity and also strike southwards from this newly created salient to take the hump of Miteirya Ridge. This was to be a night attack and 13 Corps would send in two brigades of New Zealanders while 30 Corps deployed 5th Indian Brigade (from 5th Indian Division). Crucial armoured support for the Kiwis was to be provided by 1st Armoured Division which would come up after first light – both Corps were to be on their objectives by 04.30 hrs. To reach their target the New Zealanders had to cover some six miles of ground in the dark. The attack, even once the enemy was alerted, was driven home with great élan but, in the smoke and dust of a moonlit battle, many enemy posts were left un-subdued. Some units became scattered and digging into the unyielding rock proved near impossible. Supporting arms, a few vital anti-tanks guns, were got up but much had not arrived. The remaining infantry sought to consolidate and, above all, dig in.

> The click of a rifle bolt sounded a few yards in front. It acted like a signal. The patrol
> hurled grenades and attacked. One of our corporals was killed as he stood up, and a
> private was shot in the foot; the remainder rushed in, passed a machine gun post and
> found a German shamming dead.[25]

30 Corps' attack met with stiff resistance and there was some disorder; supporting armour was still distant. Italian defenders from Brescia and Pavia Divisions had been caught off-guard and numbers of them bolted to rear. A passing column of German tanks fell upon the NZ 22nd Battalion, swiftly dealt with the AT guns exposed on their portees and compelled several hundred survivors to capitulate. Efforts were made to get the British armour mobile, and tanks were able to support a renewed assault by 5th Indian Brigade which partially succeeded in securing objectives on the ridge. Efforts to bring up supporting arms were frustrated by fire from enemy posts missed in the first rush. Only with the aid of a barrage were the reserve units able to begin filtering through.

With hindsight the Auk had done remarkably well considering the disadvantages under which he laboured and the blueprint for eventual victory had already been laid down. Some time earlier in writing to the CIGS he had referred to the matter of his own future as C in C:

> Personally I feel fit to carry on and reasonably confident of being able to turn the tables
> on the enemy in time. All the same there is no doubt that in a situation like the present,
> fresh blood and new ideas at the top may make all the difference between success and
> stalemate.[26]

With the Italians in disarray, Rommel had to assemble German units for the inevitable counter-attack, command of which was entrusted to Nehring. 4th New Zealand Brigade, with little or no support, was eventually overwhelmed and the western end of the ridge lost. Next day, 16 July, the Germans attempted to drive off 5th Indian Brigade, who repulsed this and a subsequent attack. On the 17th Australian troops attacked southwards towards Miteirya Ridge, taking hundreds of Italian prisoners but were halted by heavy shelling and a German counterstroke. In these actions, the New Zealand Division had fought hard and well but at considerable cost. They had stormed and taken their objectives but felt badly let down by their comrades in armour whom they blamed for leaving them so desperately exposed.

Back in Jerusalem, on 16 July, Countess Ranfurly had been doing a little combat training of her own:

This evening 'Abercrombie' lent me his 'Silver Lady', a special Smith and Wesson with a light trigger. It is perfectly balanced. 'There are twenty-five dummies in the chain of cellars below us,' he said, pointing with his thumb at the floor. 'They are hidden all over the place. Go ahead and don't forget to reload. At the bottom of the steps I opened a door as he had taught me: with my gun arm against the door itself. I saw three dummies and fired. Another ran across the room on a wire and then another sat up on a bed in the corner. They were hidden in every conceivable place, behind the doors and pillars. They jerked down from the ceiling on strings. Once I forgot to reload before entering a new room. 'You bloody fool,' growled a voice behind me. 'You deserve to be dead.' When I had finished we counted the bullet holes. I had hit seventeen out of twenty-five dummies. Then we went through it again with a tommy gun; the noise was terrific.[27]

The Auk now felt a further heavy blow in the centre might shatter them altogether. Overall, the Allied position was considerably better. Both the Australians and South Africans were in good shape, though the 5th Indian and New Zealand Divisions were reduced to a mere two brigades each. 1st and 7th Armoured Divisions, the latter being developed as a mixed battle-group, were in strength. 7th Armoured had a hefty contingent of over sixty Grants in addition to Crusaders and Honeys. 161st Indian Motor Brigade and 23rd Armoured Brigade were arriving to swell the muster. The British might have initially lagged behind the Germans in developing the ability to recover damaged machines under battlefield conditions but this was changing:

There is one magnificent story of one REME recovery section who were ordered 'under pain of death' to get right up with the forward troops during the night, and be ready to recover casualties when hell broke out next morning. The section did as ordered, and when dawn broke both the enemy troops and our own troops looked from their positions to see the REME section plumb in the centre of no-man's-land! it got back safely, too.[28]

For this fresh attack the main impetus fell on 13 Corps, to fracture the Axis at Deir el Shein and Deir el Abyad then drive west. A feint would be launched in the south and 30 Corps would ensure vigorous local action in its sector to keep enemy forces there tied down. Gapping the minefields was entrusted to the infantry, though both brigades were relatively inexperienced in this most difficult of tasks. Gott's plan appeared sound but a key assumption was that the minefields could be detected and gapped in time to allow 23rd Armoured Brigade, whose role was to charge forward to the further objective, to pass through. Despite the weight of artillery brought to bear, the New Zealand attack came to bear a sad resemblance to that earlier tragedy. The infantry managed, in a night attack, to gain their objectives but were left dispersed and without essential fire support. At first light Axis armour struck back, easily eliminating the few AT guns available; the denouement was inevitable. Infantry were overrun, artillery communications broke down and the brigade suffered some 700 casualties. 2nd Armoured did attempt relief but was stopped by a mix of un-cleared mines and Axis fire.

161st Indian Motor Brigade's attack 'also experienced varying fortunes'. After hard fighting, the assault battalions were either short of their objectives or driven off by vigorous counter-attacks. Only when the reserve battalion was thrown in did the attack make headway. Major-General A. H. Gatehouse was now in command of 1st Armoured Division, as Lumsden had been wounded earlier. He was doubtful over committing 23rd Armoured Brigade when it became clear the mines had not all been cleared and a viable gap had not been created. Gott would not countenance calling off this part of the plan, however, as he believed the enemy to be significantly wrong-footed. He therefore proposed that the line of advance should shift southwards to cross an area believed, or rather hoped, to be free of Axis mines.

Two tank regiments were sent in. Both were heavily shelled and struck a host of unexpected mines covering their supposedly clear approaches. Serious loss was incurred before the objective was reached and then the survivors were furiously attacked. When 21st Panzer was thrown into the fight, the battered remnants withdrew, leaving forty tanks wrecked and more badly damaged. An attempt by 2nd Armoured Brigade to get through to the New Zealanders isolated in the El Mreir Depression foundered in the face of intense fire, a further twenty-one tanks were lost in the broil. Another night action, on 22 July, again launched by 5th Indian Division, aimed at finally securing the deadly Point 63 on Ruweisat Ridge, failed after a gallant and costly attempt. The infantryman's frustration with his seemingly Olympian comrades in armour was largely based on ignorance of the tactical role and capabilities of Allied tanks. Observers like Robert Crawford who, as part of the logistical chain, could exercise a degree of understanding and objectivity were considerable less jaundiced:

> Their normal day in the forward area began before dawn, when they rose in time to get the tanks out of laager and deployed before daylight. No hot meal could be made, because all lights and fires were forbidden during the hours of darkness, while the tanks were in laager ... The tanks moved out just before dawn, and spent the remainder of the hours of daylight deployed. If things were quiet, they prepared a hot meal at their battle station. But this was unusual rather than normal ... When tank combats took place, our tank crews would watch the German tanks being refuelled and restocked with ammunition, behind a screen of anti-tank guns. Our tanks were impotent to do anything about this, as the anti-tank guns had them outranged ... After the German tanks were ready, battle would be joined. Normally, it was a case of the German tanks trying to plaster our under-gunned tanks from beyond the effective range of our tank guns; we, for our part, tried to use our greater powers of manoeuvre by darting in and out, firing as we went.[29]

On 30 Corps' front, 22 July, the Australians again attacked. Fighting centred as before on the twin eminences of Tel el Eisa and Tel el Makh Khad. Early gains prompted a savage riposte and the Australians battled hard to hold ground won. Though they had some armoured support from 50th RTR, equipped with Valentines, liaison between the two arms was again patchy and twenty-three machines were knocked out for paltry return. Despite these costly reverses, Auchinleck was not yet ready to concede a stalemate, persisting in the belief the Axis were on the cusp of disintegration. This time, on 26 July, an attempt was to be launched by 30 Corps, beefed up with additional armour and infantry, to advance through the gap between Miteirya Ridge and Deir el Dhib. For its part 13 Corps, battered by previous exertions, would mount a convincing, full-scale diversion to the south.

To the South Africans fell the task of gapping the enemy's minefields south-east of the ridge. By 01.00 hrs the Australians were to have seized the eastern flank and then advance north and west. An infantry brigade would pass through the gaps to Deir el Dhib, gapping any further minefields encountered. Then it would be the turn of the armour to strike westwards. Some initial success was soon shrouded in a mist of confusion. The armour did not come up and, once again, the attacking infantry were left vulnerable, an opportunity the Germans never failed to exploit. 6th DLI and 5th East Yorks were overrun, as latterly were the survivors of 2/28th Australian battalion. As before, heavy fire prevented supporting arms from getting through, armoured support was ineffective and costly.

> For here the lover and killer are mingled
> who had one body and one heart.
> And death who had the soldier singled
> has done the lover mortal hurt.

Keith Douglas[30]

Stalemate
Major Peter Clegg MC went through First El Alamein:

> You will know that the first battle of Alamein was all important; if it had not been won the later battle could not have taken place and the wealth of arms and ammunition being stockpiled in readiness for it would have fallen into enemy hands and enabled the Axis forces to have swept through the whole of the Middle East.[31]

Fresh raids by LRDG/SAS accounted for further enemy aircraft and Desert Air Force continued to bomb Axis positions without respite. Though these Special Forces actions were, in relative terms, mere pinpricks they did reduce the numbers of Axis aircraft and forced Rommel to divert resources into defending his airfields. Besides, this was precisely the type of Henty-esque derring-do the Prime Minister adored. Not only Churchill was impressed. Soldiers of 8th Army were not immune from the charisma of these fabled desert warriors:

> Of course, the super-saboteurs were our long range desert patrols. These were the super 'Desert Rats'. Stories were legion about their exploits ... No men were braver or fitter than those in these groups. Occasionally we actually saw them move out into 'the blue', but mostly they were as legendary as Lawrence of Arabia. They stayed out behind enemy lines for months at a time ... They were led by men of unrivalled knowledge of the Desert, and did untold material damage to German supplies, but their main contribution was in boosting our morale and lowering the German morale correspondingly; whenever news came round their exploits, our tails went up like anything.[32]

By the end of July both sides were played out, swaying like punch-drunk fighters. Generals on both sides had demanded great sacrifices from their men and these had been freely made. Driver Crawford of the RASC, who witnessed the 'tankies' in action was again more even-handed, even admiring in his assessment:

> In the earlier days they were outgunned time after time, but nothing could keep down their irrepressible spirits. How they fought in their 'cooking boxes' for hours on end I do not know. They would return from a foray wearing nothing but shorts, sun-tanned and begrimed, and looking like men from another world.[33]

As the front lines hardened, great belts of mines girded extensive positions and impeded any amount of free movement. Some writers have likened the process to the stalemate of trench warfare in the previous conflagration. It remained to be seen who might break the deadlock. Rommel had described the desert fighting as war without hate, and 8th Army observed its prisoners to be:

> … a curious mixture of arrogance, belief in Hitler and surprise that the British had ever gone to war with them; they openly boasted that they were the finest soldiers in the world, and then added that the British were easily second best.[34]

The Germans were sometimes less punctilious toward Imperial troops who might not conform to their notions of racial superiority. Driver Crawford again:

> The enemy, having captured a Ghurka, shaved him and sent him back to the Ghurka lines. Shaving is, of course, against the Ghurka religion and is considered one of the greatest shames which can befall them. After telling his comrades what had happened, the Ghurka is alleged to have committed suicide. For the whole of that day the British officers were only just able to restrain the Ghurkas from going out to the enemy. The British officers cajoled and finally threatened the Ghurkas with all kinds of punishment … When night came the Ghurkas lines emptied as though by the wave of a wand, and nothing was heard for some minutes. Then a great hullabaloo took place in the enemy lines, and the Ghurkas stole quietly back to their old positions. It was never known how many of the enemy died that night …[35]

7

Alam Halfa:
August – September 1942

Here with the desert so austere that only
Flags live, plant out your flags upon the wind,
Red tattered bannerets that mark a lonely
Grave in the sand.

R. N. Currey[1]

Swansong for a Rare Bird

Observers now wondered of Auchinleck: 'Has he anything left to offer?'[2] Both he and Dorman-Smith were painfully aware the 8th Army was not placed to deliver a decisive blow. Though Rommel had been halted this was only a check and not a reverse. Allied efforts to assume the offensive in July had been, at best, disappointing. Auchinleck's appreciation of 1 August, while conceding that major offensive operations were, for the moment, out of the question, provided that both army corps would undertake vigorous raiding, involving land, sea and air resources, utilising the buccaneering talents of the LRDG and SAS. Such an active defence would disrupt Rommel's fragile supply lines and prepare for the day, probably not before mid-September, when a serious blow could be delivered. General Gott prepared a further appreciation, focused on the need to counter an Axis offensive which was feared for August. He identified the high ground of Alam Halfa Ridge as 'vital for any advance down the Coast to Alexandria – they [Alam Halfa and Gebel Bein Gabir] are also vital to us for holding our present positions'.[3] Gott, in fact, correctly anticipated Rommel's subsequent plan:

An attack with Alam el Halfa as his first objective, going round anywhere south of the Alam Nyal ridge – subsequently cutting the road in the Hamman area and thrusting straight for Alexandria.[4]

Gott made full use of Ultra intercepts to assess Rommel's likely strength and Auchinleck left the detailed working up of Dorman-Smith's broad-brush appreciation to him. In concept, Alam Halfa was Gott's battle.

Auchinleck, when penning his own further appreciation a day later than the first, took all of his subordinates thinking into account. In essence, the plan for the forthcoming offensive comprised the following elements:

1. A major blow in the north.
2. Diversionary activity and phoney preparations to the south.
3. Disruption of enemy supply and communications.
4. To create a defended zone behind the main El Alamein line to defeat any Axis thrust from the south.
5. To ensure armoured forces were fully prepared to exploit any breakthrough(s).

This was to prove Auchinleck's legacy. Far from being washed up he had, with his subordinates, produced the blueprint for final victory in the Western Desert, even though full credit has traditionally gone to his successor. The lessons of Gazala were plain. A series of isolated brigade boxes with little capacity for mutual support and a lack of defence in depth had provided Rommel with a perfect target. Breadth and depth were the keys to fresh planning. In the north, from Alam Nayil to the coast, a dense fortified zone was to be prepared. Far thinner defences were employed further south to provide Rommel with the necessary incentive. These minefields would merely delay rather than frustrate. Two brigades from 7th Armoured Division, 4th Light Armoured and 7th Motorised were deployed as a screen. Their designated task was essentially to impose delay, to avoid being drawn into a battle of annihilation and lead the enemy on toward their own nemesis.

Auchinleck had never been able to develop an easy and clear understanding with his subordinates. Dorman-Smith, for all his undoubted abilities, was more a part of the problem. The instructions given to 30 Corps appeared ambiguous: was 8th Army defending or attacking? To the Australians the idea of thinning out their positions in the Tel el Eisa salient did not appeal at all. Morshead would be pushed into explaining reasons he did not himself understand as to why his officers and men should give up such hard-won ground. Gott had no such qualms and proposed the New Zealanders would hold Alam Halfa. Inglis could certainly see the logic but was unhappy in the detail, feeling the two brigade-sized boxes were vulnerable. Gott in turn accepted the validity of these concerns and, importantly, there was time for Inglis and Brigadier 'Pip' Roberts commanding 22nd Armoured Brigade to fully confer and develop a better understanding. 8th Army thus prepared for Rommel, had not, however, prepared for Churchill.

On 3 August, Churchill had left England bound for Cairo. He was not alone; Brooke, Wavell and Field Marshal Smuts were to join him. Though the Prime Minister had suffered immense frustrations over seemingly endless delays and disappointments, he had always been impressed by Auchinleck's many qualities and soldierly bearing. Nonetheless in the words of the OH:

> Mr Churchill and the C.I.G.S. now carried out a brisk programme of interviews and inspections in Cairo and the Western Desert. They met many senior army and air officers, including in particular General Gott, and visited the Australian and South African Divisions. On 6th August Mr. Churchill discussed his impressions with General Smuts, Mr. Casey and General Brooke. He concluded, and his advisors agreed, that a drastic and immediate change should be made to impart a new and vigorous impulse to the Army and restore confidence in the High Command.[5]

Whatever his limitations, Auchinleck shouldered an immense burden from which he had never flinched. He may not have defeated Rommel but he had stopped him dead in his tracks. He now recognised the need for a fresh pair of hands and favoured Gott. He opined that the officer appointed to command 8th Army must be:

> ... a man of vigour and personality and have a most flexible and receptive mind; he must also be young, at any rate in mind and body, and be prepared to take advice and learn unless he has had previous Western Desert experience.[6]

The 'chill' as Dorman-Smith described the atmosphere[7] could clearly be felt when the Prime Minister arrived at Desert HQ; the Auk had no gift for courtly diplomacy. The interview which followed in the stuffy, fly-laden heat of the operations room was not a happy one. Dorman-Smith felt he and Auchinleck were alone with a 'caged gorilla'.[8] Progressing to 13 Corps the Prime Minister fastened on Gott and spent some time alone with him, forming a favourable impression. Gott's excellent fighting record, high personal courage and soldierly manner impressed Churchill at a time when he was clearly utterly disenchanted with the pairing of Auchinleck and Dorman-Smith. The mere fact the Auk, like Brooke, favoured Montgomery probably helped the PM decide upon Gott as new 8th Army commander.

For Auchinleck, the die was cast and he was to be replaced by Alexander, an excellent choice, a general who was imbued with an innate flair for difficult diplomacy. Churchill expected his new C in C to lead the onslaught against the Axis personally and proposed to hive off the 'northern' Iraq/Iran sector, leaving the C in C Middle East better placed to concentrate his energies in the Western Desert. Dorman-Smith and others who Churchill saw as tainted with the Auk's brush were to be cleared out. On 7 August Gott carried out his final briefing as a corps commander, ensuring his officers in 13 Corps knew exactly what was expected of them in the coming battle.

Gott then prepared to fly to Cairo, hoping for a few days' leave before taking up the command he would never exercise. Random fate relegated Gott to one of history's tantalising 'what ifs'. His plane crashed and he was killed.[9]

Alexander's instructions were plain and as set out in a directive on 10 August:

> Your prime and main duty will be to take or destroy at the earliest opportunity the German-Italian Army commanded by Field Marshal Rommel together with all its supplies and establishments in Egypt and Libya.
>
> You will discharge or cause to be discharged such other duties as pertain to your Command without prejudice to the task described in paragraph 1 which must be considered paramount in His Majesty's interest.

A New Broom

Monty was nevertheless very much the new broom. Unlike his predecessor he was very much part of the UK military establishment and knew which officers he wanted – men who he already knew. He was not shy over getting rid of those who did not fit the bill. Alexander had made it plain that there would be no further retreats and that established divisional formations would stay as they were. Both of these pronouncements produced collective sighs of relief. Morale was not low but it was obfuscated by uncertainty. This would now disappear:

> General Montgomery ... set to work at once to inspire confidence and enthusiasm in his Army. His address to the officers of Army headquarters made a tremendous impact, of which word soon spread. The defence of Egypt lay at El Alamein, he said, and if the 8th Army could not stay there alive it would stay there dead. There would be no more backward looks.[10]

One of Monty's most remarkable and admirable traits was the air of absolute confidence he exuded, regardless of circumstance. Here was a commander who knew his business inside out, who had an almost Cromwellian faith in himself and his men. In a whirlwind tour of the troops Monty cleared away the fustian and made plain his intentions. If Rommel attacked, 8th Army was ready. When that battle was won, another and offensive engagement would follow and this time the Allies would 'hit Rommel and his army for six right out of Africa'.[11] When Monty said it, people believed him.

> I introduced myself to them [HQ staff] and said I wanted to see them and explain things. Certain orders had already been issued which they knew about, and more would follow. The order 'no withdrawal' involved a complete change of policy and they must understand what that policy was, because they would have to do the detailed staff work involved. If we were to fight where we stood the defences must have depth; all transport must be sent back to rear areas; ammunition, water, rations etc. must be stored in the forward areas. We needed more troops in the Eighth Army in order to make the 'no withdrawal' order a possibility. There were plenty of troops back in the Delta, preparing the defence of that area; but the defence of the cities of Egypt must be fought out here at El Alamein.[12]

With Gott's death a new corps commander was needed and Monty drafted in Lieutenant-General Brian Horrocks with whom he had previously worked while leading South-East Command.

He had in fact given significant thought to the coming 'modern' defensive battle. He had also decided to retain de Guingand, whom he knew well, in place. A wise choice as the chief of staff possessed a flair for diplomacy which his commander most certainly did not:

I had pondered deeply over what I had heard about armoured battles in the desert and it seemed to me that what Rommel liked was to get our armour to attack him; he then disposed of his own armour behind a screen of anti-tank guns, knocked out our tanks and finally had the field to himself. I was determined that would not happen if Rommel decided to attack us before we were ready to launch a full-scale offensive against him. I would not allow our tanks to rush out at him; we would stand firm in the Alamein position, hold the Ruweisat and Alam Halfa Ridges securely, and let him beat up against them. We would fight a static battle and my forces would not move; his tanks would come up against our tanks dug-in in hull down positions at the western end of the Alam Halfa Ridge.[13]

Montgomery was scathing about his predecessor; graciousness was not among his virtues. He tended to be fiercely even cruelly intolerant of others' perceived failures and remarkably silent as to their qualities:

Gross mismanagement, faulty command and bad staff work had been the cause of the whole thing. But the final blame must rest on General Auchinleck for allowing an inexperienced general like Ritchie to mishandle grossly a fine fighting army, and for allowing a policy of dispersion to rule.[14]

He was hardly less critical of the present officer cadre in general:

I was watching the training very carefully, and it was becoming apparent that the Eighth Army was very untrained. The need for training had never been stressed; consequently no one ever did any training, most of the officers had come to the fore by skill in battle and because there was no one any better who could be promoted; these officers were not skilled trainers.[15]

As part of his new broom approach Montgomery proposed to concentrate the whole HQ function at Burg el Arab and promote closer liaison with the Desert Air Force. This had rather slipped during the course of the recent fighting:

Now the two Services were to work in double harness, and, as will be seen, in their first big test – at Alam el Halfa – their mutual confidence was to be renewed in an unmistakable manner.[16]

As Gott had predicted, the blow would fall in the south, a lightning rush through the moonlit dark of the empty desert, sweeping for nearly thirty miles, past the bastion of Alam Halfa to expose 8th Army rear areas – this to be achieved by dawn and ambitious in the extreme. Rommel's right would be covered by his German and Italian mobile formations while Ariete and Littorio Divisions (Italian XX Corps), both armoured, moved on the left. 90th Light, which had been out of the line to recuperate would take the northern shoulder of the assault.

Surprise, speed and guaranteed mobility were the harbingers of success. Build-up would be accomplished in the hours of darkness with panzers hidden beneath camouflage during daylight. To keep 8th Army guessing the Italian forces in 30 Corps' sector would mount diversionary raids. This was, of course, precisely what Auchinleck and now Montgomery had been expecting:

> I decided to hold the Alam Halfa Ridge strongly with the 44th Division and to locate my tanks just south of its western end. Once I was sure that the enemy main thrust was being directed against the Alam Halfa Ridge, I planned to move the armour to the area between the west of the ridge and the New Zealand positions in the main Alamein line. I was so sure that the movement of my own armour would take place that I ordered it to be actually rehearsed; and when it did take place on the morning of 1st September I had some 400 tanks in position, dug in, and deployed behind a screen of 6-pounder anti-tank guns. The strictest orders were issued that that the armour was not to be loosed against Rommel's forces; it was not to move; the enemy was to be allowed to beat up against it and to suffer heavy casualties.[17]

Alam Halfa was, as both sides saw, the key. If Rommel could get safely past, his offensive stood a very good chance of achieving success. If he could not, if the Allies remained in possession, then his position would become untenable. The ridge completely dominated his lines of communication. Defences at Alam Halfa were beefed up accordingly and the newly arrived 44th Division was brought up with two brigades 131st and 133rd deployed, supported by divisional artillery, both field and anti-tank. 22nd Armoured Brigade was massed at the western end. Alam Nayil was garrisoned by Freyberg's New Zealanders together with 132nd Brigade. Behind, to the north, stood 30 Corps reserve formation, in the shape of 23rd Armoured Brigade. Eastwards, toward Point 87, was stationed 8th Armoured Brigade. Further south the deployment of 4th Light Armoured and 7th Motor Brigade had already taken place. As described above, their role was to delay rather than engage; 7th

Armoured Division would snap at the flank and heel of any eastward attack. The noose was laid. It merely remained for the Fox to obligingly extend his neck.

> The turned-back left flank of the New Zealand Division formed a stiff shoulder which could remain in place without the support of the relatively weak 7th Armoured Division to the south. In rear of the New Zealand Division's position was the Alam el Halfa Ridge, originally chosen by General Auchinleck to be a defended locality, and now strongly fortified and held by the 44th Division. General Horrocks's plan was for the New Zealand and 44th Division to hold their ground to the last, while in the south the 7th Armoured Division, on its wide front, was to delay and harass the enemy as much as possible. It was so likely that the enemy would try to seize the Alam el Halfa Ridge that the 22nd Armoured Brigade was placed in dug-in positions at the western end, where the fire of its tanks and the 6-pdr anti-tank guns of its motor battalion could be united with that of the supporting artillery in a strong defensive fire plan.[18]

The Battle of Alam Halfa

As ever, Rommel's prime concern was petrol. Insufficient supplies could be found to enable the attack to proceed on 26 August. Kesselring promised to release some 1,500 tons from his Luftwaffe stocks and the Italians promised more, their ships due to reach North Africa on 30 August. Consumption had been greatly in excess of the amounts arriving by sea, and stocks of all kinds – particularly fuel and ammunition – were running dangerously low. Rommel reported on the 22nd that, if the Panzerarmee was to attack at the end of August, shipments of about 6,000 tons of fuel and 2,500 tons of ammunition must reach Libya by specified dates between 25 and 30 August. Comando Supremo promised to do everything possible, and sent seven ships, carrying 10,000 tons of fuel, half for the Panzerarmee and half aviation spirit for the Luftwaffe. In the event four of the seven ships were sunk. Despite these depressing shortfalls Rommel could not afford to wait, the offensive would begin on 30 August regardless.

This then was be the date fixed for the attack and everything would hinge upon whether the initial objectives were gained during the night of 30/31 August: '… the DAK had seven hours in which to go thirty miles and be ready to advance again to the attack'.[19] As the tanks rumbled forwards in the light cloak of desert night they blundered into unseen British minefields of substantial depth. As pioneers moved forward to begin gapping, a storm of fire descended. Desert Air Force swooped and added a deluge of bombs. The two British harassing formations performed their roles perfectly. When the harsh glow of dawn spread over the bare landscape DAK was still far to the west of its initial objectives. Any element of surprise was now lost. Speed and élan would give way to attrition.

Sir Edward Boulton, Baronet served with Intelligence, attached to 30 Corps:

> I went through both the battle of El Halfa and that of Alamein as GIII Intelligence to
> 10th Armoured Division. In the former we were dug in at El Halfa giving the enemy the
> choice of going straight through to Alexandria, in which case we could have cut off their
> supply column or to attack our dug in tanks, which in fact they did. One German tank
> succeeded in getting up a narrow wadi to the perimeter within twenty yards of my ACV
> and we had to move off at speed with the canvas flaps flying at both sides.[20]

For the Desert Fox there was no good news. Two of his experienced senior officers were down, von Bismarck, commanding 21st Panzer had been killed by a mine and Nehring wounded by bomb blast. Bayerlein assumed temporary command of DAK as the drive eastwards struggled to gain momentum. Even at this early stage Rommel contemplated calling a halt but instead modified his plan of attack. Now, the panzers would not seek to pass to the east of Alam Halfa but turn north, aiming for Point 132 on the line of the ridge while the Italians made for Point 102 at Alam Bueit. If a breakthrough could be achieved then the Axis forces could continue their drive to the coast passing the eastern edge of Ruweisat Ridge. At this time however, say noon on the 31st, both Ariete and Littorio were still held in the minefields and 90th Light halted around Deir el Munassib. It was time to tighten the noose.

As Colonel Green observed, the ability of troops to rise to every fresh challenge was dictated by their physical state at the time:

> We spoke about fatigue. The distance between fear and courage is narrow. If you are fit,
> wide awake and on the ball things do not seem too bad; if you are exhausted and down,
> then nothing seems possible – just let it all end for God's sake.[21]

Monty now sent 23rd Armoured Brigade to cover the gap between the New Zealanders and 22nd Armoured. This was just the type of battle he had intended to fight, his armour hull down and in strength with the Axis doing the 'balaklavering'. Both German tank divisions now barged into this strong defence and an intense battle raged all afternoon: 'A fierce duel began in which the Royal Scots Greys, the 1st and 104th Regiments RHA, and part of the 44th Divisional Artillery joined to give the enemy tanks a hot reception.'[22] The British would not be lured from their positions and the battering cost Rommel dearly. As darkness again fell the panzers withdrew. Overall, they had achieved nothing.

Night brought no relief from prowling bombers that hammered the exposed attackers, seeking out transport and supply. The milky dark suddenly livened by the incandescent drop of flares, laying bare the bones of the desert floor, throwing vehicles into stark relief:

A most important factor which forced his [Rommel's] eventual withdrawal was the action of the Desert Air Force ... Army and Air Force worked on one plan, closely knitted together ... A major factor in the overall air plan was Tedder's decision to send his Wellingtons to bomb Tobruk behind Rommel's attack, in that his last quick hope of re-supply vanished.[23]

On 1 September, 15th Panzer attempted to outflank 22nd Armoured Brigade but found its advance barred by 8th Armoured Brigade. Other Axis armoured formations scarcely moved, the Italians still mired in mines. Trieste and 90th Light, further north, managed some limited gains, insufficient to affect the outcome. It was now stalemate; as darkness fell Desert Air Force began its nightly ministrations:

A night of continuous bombing left a pall of smoke from countless petrol fires and burning vehicles. Of this and the next few nights the DAK recorded that not only was the damage very great but officers and men were badly shaken and their fighting capacity considerably reduced by the enforced dispersal, lack of sleep, and the strain of waiting for the next bomb.[24]

Montgomery, true to his expressed doctrine, refused to be drawn but, with all Axis forces committed he could afford to deplete 30 Corps to stiffen the line at Alam Halfa. South African 2nd Brigade was shifted to a position just above the line of the ridge while 5th Indian Brigade was placed under Freyberg. From the Delta he moved up 151st Brigade (50th Division) toward the eastern rim. The noose was tightening. British armour in the south was already nibbling at Rommel's exposed flank and Freyberg was ordered to prepare for a southwards thrust. Still on 1 September the Australians mounted a major raid from their salient, 'biffing' the German 164th Division and netting a haul of prisoners, some 140 in all, though at the cost of 135 casualties sustained.

F. A. Lewis was another Allied tanker who spotted the perfect target of opportunity apparently totally unprepared:

Directly to my front at about 1,000 yards was a table and bending over it a particularly fine specimen of the Reich seemed to be very busy on some unspecified task. To his right at some 500 yards was an 88mm gun pointing straight at me, and behind it was an enormous camouflaged hangar, which was evidently being used as an MT workshop. Hardly able to believe the evidence of my own eyes, I trotted back to my tank and was soon checking up with the photographic map.

Once it was established these were definitely not 'friendlies' Lewis attacked:

... causing great glee and a powerful argument as to which target we should engage first. Obviously it should have been the 88, but I simply could not resist the tent and the figure outside it so, giving the necessary orders, the gunner was soon pumping streams of bullets at it from the machine-gun. Satisfied with the results we switched the big gun onto the 88 and at the fifth shot completely wrecked it, the long barrel sticking in the air like a signpost.[25]

The hangar was soon 'blazing furiously'.

On 2 September, the Fox conceded the game was up and began a phased withdrawal back through the maze of the British minefields. He expected to be attacked in force but Montgomery would not be drawn, confining his armour to harassment and cutting up stragglers. Though Rommel might have judged his opponent overly cautious, British attacks in July had clearly indicated that 8th Army was not yet fully ready for the offensive role. Much additional training and preparation was needed. Time, despite any urgings he might receive from Whitehall, was on Montgomery's side:

Although it was clear to General Montgomery that Rommel had shot his bolt, he resisted the temptation to start a general counter-attack. He judged the 8th Army to be unready, and going off at half-cock would only make it harder to prepare for the decisive blow he had in mind.[26]

Even Freyberg's push, set for the night of 3/4 September, had very limited objectives, intended to do no more than close the minefield gaps as the Axis withdrew. At 23.00 hrs on the 3rd the attack went in with the inexperienced 132nd Brigade suffering heavily from enemy fire: '… the enemy reaction was immediate and violent'.[27] The newcomers had 'much difficulty' in reaching their start lines, being nearly an hour late by which time the Axis had ample notice: 'There was much straggling and general confusion, which took some time to sort out.'[28] This may be something of an understatement. Brigadier Robertson was disabled by wounds and Clifton, commanding 6th NZ Brigade, was captured when he ran into enemy positions while undertaking reconnaissance.

5th New Zealand Brigade, veterans of desert warfare, reached their objectives after heavy fighting. Indeed the Maoris overran enemy rear areas, wreaking havoc. Next day the Axis counter-attacked in strength. This was seen off as was the next; guns and aircraft piled into the advancing enemy. Such was the intensity of the combat that Freyberg rightly concluded any further attempts by his Kiwis were pointless, casualties were already high. His subsequent request to withdraw survivors was accepted by both Horrocks and Monty. The latter remained sanguine:

> Moreover, it suited me to have their [Axis] forces in strength on the southern flank since I was considering making my main blow, later on, on the northern part of the front. I remember Horrocks protesting to me that the enemy remained in possession of not only our original minefields but also of some good view points from which to observe his [13] corps area. I replied that he should get busy and make new minefields for his corps. As regards the observation points such as Himeimat, it suited me that Rommel should be able to have a good look at all the preparations for attack we were making on our southern flank: they were a feint.[29]

In assessing the results of this battle the OH defines the effect on morale as being of greater importance than the material gains which were indeed insignificant:

To the Axis the battle seemed to put an end to their hopes of reaching the Delta; to the British it appeared as a clear cut victory in which Rommel had been defeated at his own game.[30]

This must substantively be correct; 8th Army had won no new ground nor destroyed the Panzerarmee Afrika but it had fought Rommel to a standstill and obliged him to withdraw. The limited offensive operation with the closing of the minefield gap as its objective had failed but:

What had been plain for all to see was the benefit of concentrating resources, which was made possible by a particularly accurate forecast of what Rommel was going to do. This meant that the enemy's striking force could be met on ground of the defenders' choice by a tremendous volume of fire: from the air with a rain of projectiles ranging from machine gun bullets to 4,000lb bombs, and from the ground with the concentrated fire of field and medium artillery, anti-tank guns and the guns of dug in tanks, notably the Grants.[31]

8th Army had scored a signal defensive triumph. The task now was to convert this new confidence into an overwhelmingly successful attack. To prepare the ground for this, the number of fighting patrols being sent out was increased – J. R. Oates of No. 5 Field Unit was a participant:

These nightly forays into No Mans' Land, and on many occasions into German occupied territory itself, yielded good results. Not only were casualties inflicted on the enemy and information gained, but in many cases weapons and stores were captured. Working on information gleaned by patrols, parties of engineers made a feature of penetrating the enemy lines, stealing dumps of mines and sowing them in enemy territory ... At first our patrols were very successful, but the Germans soon began to wire themselves in, bringing up more machine guns, mines and booby traps. These counter measures and the increasing strength of the moon made the work of patrols more hazardous. Although lacking many of the more spectacular successes of the earlier period, they nevertheless continued to harry the enemy, wearing his nerves and, by being an ever present potential menace, preventing him from using men and material for reinforcing other sectors.[32]

8

Second El Alamein: Break-in

The Night lies with her body crookedly flung
In agony across the sharp hills;
By the fitful moon her nostrils are taut, quivering;
She is tensed in cold sweat and lonely fear,
Giving sudden birth in dark, sly, trodden places
To her unlawful issue, blind hideous death.

Richard Spender

If Auchinleck's appreciation of 2 August proved the blueprint for the successful outcome of the Second Battle of El Alamein, there can be no question that the plan was made flesh by Montgomery.

> I was interested to read in 1955 a book called *Panzer Battles* by Von Mellenthin ...
> He describes Alam Halfa as 'the turning point of the desert war, and the first of a long
> series of defeats on every front which foreshadowed the defeat of Germany'.[1]

Monty was never one to pass by an observation which gilded his own laurels but there is a certain truth in Von Mellenthin's assertion. After Alam Halfa 8th Army would never taste defeat and the Axis fortunes in Africa began, inexorably, to wane towards extinction.

The Build-up

> Montgomery came to the southern sector of the Alamein front at Alam Halfa, and
> one of the first things he asked was, when did we leave England and had we had
> any post? Not a single soldier had had a letter. Had we any NAAFI? We hadn't
> even seen the NAAFI. We were scrounging as much as we could from other units –

cigarettes – and understandably, other units weren't prepared to give them away or even sell them. He wanted to know why our shirts were stained – because we had only one shirt, and there was sweat – and they were hard, like bloody cardboard. He wanted to know if we'd had any leave. Nobody had had any leave at that stage. He made sure his adjutants took note of everything. He wasn't talking to the officers – he was talking to the riflemen – he was sitting inside little dugouts with the lads.[2]

Monty believed the battle had shown his subordinates the need for a clear guiding hand at the top, a degree of certainty absent from his predecessor's tenure:

> The Eighth Army consisted in the main of civilians in uniform, not of professional soldiers ... to command such men demanded not only a guiding mind but also a point of focus: or to put it another way, not only a master but a mascot. And I deliberately set about fulfilling this second requirement.[3]

Thus, Monty exercised his own particular genius for self-promotion, a trait he shared with his adversary:

> He [Montgomery] was wearing this Australian hat, with all the badges that were around the brim and a pair of 'Bombay bloomers' – KD shorts, which were a lot wider than the normal. Now, dressed in that hat and shorts, and with his thin legs, he looked like matchsticks in a pair of boots; very high-pitched voice – and he didn't look like a general at all.[4]

The famous Australian bush hat and equally celebrated black beret, replete with badges became the Monty trademarks: '... I readily admit that the occasion to become the necessary focus of their attention was also personally enjoyable.' Boosting his own profile was manna indeed to Monty and nobody can deny it was necessary. To win, 8th Army had to believe in its commander as one who could outfox the Fox: 'What started as a private joke with the tank regiment which gave it [the badge] became in the end the means by which I came to be recognised throughout the desert.'[5]

> Montgomey was what I call a bit of a bullshitter, but I think that was part of his act, and very effective, I think. He had to publicise himself and build up a reputation

against Rommel, whose reputation was extremely high. We all thought the world of Rommel. If you were opposite Rommel, you expected something to happen. He did have a very demoralising effect on British troops; he was a bloody good general.[6]

Monty was ruthless in jettisoning officers he felt were below standard. He had already brought in Horrocks to command 13 Corps and he now replaced Ramsden with Leese, an officer he knew well 'and I never regretted that choice'. 10 Corps, which he was building up as an Allied response to DAK, was grudgingly entrusted to Lumsden, currently commanding 1st Armoured. Lumsden was a less certain appointment, an officer of whom Monty had no prior experience and he had reservations. Having imported two new senior commanders from the UK, however, he or rather Alexander, felt a promotion 'from within' was politic. A. F. J. Harding (latterly Field Marshal) was moved up to lead 7th Armoured Division.

As gunnery would be a vital element in the forthcoming offensive, Monty sent for Brigadier S. C. Kirkman:

> When I told this to a senior officer at GHQ, he remarked that the present man was a delightful person and was also a golf champion. I agreed he was delightful but added that unfortunately the game we were about to play was not golf.[7]

Monty also brought on some highly competent staff officers: Brigadier Sir Brian Robertson (1st Baron Oakridge), Lieutenant-Colonel Graham and Brigadier Belchem. He appointed Brigadier B. T. 'Bill' Williams as his intelligence chief: '... it was a conversation with him which gave me the idea which played a large part in winning the Battle of Alamein'.[8]

Some 30,000 Egyptians now laboured to supply Middle East Command and every output reduced the need for supply by sea. The range and quantity of items manufactured was prodigious:

> An immense variety of work ... in June 1942 the workshops [at Abbasia] had over 900 separate jobs in hand, from notice boards to AA mountings, from meat-safes to carriers for sterilised blood-bottles, from 12,000 crates for Molotov cocktails to 25,000 trestle tops for tables. Shell and ammunition gauges and extractors of all kinds, fire ladders, open sights for 25 pounders, chairs, covers for machine guns, magnetic detectors of A/T mines, hospital trolleys, jigs, pistons, saddlery, yakdans (the sheepskin

jacket beloved of Eighth Army officers), swivelchairs for tanks, tool chests, steel tent pins, special armourers' instruments etc. were only a few of these varied and special requirements.[9]

To deliver his decisive blow Montgomery, who would not be rushed, could deploy three armoured divisions, two armoured brigade groups, a single brigade of infantry tanks, seven UK and dominion infantry divisions, two Free French and one Greek brigade groups. Rommel, by contrast, and in terms of his German units, could deploy only two armoured divisions, one motorised; one partly-motorised with a single parachute brigade. The Italians added two armoured divisions, one motorised, four infantry and one parachute. The disparity was far greater than this bare summation may suggest. Axis formations were under-strength and suffering acute shortage of supply. The Allies were building up a marked superiority in both armour and ordnance, including anti-tank capability. The new professionalism which Montgomery had introduced manifested itself in the close and meticulous preparation for the coming fight. V. L. Bosazza, serving with a South African survey unit explains:

> In September our artillery drew attention to the fact that the Axis guns, particularly their 88s, either did not have alternate positions or did not use them. A British survey company officer came up and helped us with unmarked triangulation stations far forward. At the same time four tubular scaffolding towers were erected to observe enemy positions. With help from aerial photographs we gradually built up an accurate plot of the order of battle of almost the entire enemy artillery. When we went forward after the battle I especially visited the 88mm gun sites and there were dead around each gun, hit by our 5.5in medium gun on the night of 23/24 October.[10]

10 Corps was a new formation and was born from Montgomery's desire to create a strong reserve, well provided with armour. His initial intention was to pull together 1st, 8th and 10th Armoured Divisions with the New Zealanders. However 8th Armoured, which could not be given a motorised infantry brigade, was split up instead. Freyberg's Kiwis were attached to 30 Corps to take part in the first phase of the attack – the break-in. For the forthcoming battle, brigade groups were abandoned with the exception of the French and Greek units. Divisions would remain as distinct entities and fight as divisions.

In principle, brigades would not be detached, though inevitably this did occur as expediency dictated.

With the arrival of the long-heralded Shermans, 8th Army would have tanks equal to the best of their opponents. That dangerous gulf which previous failures had opened up between armour and infantry had yet to be bridged but some, like driver Robert Crawford, maintained their admiration for the tankers:

> We all liked the armoured brigade men. They had a touch of something that was different. They were proud of themselves and prouder still to claim the title of 'Queen of Battle', which had been held previously by the cavalry. We liked their buccaneering way of going about. They had confidence and cheekiness sticking out a mile ... The officers were the most unmilitary looking men in the whole British Army. They wore little or no military uniform! Invariably they wandered round a golfing jacket and a pair of grey flannel bags [trousers]. Sometimes they deigned to wear a forage cap and could thus be distinguished as belonging to the army. But other than that they looked like so many civilians wandering about. It was quite a common sight to see the same figures going off with shotguns, when the brigade was at rest stations, for a day's shooting in the Desert![11]

On the Other Side of the Hill

Defence in depth was a concept the German Army understood well and one which it had perfected during the Great War. The front was defined by coastline to the north and impassable desert to the south. This line could not be outflanked therefore it must be breached in a grinding battle of attrition. Rommel had provided a double mesh of mines all along the front. The belts were, at intervals, linked to form boxes. The defenders' role in any sector was simple, to hold the line for long enough to allow the armour time to come up. Part of his difficulties lay in that he had insufficient German troops to form the static garrison and he had proven doubts over some if not the majority of Italians. To stiffen the collective spine of his allies, Rommel mixed units along the line, down to battalion level, so that every Italian formation had intervening German troops to act as a brace.

His armour he kept to the rear, 15th Panzer in the north, 21st to the south. Littorio Armoured Division was attached to the former and Ariete deployed before the latter, thus splitting Italian XX Corps. Both 90th Light and Trieste Motorised Division were left in the north, westwards along the coastline. From the Mediterranean shore to Miteirya Ridge 164th with Trento Divisions held the line. Southwards, as far as Deir el Shein and Ruweisat Ridge, was the responsibility of Bologna Division. Southwards again, Brescia was deployed around Bab el Qattara. These two Italian formations were stiffened by dispersed battalions of *fallschirmjager* drawn from Ramcke's Brigade. Down to Qaret el Himeimat Italian paratroopers from Folgore and infantry of Pavia Division manned the front.

If the Allies were learning how to take on the panzers and now possessed at least some of the tools to do so effectively, the Axis advance could still be a sobering, indeed awe-inspiring sight as 'Pip' Roberts commanding 22nd Armoured Brigade describes when recalling Alam Halfa:

> On they [the panzers] come, a most impressive array ... It is fascinating to watch them, as one might watch a snake curl up ready to strike. But there is something unusual too; some of the leading tanks are MkIVs and Mark IVs have in the past always had short-barrelled 75mm guns used for close support work and firing HE only, consequently they are not usually in front. But these Mark IVs have a very long gun on them; in fact it looks like the devil of a gun; this must be the long-barrelled stepped-up 75mm gun the Intelligence people have been talking about.[12]

In line with established practice, the leading edge of the first dense belt of mines was held by outposts only, with additional positions in the mine-marshes. These were liberally sown with anti-tank and anti-personnel mines, complicated by a deadly spread of booby traps. There were as many as 445,000 mines in total, the majority intended to disable enemy armour. The outposts were not garrisoned in strength, platoon or company sized units only, with a solid supply of anti-tank and machine guns. At a distance of perhaps one and a quarter miles behind lay the principal minefields, fronted by very strong defences. One battalion would be responsible for a section of the line, say a mile wide and over three times that in depth. More and numerous anti-tank guns and plentiful machine guns studded these positions. The whole defended zone was anywhere between two and a half and four miles deep with the main gun line behind. Regardless of 8th Army's numerical superiority and weight of armour, a very tough nut to crack.

In line with his rightly held obsession with training Montgomery drilled his men hard for the coming contest. Major-General Douglas Wimberley, commanding 51st Highland Division, was a firm believer:

> We were in a fortunate position, only a small proportion of our fighting troops were in the line at one time with the Australians, and we were able to give our troops preparatory training for the forthcoming battle. I was allotted an area of open desert and here with the aid of sappers I laid out an exact replica of the enemy defences. Then I took my men, a brigade at a time, and practised every battalion in the exact job it was to do in the initial attack.[13]

Dummy trenches were laid out, the artillery plan was practised, signals and sappers went about their specialist trades as they would during the attack and models of every enemy outpost to be overcome were made and studied. No one could ever call Monty a mere opportunist.

An attack upon the forward outpost line would certainly be heralded by a massive artillery bombardment followed by infantry assault. Though this might gain some ground such deep defences would slow the attack and give clear note of where it was directed. Surprise would be gone before the main positions could be assaulted. Clearly the purpose of infantry would be to blast a gap through which Allied armour could deploy. The depth of these defences and the potency of the anti-tank guns could contain and slow an armoured thrust until Axis tanks could be brought up to seal the breach. With such thorough preparations, Rommel had done everything possible to safeguard his army and prepare for the blow that must fall. By this time he was a sick man, lesser mortals would have been ground down long before; only an iron will kept him in harness. Nonetheless, he was obliged to take sick-leave and return to Germany while General Stumme assumed temporary command in the field.

Stumme, if he was wary, was not unduly pessimistic. He was, of course, painfully aware of chronic shortages in supply and cautioned against unnecessary consumption of fuel or ammunition, and that stocks of both had to be conserved as far as possible. He knew an offensive must be launched soon but incorrectly thought the weight of preparation in the chosen sector would provide ample warning. As reported early in October to Kesselring: 'Pz Army thinks that the main weight of the enemy attack will be south of Ruweisat, and perhaps also on either side of the coast road.'[14] Aside from patrolling and desultory flashes of artillery, October was a relatively quiet month which enabled the Axis to concentrate on developing their defences to a most potent level. Stumme would use his infantry to contain the break-in while deploying his armour on the flanks to pinch out the enemy salient and surround the attackers: 'It may be necessary ... for battle groups of Afrika Korps and XX [Italian] Corps to move east through our minefields to launch a concentric attack, in order to make the pincer movement as effective as possible.'[15] The Panzerarmee Afrika was not about to stoically accept its destruction. These men were veterans who had proved themselves many times in action. They had suffered reverses but never tasted defeat. Even if Rommel was not with them physically, the legacy and glow of his genius remained.

'Bertram'

The object of the [Allied] deception plan [Operation 'Bertram'] was twofold:

To conceal from the enemy as long as possible our intention to take the offensive.

When this could no longer be concealed, to mislead him about both the date and the sector in which our main thrust was to be made.[16]

In the case of Operation 'Lightfoot' as the break-in phase of the planned battle was called, deception was a significant part of overall preparation. In the north, 30 Corps sector, where the main attack was planned, a great mass of dummy vehicles, tanks and guns had been fabricated to create an impression of density. Immediately prior to the attack, under cover of darkness, these were replaced by the real thing and dummies transported to rear. At the same time, Lieutenant-Colonel Charles Richardson, 8th Army wizard masterminding the whole show, had to conceal the vast supply dumps being created. That these were satisfactorily kept hidden was a masterpiece of disguise brought into being by Lieutenant-Colonel Geoffrey Barkas (in 'civvy-street' a film-set designer), director of camouflage at GHQ Middle East.

Sergeant John Longstaff of 2nd Battalion, Rifle Brigade remembered both the deception and preparation:

We were told that the last battle of the Alamein line – of Rommel's attack – would take place right in the sector that we were in front of – at Alam Halfa. We had something unique. We had magicians in charge of our camouflage. Large tins that had held potatoes were made to look as if they were anti-tank guns, vehicles were made with hessian to look like tanks – tanks were made to look like vehicles. Petrol supplies were made out of any old rubbish. Water points were made where there were no water points.[17]

Dumps, such as that at Imayid, covered very large areas, in this case some three square miles. Dummy vehicles were again employed to conceal the crates of ammunition within the timber and canvas frame, fuel cans were hidden in existing ostensibly abandoned trench lines. The distinctive 25-pounders with their equally recognisable quad tractors to be concealed in the forward areas were artfully disguised by fixing a false section to the tractor making it resemble an ordinary truck and by bunching gun and limber then placing a fake screen over them.

We were engaged in 'creating' a concourse of tanks and lorries and even an HQ to confuse the enemy reconnaissance planes. It was all done by hessian, some string and some very light wood, poles etc. The dummy camp and vehicle sites were erected at night with the help of moonlight and during daylight gave the appearance of busy military areas to very high-flying enemy planes. Vehicles travelled around and about creating clouds of dust and in early morning every encouragement to brewing up amongst the dummy bivouac was given, and of course, round the vehicles, or tanks, outlined in hessian, supported by thin wooden poles or 'cats' cradles of strong twine.[18]

To provide an impression that the main effort was to be directed toward the southern sector part of the overall deception involved the construction of twenty miles of dummy 'Diamond' water pipeline:

The pipe-trench was excavated in the normal way. Five miles of dummy railway track, made from petrol cans, were used for piping. The 'piping' was strung out along the open trench. When each five-mile section of the trench was filled in, the 'piping' was collected and laid out alongside the next section. Dummy pump houses were erected at three points; water points and overhead storage reservoirs were made at two of these points.[19]

Montgomery deemed Operation 'Bertram' a clear success but as with most such operations this is hard to evaluate. Nonetheless, Axis intelligence remained convinced the main blow must fall in the south. One vital area, wherein 8th Army's performance improved exponentially, was that of signals and wireless communication. Ultra intercepts betrayed every Axis move and Rommel's ears had been clipped with the elimination of his elite interceptors. 'Ghost' radio traffic was added to the web of deception to mask and confuse troop movements.

Preparation

Monty was never one to accept that ideas of genius emanated from any genius other than his own: 'The gossip is, so I am told, that the plans for Alamein ... were made by Alexander at GHQ Middle East and that I merely carried them out; this is not true.'[20] Thus Monty hastens to confirm that the planned breakthrough was all his own work. This is equally fallacious for, as we have seen, much of the concept derived from earlier appreciations penned by his predecessors, including Auchinleck, Dorman-Smith, Gott and Ramsden. He then, rather disingenuously, confirms that, 'all the plans for Alamein and afterward were made at Eighth Army HQ'. This is quite right but the intimation is that the whole scheme was Monty's alone. He goes on to insist the initial plan was 'made in the first days of September; immediately after the Battle of Alam Halfa was over' – Monty makes no mention of the vital conceptual work undertaken in August. Leese with 30 Corps would be responsible for the main effort in the north where infantry would 'punch' two corridors through Axis defences along which Lumsden could send 10 Corps armour. The intention was that Allied tanks would pour through the gaps and draw Rommel's panzers into a melee, where they would be irretrievably ground down.

Horrocks, in the southern sector with 13 Corps, would 'break into the enemy positions and operate with 7th Armoured Division with a view to drawing enemy armour in that direction; this would make it easier for 10 Corps to get out into the open in the north'.[21] The Desert Rats were not to get drawn into a mauling or engage in attritional 'dogfights'. They were to husband their strength for pursuit once the breakout was achieved. Monty allows himself full credit for the idea of delivering the main blow in the north and avoiding the tried tactic of the flanking attack from the south: 'I planned to attack neither on my left flank nor on my right flank, but somewhere right of centre; having broken in, I could then direct my forces to the right or to the left as seemed most profitable.'[22]

Leese was to put four divisions into the attack. Nearest the coast Morshead's 9th Australian would have the extreme right, breaking in eastwards from Tel el Eisa. Next, Wimberley's 51st Highland Division, charged with assaulting towards Kidney Ridge. Then Freyberg's 2nd New Zealand Division would strike towards the western extremity of Miteiriya Ridge with, on the far left, Pienaar and 1st South African Division attacking the centre. The front stretched for four and a half miles with a depth, on the right, of five and a quarter shrinking to two and three-quarter miles on the left. Horrocks was to launch his offensive, diversions aside, on a narrower front with Harding's 7th Armoured and Hughes' 44th Divisions striking out south of Ruweisat Ridge. In the main this was to convince the Axis that the main blow was indeed falling in the south and to fix 21st Panzer's full attention here. Secondary objectives included attacks on Himeimat and Taqa Plateau but these were not to be pressed home in the face of strong opposition.

Sergeant Longstaff was involved in the work of gapping British minefields:

> Our 2nd Battalion lads had the responsibility of going up on the 22nd October to take a position and to start making a gap through a British minefield. They went out without any mine detectors, digging their bayonets into the ground to discover mines, then putting a bandage on a steel post. As soon as they found a mine, they'd tie a wire to it, then somebody would yank the mine out; they were generally Teller mines, and one Teller mine could put a British tank out of action.[23]

On the 18th of the month, with just five days to go till the launch of 'Lightfoot', bombing raids began in earnest. Tobruk was further damaged. Next day Daba was bombed again together with troop concentrations, road and rail traffic along the coast. Sidi Barrani, Tobruk, Daba and Fuka fields were repeatedly hit. During the night of 21/22 October Allied bombers ranged over installations on Crete. The overall strategy was for Desert Air Force to win hegemony in the air then switch to close operational support. The bombers would fly in support of the opening bombardment, seeking out those guns still able to reply. Wellingtons, suitably equipped, would jam enemy radio signals thus leaving the Axis 'blind' during those critical opening hours.

Training continued to remain, in Monty's view and rightly, a major deficiency. His view of many of his subordinates was dismissive: 'many were above their ceiling'.[24] Monty had little tact and no mercy for those who came within his sights. This level of waspish tunnel vision would cause considerable difficulties with Eisenhower later on. He identifies his concerns over insufficient training as the main reason why, on 6 October, he rather radically changed tack: 'If I was not careful, divisions and units would be given tasks which might end in failure because of the inadequate standard of training.'[25] He decided to turn the key objective on its head. No longer would the intention be to draw Rommel's armour into a dogfight and leave the infantry to be mopped up at leisure. This new plan focused on a methodical destruction of the fixed defences and troops within with enemy tanks being kept at a distance so they could not effectively intervene:

These un-armoured divisions would be destroyed by means of a 'crumbling' process, the enemy being attacked from the flank and rear and cut off from their supplies. These operations would be carefully organised from a series of firm bases and would be within the capabilities of my troops. I did not think it likely that the enemy armour would remain inactive and watch the gradual destruction of all the un-armoured divisions; it would be launched in heavy counter-attacks. This would suit us very well, since the best way to destroy the enemy armour was to entice it to attack our armour in position.[26]

Monty found the inexperience and lack of training among his formations as the perfect excuse for restricting what would have been an unsound and overly ambitious plan. Alam Halfa had clearly shown that the way to deal with the panzers was with a wall of fire from AT guns and dug-in armour. The days of 'balaklavering' were gone.

This was a variant on the break-in battles of 1918. British armour, rather than breaking out or hurling itself into the attempt, would act as a blocking force to prevent Axis tanks coming up:

I would then turn the enemy minefields to our advantage by using them to prevent the enemy armour from interfering with our operations; this would be done by closing the approaches to the minefields with our tanks and we would then be able to proceed relentlessly with our plans.[27]

It was axiomatic to the success of this plan that 30 Corps could achieve the necessary break-in and open viable corridors for 10 Corps armour.

Speed was of the essence and Monty proposed that the funnelling of tanks into the passages should occur before it was confirmed the breaches were fully viable. This was the tankers' looming nightmare. If the tanks, bunched invitingly, were lined up and static on the morning of D+1, 24 October, they were sitting ducks. Infantrymen had been quick to castigate their armoured brethren for faint-heartedness but this was generally unfair. Tanks had severe limitations in exposed terrain and Monty's idea that, if the gaps were not cleared by dawn, the tanks should simply fight their way forwards raised hackles of alarm: 'It will be seen later how infirmity of purpose on the part of certain senior commanders in carrying out this order nearly lost us the battle.'[28]

Rommel's 'corsetting' of potentially 'unreliable' Italian units with a regular stiffening of Germans offered the possibility of employing 'crumbling' tactics primarily against the weaker partner and opening gaps in the line by destroying the Italians first; 'unreliable when it came to hard fighting'. Monty had issued general orders on morale on 14 September promising 'a real rough house'. These were followed, on 6 October, with further orders on leadership which emphasised the need to avoid mass surrendering by units simply because they were 'cut off or surrounded'. If a formation was in this invidious position they should dig in and fight it out regardless; 'by doing so they will add enormously to the enemy's difficulties'.

Barney O'Kelly was one of those monitoring Axis dispositions:

> DAK always believed, in static situations, in keeping the minimum force in the line, giving the others every opportunity for rest and refreshment. So here on the Alamein line, our information was that generally one armoured formation occupied the forward area, in the vicinity of the coast road, while the other indulged in sea-bathing in the rear. It was important for the success of our plan, despite our numerical advantage in tanks, that we should be able to deal with one panzer division at a time, and therefore they should, if possible, be kept apart.[29]

On 19 October, the general briefed senior officers from 13 and 30 Corps then addressed those of 10 Corps the day after. He predicted that the battle would last for twelve days (originally he proposed ten but erred, wisely on the side of caution). He reminded his officers of the task in hand and the tools they now possessed. He explained both the original and modified plans with his reasons. He pointed to the Allied superiority in guns and armour and rehearsed each element of the plan. He defined how the crumbling operation would play out and stressed the need for resolute and continued action. He cautioned against expectations of a speedy and easily won victory. This battle would produce neither.

Curtain-Raisers

As early as 22 August, a major raid had been launched against Rommel's supply base at Tobruk. Similar if less ambitious attacks were put in against Benghazi and Jalo. On 30 September the inexperienced 44th Division launched its 131st Brigade against the Deir el Munassib. The objectives were two-fold: to improve fire positions for Allied guns and also to draw the enemy's suspicions southwards. The attack was well supported both on the ground and in the air. Some ground, on the northern rim of the depression, was gained but the attack in the south stalled against stiff opposition put up by the Italian paratroopers of Folgore. Ernest Norris was serving with the QOR and the battalion's inexperience quickly led to difficulties:

> The creeping barrage was too far in front of us but we couldn't change that. We fixed
> bayonets, formed up in line and were given the order, 'Forward'. At the time I felt
> pretty good, proud even. Our barrage was going on ahead and it gave us a feeling of
> protection. Then suddenly the barrage stopped; you feel so naked you can't describe
> it.[30]

Axis fire and the deceptive flare of tracer zipped through the still night air, men fell: 'Captain Clarke was mortally wounded and I heard him call out: "Carry on, Mr Cole-Biroth. I've been hit." Then my Bren gunner screamed and went down. I mentally panicked.' A fearful baptism of fire; soon most of the officers were down:

> We were so close to the enemy that they could see us clearly and they began mortaring
> us. And as we'd gone past enemy machine-gun posts in our advance we were being
> fired on from behind as well as in front. We couldn't move forwards or backwards

but we tried to reply to their fire as best we could. Eventually we heard voices and we knew the enemy was coming for us. Then we saw them standing above us and making signs to throw our rifles down and come out. And that's what we did.[31]

For everyone, a period of waiting preceded the offensive. For senior commanders the die was effectively cast. Units were involved in moving up toward their battle positions but most found they had time on their hands. Time to rest and prepare, to play cards, to write letters home. It was an uncertain interval this period of waiting, where the worm of fear lurks in shadows, where the act of letter writing takes on a very particular significance. For those battalions of 30 Corps who would be spearheading the assault, the long daylight hours of 23 October were spent in hot, cramped and tedious anticipation, huddled in their slit trenches. Monty, as ever, breezed confidence. His tactical HQ was located on the coast north of Alamein in close proximity to those of his subordinates Lumsden and Leese. From there, on the eve of the offensive, Monty issued a 'Personal Message from the Army Commander':

When I assumed command of the Eighth Army I said that the mandate was to destroy ROMMEL and his Army, and that it would be done as soon as we were ready.

We are ready NOW. The battle which is now about to begin will be one of the decisive battles of history. It will be the turning point of the war. The eyes of the whole world will be on us, watching anxiously which way the battle will swing. We can give them their answer at once 'It will swing our way'.

We have first-class equipment; good tanks; good anti-tank guns; plenty of artillery and plenty of ammunition; and we are backed by the finest air-striking force in the world. All that is necessary is that each one of us, every officer and man, should enter this battle with the determination to see it through – to fight and to kill – and finally, to win. If we do all this, there can be only one result – together we will hit the enemy for 'six', right out of North Africa.

The sooner we win this battle, which will be the turning point of this war, the sooner we shall get back home to our families.

Therefore, let every officer and man enter the battle with a stout heart, and with the determination to do his duty so long as he has breath in his body. AND LET NO MAN SURRENDER SO LONG AS HE IS UNWOUNDED AND CAN FIGHT. Let us all pray that 'the Lord mighty in battle' will give us the victory.[32]

9
Second El Alamein: 'Lightfoot'

Nothing grows in the sand-flats
Beside the salt lake at El Alamein,
The water is still and rust-pink,
And the flat sand rim is crusted with salt.

John Jarmain[1]

A German gunner, Martin Ranft, serving with 220th Artillery Regiment, recorded an initial view from the Axis side of the hill:

El Alamein was my home for quite a while, because we were stopped. On the 23rd October, nine o'clock in the evening, that's when we heard that terrible artillery fire from the British line. I was facing the front line and suddenly the whole sky was red with gunfire. The shells were howling over you and exploding all around you – it was just horrible; we thought then that the world was coming to an end.[2]

Lightfoot: The First Blow
Churchill would at last have his decisive battle:

At 22.00 hrs on 23rd October three simultaneous attacks were to be made –
by 30th Corps, to secure before dawn on 24th October a bridgehead (objective 'Oxalic') beyond the enemy's main defended zone, and help 10th Corps to pass through it:
by 13th Corps, to penetrate the enemy's positions near Munassib and pass the 7th Armoured Division through towards Jebel Kalakh. This division was, however, to be kept 'in being' it was not to be exposed to serious losses in tanks:

also by 13th Corps, using the French forces, to secure Quaret el Himeimat and the el Taqa plateau.[3]

Perhaps the most enduring image in the popular consciousness of the El Alamein battle is those dramatic, stabbing flames of massed artillery that presaged the attack by 30 Corps on the night of 23 October. At 21.40 hrs the guns spoke. Allied medium guns sought out the Axis batteries beyond the reach of the 25-pounders, 96 rounds were awarded to each in an intense two-minute deluge, some 1,800 shells in all; an inferno of fire:

The prelude to the battle was a nightmare period of dumping ammunition at the gun position we were to occupy, on the eve of the battle ... Working conditions were appalling; the Alamein position had been fought over several times and the whole area was littered with decomposing corpses, some unburied and others whose graves had been uncovered by the wind. The stench of putrefaction was all-pervading and the air thick with dust and horrible desert flies, bloated from feeding on the corpses. The fine dust stirred up by the constant passage of vehicles during each night penetrated everywhere and a handkerchief tied over the moth was useless. The flies were the worst scourge ... Zero hour for the battle was some time just after dark on the night of 23rd October, and the gunners task was to start with fire at the enemy's positions, and especially their artillery emplacements, and then go over to a creeping barrage of fire, timed to fall just ahead of our highland infantry.[4]

As artillery boomed, leading companies in each of the four attacking divisions moved off from their start lines. The infantry advanced, covering 100 yards every two minutes, several yards between each individual. Most had around a mile and a half to cover to reach the edge of the first minefield. As they moved behind the barrage, great clouds of choking dust and cloying fumes cloaked the battlefield so men would feel they were marching literally into the fog of war:

My most vivid memory of the battle was the opening of the barrage of over eight hundred guns at 21.40 hours on 23rd October. I was a regular commanding my battalion – a TA battalion of 'heavy' infantry – was in reserve but waiting to go into action and we were therefore naturally somewhat tense. To me the sudden lighting up of half the horizon behind us and the crash of the guns was awe-inspiring in the extreme and gave me a feeling of confidence in the Royal Regiment [Royal Artillery] that I have never forgotten.[5]

Figures loomed eerily in the shrouded night as the demonic fury of the guns split the air, stabling like forked lightning. The smack and thump of shells a doleful chorus as men moved forward as though on exercise. Shock and awe of bombardment would ensure the enemy kept their heads down in the first instance. Searchlights intended to act as beacons punched through the murk, tracer zipped like bright and deadly fireflies. The cakewalk would not last. Capturing this vital passage before dawn was the key objective; tanks had to be guided through and the break-ins consolidated. For armour to be caught in the open during daylight, strung out like a gunner's dream, was a most unattractive prospect.

> Stay with me, God. The night is dark,
> The night is cold: my little spark
> Of courage dies. The night is long;
> Be with me, God, and make me strong.

Anonymous[6]

Even for experienced desert veterans like Sergeant Longstaff, the offensive was something remarkable:

> It was eerie seeing the flashes of our guns on 23rd October at ten o'clock. The gunners seemed to be firing rapid fire with 25 pounders. The sky had to be seen to be believed. Round about seven o'clock that night, we received orders to march. B Company under John Francis was to lead the battalion. We were now through the second of the British minefields, which meant a journey of about two or three miles through a narrow gap, no wider than say two tanks could get through. These gaps had been made by the Rifle Brigade and the Royal Engineers – and they did damn good work.[7]

It was essential that the first phase saw the enemy's outposts cleared, taking a bite perhaps a mile beyond the forward edge of the Axis mines. The gunners were assuming infantry would be on these objectives, (collectively labelled the 'Red' line) five minutes before midnight. For two hours thereafter there would be a planned hiatus in the advance while the infantry prepared to take on the main defensive positions. It was intended these would be overrun and neutralized by 02.45 hrs and the 'Blue' line, over two miles distant, gained. This would leave a breathing space of three hours before dawn in which time the attackers would dig in and consolidate, their anti-tank guns and mortars ready to respond to the inevitable counter-attacks. Behind them, rumbling forward from 02.00 hrs, armoured formations would begin to move through gaps breached by their sappers. Operational orders stipulated tanks were never to operate at less than squadron strength, nor should they attempt un-cleared minefields, reserves should be kept in hand to meet enemy moves after dawn.

> I knew that death is but a door.
> I knew what we were fighting for:
> Peace for the kids, our brothers freed,
> A kinder world, a cleaner breed
>
> Anonymous[8]

Once all objectives had been gained, there would be no respite for the Axis. Fighting patrols would be sent forward to biff the enemy and spike his remaining guns. All efforts would be made to get the tanks through; this was the second essential. The first was for the infantry to secure the break-in but this was incomplete if the armour did not follow. Both asked a great deal of the men involved. Battles, described in general staff terms, have a pleasing simplicity. The reality is always altogether different and the desert offered only a bare, desolate terrain unmarked by recognizable features, churned into a cloying soup. Once the ground had been taken and held, Morshead's Australians were to break out and advance further in the northern sector, Freyberg's Kiwis to burst southwards towards Deir el Shein, shadowed by the South Africans.

> What made an impression on me were not victories, large scale battles, but incidents which left an indelible impression. Such as the poor devil with his legs blown off spitting out a mouthful of sand and with it the morphia pills which had been given to ease his agony. Private Bradshaw laughing and shouting excitedly because his rifle had blown up and blown off his finger when he had fired his sand-filled weapon at a diving Messerschmitt.[9]

Close cooperation with the Desert Air Force was maintained throughout:

Air Vice-Marshal Coningham's plans for 23rd/24th the first night of the offensive, were to illuminate and bomb gun positions and concentrations, attack with low flying night fighters, jam the R/T communications of the enemy's armoured formations by specially equipped Wellingtons, and create confusion by dropping dummy parachutists and laying smoke. At daybreak on the 24th day-bombers and fighter bombers would attack prearranged targets. And thereafter, with smoke-laying aircraft, were to be on call to meet the army's requests for air support.[10]

In reality, a great, massed bombardment was not entirely possible and the image of every gun along the front firing in unison, while compelling, is untrue:

> For seven minutes the enemy's forward defences received a tremendous pounding by the full weight of 30 Corps artillery. Then, at zero plus 7, the fire support began to vary with each division's needs; it consisted mainly of concentrations lifting at given times from locality to locality, except in two places where it took the form of a barrage. The whole elaborate programme lasted about 5½ hours.[11]

There was a paucity of guns in the north so the bombardment was delivered in bursts, with the main weight of fire supporting Wrigley's 20th Brigade on the left. As the brigade attacked, with two battalions 2/17th (right) and 2/15th (left) up, the Red line objectives were taken as planned. 40th RTR was then to pass through with 2/13th Battalion following. The armour was held back but the infantry pushed on, not wishing to sacrifice its artillery shield. But now, the going became much tougher as resistance stiffened and casualties mounted. The advance stalled. Five long hours passed till the tanks came forward, too late to prevent the curtain of night giving way to the grey of dawn and still 1,000 yards short. It was time to dig in with the exposed armour falling back to more secure, hull-down positions.

> There was a terrific explosion, and something flew past my head; it was a leg with a boot on it. A round of HE had taken Chalky White's leg off. He was looking at me with astonishment and pointing to the raw, bleeding stump with the white bone sticking through. I went towards him with the idea of helping him, I think; just then the machine gun opened up again and poor Chalky got it full in the face.[12]

On the northern flank of the division, Godfrey's 24th Brigade was not seriously engaged, apart from mounting diversions and lending a battalion as reserve. 26th Brigade (Whiteley) was detailed to take and cover the northern shoulder. By midnight the Red line objective had been secured by 2/24th Battalion and 2/48th passed through on schedule. Despite heavy fighting, these reached the Blue line by the allotted time. Such precise reporting gives no true note of the horror and confusion which reigned on the field that night:

> A bullet smashed into my hand causing me to drop my rifle. I felt something boring into my shoulder and a taste of blood in my mouth. Nearly everyone seemed dead or dying, and I ran away from the senseless slaughter, unable and unwilling to stay and let myself be shot full of holes like a colander.[13]

The highland regiments of the British Army have always enjoyed a high reputation and Wimberley, rightly, had every confidence in his men. Though new to the desert they had trained hard and were ready. Nonetheless, their task was a most formidable one. They would have to fan out from the start line to attain their final objectives with a frontage of nearly double, the whole studded with very strong defences. In recognition of this, extra halts had been added on Green, then Red, on to Black and finally the Blue lines. Each of the defended areas was labelled with a homely Scottish name. More than in any other sector this was to represent a Great War battle. The troops even had the Saltire, outlined in scrim cloth, across the rear of their packs. Each carried sufficient ammunition and rations, plus entrenching tools and materials for a full twenty-four-hour period.

> I'm but the son my mother bore,
> A simple man and nothing more.
> But – God of strength and gentleness,
> Be pleased to make me nothing less
>
> Anonymous[14]

It was just after 10 p.m. that the rant of skirling pipes heralded the highlanders' advance, General Wimberley to the fore:

As we motored forward it was amazingly quiet. In fact, with memories of the 1914-1918 War, I thought it was really too quiet to be true. One thousand guns were to start firing at 2140 hours and in the stillness that preceded the storm I stood at one of the gaps in the wire and watched my Jocks in the moonlight. Platoon by platoon they filed past, heavily laden with pick and shovel, sandbags and grenades – the officer at the head, his piper by his side. There was nothing more that I could do now to prepare for the battle, it was only possible to pray for their success, and that the Highland Division would live up to its name and the names of those very famous regiments of which it was composed.[15]

Murray's 152nd Brigade was tasked to hold the front line and continue the business, begun on previous nights, of clearing and marking routes in the western openings of the three designated tracks: 'Sun', 'Moon' and 'Star'. The job facing Houldsworth's 154th Brigade was daunting; nearly three quarters of the front was their battleground. Advancing on the left of the line, and on the right of the brigade frontage 1st Black Watch and 7/10th Argyll & Sutherland Highlanders would come up against 'Stirling' a very heavily fortified locality. To their left, two companies of 5th Camerons would advance to the Red line and 7th Black Watch would leapfrog to seek out the Kiwis on Miteiriya Ridge. Into the gap between the Camerons and Argylls, 50th RTR would deploy and seize a further stronghold, 'Nairn' and then press on towards the Blue line:

The line had broken up into blobs of men all struggling together; my faithful batman was still trotting along beside me. I wondered if he had been with me while I was shooting. My runner had disappeared, though; and then I saw some men in a trench ahead of me. They were standing up with their hands above their heads screaming something that sounded like 'Mardray'; I remember thinking how dirty and ill-fitting their uniforms were and smiled at myself for bothering about that at this time.[16]

On the right of 154th Brigade, Graham's 153rd would attain the Red line with 5th Black Watch who would then pass the baton to 1st Gordons tasked to assault another very strong position, 'Aberdeen'. Sergeant Covell of the Gordons recalled the high morale of the storming highlanders:

At about 7 o'clock that night we collected all our equipment and moved up to the start line. All you could hear was the sound of people laughing and talking all around us. Everyone was in very high spirits and looking forward to getting their own back after the last do at St. Valery ... When the Black Watch moved forward we followed and then went through them. There was a lot of opposition from machine gun posts, but we soon mopped them up with bayonet and grenades. We took our objectives and held onto them like grim death until the tanks came through.[17]

On the left of the brigade advance, 5/7th Gordons would undertake the job of capturing yet another Axis bastion, 'Strichen'. As the pipes sounded their familiar clarion call to battle, 5th Black Watch stormed forward into an intensifying enemy fire that claimed, among others, the life of nineteen-year-old Piper MacIntyre. As the dust and murk descended, lit by flashes of detonations and livened by the crack of rounds, cohesion slackened and the Green Line was mistaken for the Red. The Gordons could not immediately advance as heavy shelling was splintering the dark some 300 yards ahead; 'our guns or theirs' the not unfamiliar cry: '... when I discovered there was no one on my left either, my anger turned to fear ... a nauseating wave of terror went right through me'.[18]

Michael Carver, later to write his superlative history of the battle, witnessed the 'Jocks' advance:

Suddenly the whole horizon went pink and for a second or two there was perfect silence, and then the noise of 8th Army's guns hit us in a solid wall of sound that made the whole earth shake ... Then we saw a sight that will live forever in our memories – line upon line of steel helmeted figures with rifles at the high port, bayonets flashing in the moonlight, and over all the wailing of the pipes ... As they passed they gave us the thumbs up sign, and we watched them plod on towards the enemy lines, which by this time were shrouded in smoke.[19]

Some minutes behind schedule the advance continued as did some confusion. 'Braemar' which was 1,000 yards west of 'Kintore' was stormed and almost overrun. This put them almost on the Black line but losses had been severe. One company, detached in support of 'A' Squadron 50th RTR, dealt with 'Kintore' then the armour raced on to engage 'Aberdeen' only to fall foul of un-cleared mines. The other Gordon battalion had encountered similar difficulties short of the Red Line. Axis machine guns began their rapid, staccato rattle, spitting fire from 'Keith' and 'Strichen' both covered by mines. The advance was slowed. One company, attempting to flank a first minefield, became meshed in another. The net result of these accumulated obstacles was that the brigade had scarcely been able to penetrate much beyond the Red line when dawn broke.

> In front of me a terrified Italian was running round and round with his hands above his head screaming at the top of his voice. The men I had signalled started to come out. Suddenly I heard a shout of 'Watch out!' and the next moment something hard hit the toe of my boot and bounced off. There was a blinding explosion, and I staggered back holding my arm over my eyes instinctively. Was I wounded? I looked down rather expecting to see blood pouring out, but there was nothing – a tremendous feeling of relief. I was unhurt. I looked for the sergeant who had been beside me; he had come to take the place of the one who had fallen. At first I couldn't see him, and then I saw him lying sprawled out on his back groaning. His leg was just a tangled mess.[20]

1st Black Watch was on the right of Houldsworth's Brigade, hugging the fiery screen of the barrage. The Red line was reached but moving forward from there entailed much bitter fighting. They reached and even passed their final objectives which included 'Perth', another strong bastion. Doggedly, the attacking company battled through the insidious web of anti-personnel mines, despite very heavy loss. 7/10th Argylls pressed on beyond the Red line into the teeth of furious enemy fire:

> One of the most memorable and still chilling and nightmarish things is hearing the voices of those who'd been badly wounded, their voices raised in terror and pain. I can remember one particular sergeant who's always seemed to me almost a kind of father figure ... He was badly wounded and hearing his voice sort of sobbing and calling for his mother seemed to be so demeaning and humiliating and dreadful.[21]

Companies were shredded and the tanks of 'C' Squadron 50th RTR slow in coming up. 'Stirling' remained unvanquished as the survivors dug in. With dawn, chances of successfully taking the position evaporated. On the left, 5th Camerons reached their Red line without difficulty; 7th Black Watch passed through but sustained very heavy casualties before reaching Black. Captain Cathcart led a much-reduced company onto Miteiriya Ridge and took 'Kircaldy', a remarkable feat of arms, though the cost was high indeed. The wounded Cathcart was able to establish a link to the Kiwis on the depleted unit's left. Even this proved difficult due to the severity of losses incurred.

> I suddenly felt furious; an absolute uncontrollable temper surged up inside me. I swore and cursed at the enemy now crouching in the corner of the trench; then I fired at them at point blank range, two, three, and then click! I had forgotten to reload. I flung my pistol away in disgust and grabbed a rifle – the sergeant's, I think and rushed in. I believe two of the enemy were sprawled on the ground at the bottom of the square trench. I bayoneted two more and then came out again.[22]

It was 02.30 hrs before the armour moved and then only to encounter yet more un-cleared mines. As the vehicles crawled forward they were met by heavy and accurate fire which knocked out several. Wimberley's division had attacked with great élan and the highlanders had advanced upon their objectives with outstanding courage and resolution. Despite such gallantry the overall position was not satisfactory. With the exception of the extreme left, final objectives had not been secured, the main defensive line was un-breached and a number of strongpoints survived in rear: 'Kintore', 'Stirling' and 'Strichen'. The armour had not been able to punch through and the swirling chaos of dust-laden darkness cast a pall of confusion over the field.

> Help me, O God, when death is near
> To mock the haggard face of fear,
> That when I fall – if fall I must –
> My soul may triumph in the Dust

Anonymous[23]

Freyberg's New Zealanders were old desert hands and had learnt much from earlier fights. His front was less extensive than that allotted to Wimberley, one and a half miles widening out to twice that. Freyberg planned to husband his resources, deploying one battalion from each of his two brigades to seize the Red line objectives. When this was consolidated, a two hour pause being allowed, the other two battalions from each brigade would push on, halt briefly then drive on toward their objectives over Miteiriya Ridge. The Maoris were detailed to follow behind both and mop up as they advanced. 5th

Brigade (Kippenburger) on the right would be supported by Royal Wiltshire Yeomanry, while Gentry's 6th Brigade would have the Royal Warwickshire Yeomanry.

The guns, with additional batteries from 10 Corps, delivered timed barrages against the enemy's known strongpoints with only a token fire across the front. As Kippenburger's infantry surged forward, the 23rd Battalion suffered heavy loss past Red, though ably supported by the following Maoris. 21st Battalion, passing through 23rd advanced steadily and gained their objectives, digging in on the leading edge of the ridge. Contact, as mentioned above, was established with the Scots on their right, fighting patrols probing forwards. Gapping, as ever, proved problematic and heavier weapons were slow in getting up. On the brigade's left flank, 22nd Battalion suffered casualties from the same redoubt that had troubled the 23rd though the position was outflanked and dealt with. With this hurdle overcome, the Kiwis took their objectives and, despite being heavily mortared, were able to send out fighting patrols. Behind the infantry patient work of gapping went on, beset as ever by difficulties but a cleared route to the forward positions was finally opened before dawn.

Gentry's left-hand battalion, the 24th, ran into heavy enemy fire and took casualties before they even reached the Red line. As 26th Battalion came forward on the right they suffered under intense shelling, possibly 'blue on blue' in the modern idiom. Nonetheless, they attained their objectives on the ridge, unlike 25th Battalion which ran into serious opposition and, though they came up to the ridge, were not able to move across the crest and dig in on the western slopes. While the New Zealanders had attained nearly all of their objectives, the line remained incomplete with a considerable gulf between 25th and 26th Battalions, nor, at this point, was their any trace of the South Africans. At length, heavier weapons were brought up and the Maoris battled their way forward to the ridge. Barney O'Kelly again:

The 'I' officers and NCOs had a little tipple in the van to drink success to the operation, and our poet, Corporal Hughie Scholes, recited a pastiche of Henry's speech before Agincourt, suggesting that gentlemen in England then abed would hold themselves accursed they were not here etc.[24]

Behind the Kiwis, Yeomanry armour rumbled forward. The Wiltshires, who were on the right, successfully negotiated the ridge but lost nine machines to mines. Their advance was met by a stiff counter-attack from Axis tanks and the survivors withdrew behind the rise. The Warwickshires had a similar experience, gaining the ridge by 04.00 hrs but falling foul of more mines before going hull down. Initially in reserve, 3rd Hussars moved up after being heavily shelled and took station to the right of the Warwickshires. For the most part, the ridge was now in Allied hands, yet no sign of more armour passing through. The undetected mines on the crest and beyond had scuppered any chances of the Yeomanry getting forward. It was indeed a job very well done but did not offer any immediate prospect for exploitation. The late arrival of support weapons naturally left the infantry feeling vulnerable:

> The inferno that was the great battle of Alamein continued unabated. The appalling din of guns firing and shells bursting, the grim sights of mangled men and twisted corpses, the nauseating smell that was a mixture of sulphur and rotting human flesh, the mental strain from sleeplessness and responsibility, the fear of breaking down in front of the men; all these became everyday things. I suppose that we grew accustomed to them, for as time went on we noticed them less.[25]

In the sector allotted to Pienaar, he adopted a similar deployment to Freyberg. His 2nd Brigade was on the right, 3rd to the left. A scratch force of armoured cars and A/T guns was deployed with 1st Brigade on the extreme left to secure an open flank. Heavier armour, from RTR, with 2nd Regiment Botha was to keep pace with the advance in the centre, provide support and seize such opportunities as events might offer. The divisional guns, with extra batteries, would provide full fire support with the addition of smoke to facilitate regrouping during the pauses. The brigades attacked with one battalion 'up' and two waiting to strike beyond the Red line. It was the 1st Natal Mounted Rifles from 2nd Brigade who took Red but the Cape Town Highlanders following were badly mauled by intense enemy fire. Their difficulties led to delays in the continuing barrages. Despite this, the advance was successfully resumed and Miteiriya Ridge was gained before dawn. Left of the Highlanders, 1st/2nd Field Battalion had a stormy passage, taking many casualties and halting a mile east of their final target.

Though O'Kelly and his comrades in Intelligence snatched some fitful sleep, 'even at our safe distance it was impossible not to be aware of the sweat and darkness and horror of the night; in so much intelligence work one was deeply involved but physically remote'.[26]

Leading 3rd Brigade's attack was 1st Rand Light Infantry, who ran into opposition barely west of their start line. Despite this they overcame the obstacle, took prisoners and reached the Red line barely behind schedule. The delay worked to the advantage of Imperial Light Horse and Royal Durban Light Infantry, as the artillery schedule caught up and both battalions were on their objectives before first light. As ever, delays in gapping slowed the divisional reserve and dawn was breaking before they approached the eastern flank of the ridge. Mercifully, they sustained no casualties. The situation overall was similar to that of the New Zealanders; most objectives had been taken but no prospect for exploitation arose. Further south of Pienaar, 4th Indian Division had performed its diversionary role admirably. Despite the very real difficulties, dust and confusion, 30 Corps had achieved a great deal, considering the plan was an extremely ambitious one. For their brethren in armoured chariots, there was no cause for celebration that night:

> I was pretty impressed the night of Alamein, when the guns opened up. It was tremendous. All our searchlights were facing upwards in the sky to make a false daylight, to make things easier. When we went through the minefields and got to the first positions, there were dead Italians everywhere. I can remember seeing a man in his trench with his mess tin in front of him. He was dead. The barrage had opened up so suddenly, it had caught them well and truly unprepared.[27]

Montgomery had intended this formation would be his answer to DAK. Its strength was impressive containing some 434 tanks of which roughly half were Shermans. 1st Armoured Division (Briggs) was to advance on the extreme left of the Australians while 10th Armoured (Gatehouse) came on through the flank of the New Zealand Division. Each of these was responsible for gapping its individual paths. The Minefield Task Forces assigned to each division would need to clear three lanes for the tanks. These would be some 500 yards apart, 1st Division had Sun, Moon and Star, 10th Division would proceed along Bottle, Boat and Hat. The monsters rumbled forth from their rearward lairs after dark.

Springbok Road running south from El Alamein marked a jumping off point. Their fuel tanks replenished, these leviathans were to be on their designated lanes by 02.00 hrs. The plan was that the leading squadrons of 2nd Armoured Brigade, from 1st Armoured Division (Fisher), and 8th Brigade from 10th Division (Custance), would be in position to break out from the infantry positions astride the 30 Corps objectives. During the course of the initial move, a distance of some three miles west to 'Pierson', 24th Armoured Brigade (Kenchington), would deploy to the left of Custance.

These three brigades still, as it was hoped, operating under the cover of darkness, would be ready to meet whatever the Axis might throw at them. As the cloak of night was whipped away, Fisher and Kenchington would motor on for another mile. The tanks' northern flank would be covered by 7th Motor Brigade (Bosvile) and in the south by 133rd Lorried Infantry Brigade (Lee). The final bound, now in broad daylight, would bring Fisher as far as the Rahman track and place Custance, after a four mile dash, just south. As the tanks ground forward, armoured cars would race ahead trying to locate 15th Panzer and to give warning of any riposte by Axis armour from the south. It was thus hoped that, fog of war notwithstanding, these three brigades could engage and neutralize any enemy tanks, though Lumsden had issued a strict order against any 'balaklavering' – the days of charging full tilt onto an Axis gun line were most definitely over:

> The leading armoured brigades were therefore to be prepared to deploy and if necessary fight through to open country. But General Lumsden warned them that they must on no account 'rush blindly on to the enemy's anti-tank guns or try to pass through a narrow bottleneck which is covered by a concentration of enemy tanks ... There is no doubt General Lumsden was very uneasy about the role given to his Corps ...[28]

This element of caution, which Montgomery was apt to decry as timorousness, would lead to friction and confirm the army commander's doubts over the corps commander's suitability for the role.

Then there were mines. Gapping, begun generally on time, did not proceed smoothly. Sun route was not opened as far as the infantry forward positions till 05.00 hrs. On Moon track, defective detectors and enemy resistance completely disrupted the programme. The enemy strongpoint 'Kintore' was not taken till 09.00 hrs which brought the sappers only as far as the second minefield and by the time this was dealt with, the third was impossible. Star was 'loaned' to the New Zealanders for a time and they were not clear until 03.00 hrs. By 04.30 hrs, the second minefield was only partly gapped and further progress was impeded by 'Strichen' which remained in enemy hands. F. A. Lewis, 'a back street cockney' was one of those in the armoured advance:

We were very silent for most of the [approach] journey until, just as we were approaching the first of our own minefields, the very skies seemed to open and become one leaping, dancing, frenzy of gun flashes as the artillery opened its barrage. Soon we were among the guns, and stopped for a few moments among a battery of sixty-pounders. A few yards to my right the long snout of one rose from it spit, and suddenly with a terrific white flash it sent its shell flying over towards the enemy; in the momentary light one could see the stark silhouette of the steel helmeted gunners standing motionless in the pit.[29]

For the tanks to advance, even where gapping was complete, was no easy matter. Navigating in the dark with the endless billowing clouds of dust settling a sticky pall over men and vehicles proved almost nightmarish. Signs were difficult to spot, vehicles blundered off the lanes. Some were disabled by mines. The crowding came to resemble a vast traffic jam, a driver's purgatory. Tanks struggled forwards, the Queen's Bays group astride Sun, 9th Lancers, with Brigade HQ on Moon and 10th Hussars group on Star. The Bays came to think they were a good deal further west than was in fact the case. Optimistically they radioed they were, by 05.00 hrs, passing through the third minefield. They were not, they were barely clear of the first. The Lancers fared little better and dawn found them just clear of the first minefield, their support troops engaged in reducing 'Kintore'. 10th Hussars were similarly discommoded by 'Strichen'. In short, though enemy action had been paltry, the entire brigade was still way too far to the east; 'the achievements of 10th Corps fell a long way short of [these] expectations'.[30]

Further south, Custance and Kenchington, with more vehicles to manage, also encountered difficulties but, by 04.30 hrs a quartet of cleared lanes had opened the tank highway onto Miteiriya Ridge. Opposition had been stiffer and the mines more numerous. 8th Brigade led the way, Staffordshires on Bottle, Sherwood Rangers astride Boat and, using Hat, 3rd RTR, armoured cars following. Enemy fire and yet more mines obliged the Staffordshires to halt on the eastern flank of the ridge. A deluge of fire also greeted the Sherwood Rangers as they traversed the crest and they too were obliged to pull back, though not without loss.

'Scuttler' Maile commanded a tank in this action:

> Coming up the ridge we were all alone. We were right out in front, one tank burning on the left, one tank burning on the right. We were being hit with HE and anti-tank rounds. The enemy guns had us at pretty close range and we were right up there on the skyline … We'd only just got there when I looked over the side and saw that one of our caterpillar tracks was off; we couldn't move now. The bow gunner was the first to notice the enemy gun facing us. He shouted: 'Look! There's a bloody big gun over there, pointed straight at us.' Then we saw it in an emplacement only 200 yards away. We got our gun on it. Everybody was jumping about. We hit him square but as we hit him he hit us. I gave the order to bale out and we threw ourselves down in the sand.[31]

Maile's tank and one other were the only ones to attain the ridge, both were now knocked out and the survivors huddled in the shell-ravaged desert – 'You didn't dare move a muscle.'

As they crouched, unarmed they could see Axis infantry converging, though the British barrage scythed a number:

> The officer was talking to us when he was hit in the back of the neck and killed. The fellow on my left, my driver, got a bit of shrapnel in his ear. He said he was feeling faint and I said: 'Don't be stupid. Wait until your head's blown off!': that was the way to keep their morale up.[32]

The Axis could not reach them but sniped incessantly; only darkness might bring relief but the Germans would be sure to rush them again. Maile was determined to break out but their line of escape was handily illuminated by blazing hulks: 'It was our only chance to get through, so we made our dash between the two blazing tanks and somehow made it without loss.'

Delays in gapping caused 3rd RTR to lose the cover of darkness as they were still labouring through the mines. They finally managed to work forwards to positions on the left of the Sherwoods. There was no prospect of the armoured cars being able to break free. Behind

Custance's Brigade, Kenchington's was stalled in the great mass of
vehicles and guns attached to the Kiwis and South Africans. Another
vast and apparently random scrum of vehicles began to build up.

Supply was both of the essence and a planner's nightmare. Those
who fetched and carried just behind the front were every bit as vital as
those ahead in the front of the front. Sergeant Harry Simpson of 7th
Black Watch was one of these:

> In the main battle of El Alamein in October 1942 it was our job to bring out the
> carriers with food and ammunition behind the main attacking lines. When the forward
> infantry had secured their positions, we had to provide them with our supplies. The
> further advanced we got, the more horrifying the experiences were. There were our
> mates, lying prostrate on the ground in a terrible state. We gave the wounded what
> help we could, and then we advanced further up. We also helped the enemy if we could
> because you felt sorry for them.[33]

Not all were grateful:

> One chap I do remember, in the odd silence you got when the guns stopped, he was
> swearing at us in Italian, so we gave him a drink of water and a cigarette. But he threw
> them on the floor, so I said to Captain Miller: 'Let's put a bullet through the bugger,'
> and we laughed like Albert – so we left him there and we carried on. What happened
> to him I don't know – and frankly, I wasn't even bothered.[34]

As the infantry divisions of 30 Corps and the armour of 10 Corps put
in their great offensive in the northern sector, 13 Corps in the south
was tasked to break through 'January' and 'February' minefields and
push its tanks beyond. For this, 7th Armoured Division deployed two
of its brigades; Roberts' 22nd Armoured and Roddick's 4th Light
Armoured. The approach was over thirteen miles and through three
lines of Allied minefields. A Minefield Task Force would then clear
four gaps through the Axis mines allowing 22nd Brigade to penetrate
some 6,000 yards beyond with 4th Light Armoured Brigade clinging
to their coat-tails.

This onslaught would begin at 22.00 hrs to coincide with 30 Corps
attack. Four regiments of field artillery would provide a covering
barrage while 131st Infantry Brigade (from 44th Division) protected
the northern shoulder with the Desert Air Force and the guns

contributing dense smoke immediately south. Further south still, on the extreme flank, Koenig's 1st Fighting French Brigade Group would seek to penetrate for ten miles and seize high ground at Naqb Rala. The Minefield Task Force was led by 44th Reconnaissance Regiment with elements from 4th and 21st Field Squadron RE, a troop of Honeys from the Scots Greys with half a dozen Scorpion flails.

> We set off; exciting, breathless and that sort of orchestral music of the continuous guns in the background. We wondered if the Jerry saw it that way! I remember seeing a captain walking behind a Scorpion, intent on supervising the job. This tank had a barrel fastened across its nose which revolved. Fastened by one end were chains which whirled round and thumped the ground ahead; supposed to blow up any mines in its path. Something seemed to worry the captain and he literally screamed at the crew and someone nearby, on edge, poor devil, some Job![35]

'January' was thought to be some 350 yards in depth and 'February' perhaps 1,000 yards. Four lanes had to be cleared and the work progressed despite the gradual elimination of the flails and some enemy fire. By 02.30 hrs the southerly lanes were cleared of mines but Axis outposts had to be tackled by infantry from 1st Rifle Brigade. By 04.00 hrs a bridgehead had been consolidated but this now left 'February' a denser obstacle and with the task force much reduced. It was thus decided to utilise two lanes only. Even this proved too ambitious, intense enemy fire descended like the dawn chorus and the attempt could not be continued. Further north, 131st Brigade's attempts had met with equal frustration; the assault on an enemy strongpoint had resulted in heavy casualties among 1/7th Queen's Royal Regiment. Koenig's Group, after hard fighting and difficulties in bringing up heavy weapons, could do no more than win a toehold south of Naqb Rala. Gains in 13 Corps sector were modest and costly while falling far short of what was hoped for.

> So we set off late one evening, two battalions, two companies up in line abreast across a thousand yards of minefields, led by an officer on a compass bearing and Lieutenant-Colonel East using a stick as a result of a First World War wound. We were to advance behind a barrage of a thousand guns. There were casualties in the platoon on my right from one gun firing short or possibly from the enemy replying. I can still remember the shriek from one of my platoon when a booby trap on the barbed-wire

literally blew him to pieces ... Eventually our leading platoon and the 1st/6th Queens
on our left arrived in the middle of the Italian positions and some twenty to thirty
Italians cheerfully gave themselves up and remained for the next twenty-four hours,
withdrawing with us at the end of that time. The remainder of the Folgore Division,
however, were made of sterner stuff and proceeded to inflict heavy casualties on us,
using mortars and machine guns, firing from entrenched positions. I remember young
O'Connell, both legs severed by a mortar bomb, screaming for help and then for his
mother before he mercifully died.[36]

The advance ground on:

... next day we moved forward through a narrow gap cleared through the enemy
minefields and took up a new position, from which we fired another formidable
box-barrage that night. During the day we came under fire for the first time from a
distant ridge, on which we could just see enemy tank turrets appearing from time to
time.[37]

The Dogfight

Dawn threw the battlefield into sharp relief, though much smoke and
dust lingered. Montgomery had to plan his next moves in the light
of what had, and had not, been achieved. It was imperative that the
northern corridor on 30 Corps front be cleared and that the Kiwis
should attempt to break out southwards from the hard-won ground at
Miteiriya Ridge. Morshead was to prepare for a 'crumbling' operation
that night. In the south, a way had to be found through the 'February'
minefield. If 7th Armoured could not get tanks through then the
infantry from 44th Division must undertake the task. Monty remained
convinced that 10 Corps armour must penetrate as far as 'Pierson', as
previously proposed. He hammered home to Lumsden, about whom he
had swelling doubts, of the need to achieve this objective, even if heavy
casualties were sustained. Freyberg, as he exploited southwards, would
need the tanks covering his flank.

Dawn and the Allied intelligence gatherers were as alert as magpies:

The next morning, first light was typical of a battle seen from an 'I' van. The 'phones
were going all the time, signals were arriving, despatch riders looking in, the gen log
building up item by item. The battle map was constantly being brought up to date
with new locations on the chinagraph, red for us and blue for them ... There was no

time for breakfast, someone brought me a mug of tea and by mid morning, the floor around my feet was ankle deep in cigarette ends.[38]

Throughout the day, Desert Air Force was heavily engaged. Axis armoured groups and aerodromes received a great deal of attention while, in the south, a squadron of British light tanks, in German hands, was destroyed by cannon-firing Hurricanes. Losses among the attacking aircraft were high and over 1,000 sorties flown. Along the front, guns bickered and Wimberley's Highlanders, aided by infantry tanks from 50th RTR, eliminated Axis outposts previously bypassed. The grinding business of clearing and gapping minefields continued, enabling 2nd Armoured Brigade to inch forwards in the teeth of savage enemy fire. By evening, however, the lead units were on the 'Oxalic' line between Australians and highlanders.

Two thrusts were planned for the hours of darkness. 10th Armoured was to push on over Miteiriya Ridge with 24th Brigade to the right and 8th to the left, 'Pierson', its earlier objective, being the goal. Each brigade of tanks would be supported by a squadron of RE to deal with mines and a single battalion from the lorried infantry would remain on the ridge, acting as a 'pivot of manoeuvre'. To provide further support, 9th Armoured Brigade, attached to the New Zealanders, would keep pace on the left flank of the 8th. This move would have the benefit of a full artillery programme and barrage, seeking out enemy guns and strongpoints. Axis battlegroups would again receive the very best of the Air Force's attentions. 'Quite early it became clear that there were frustrations on the corps front.'[39]

From the very beginning the plan began to unravel. Inevitably, mines were thicker than imagined on the western slope. Axis guns were not subdued and added their chorus of destruction as the sappers laboured. Immediately after 22.00 hrs, zero-hour, the Luftwaffe scored a mercifully rare success when they blitzed 8th Brigade at the very worst moment, in the act of assembling. Bombs rained down havoc. The resultant flames from burning vehicles greatly assisted the Axis gunners. In such circumstances, it made excellent sense for all vehicles to disperse but this destroyed the timetable. The artillery barrage disappeared, rolling westwards. By midnight, Custance felt the advance could not proceed and accordingly reported to Gatehouse who, sharing his subordinate's fears, alerted Lumsden, who concurred.

As we topped the crest the enemy opened up. The covering party rushed the post. Half of them were hit before they got there, but they captured the chaps causing us all the trouble. While they were doing this we probed for mines. Yes, there they were, our own, captured in June and re-laid by the Boche. That was a good start. I found the far end of the field and placed my light. I went over to the infantry and told the dazed corporal to get back. The prisoners carried their officer – shot in the stomach. They told he'd led the charge waving an empty pistol. A Boche prisoner told me in French there were no more mines and that the next field was a dummy. I believed him, he was in such a state; the enemy machine gun fire grew worse, the tracer appearing to fill the air and make an impenetrable wall.[40]

Montgomery's doubts about his 10 Corps commander stuck deep. Lumsden was not one of his nominees and was, if nothing else, a handy scapegoat should one be needed:

In accordance with my orders I expected the armoured divisions to fight their way out into the open. But there was some reluctance to do so and I gained the impression during the morning they were pursuing a policy of inactivity. There was not that eagerness on the part of senior commanders to push on and there was a fear of tank casualties ... The 10 Corps commander [Lumsden] was not displaying the drive and determination so necessary when things begin to go wrong and there was a general lack of offensive eagerness in the armoured divisions of the corps.[41]

This was, of course, grossly unfair and reflects more upon the Army commander's antipathy to his subordinate than upon tactical realities. De Guingand, on hearing from Lumsden, had summoned both him and Leese to 8th Army Tactical HQ for a meeting at 03.30 hrs. Monty, on being awakened, agreed:

Leese and Lumsden arrived on time and I asked each to explain his situation ... I discovered that in the 10th Armoured Division, one of the armoured regiments was already out in the open and that it was hoped more would be out by dawn. The divisional commander [Gatehouse] wanted to withdraw it all back behind the minefields and give up the advantages he had gained; his reason was that the situation out in the open would be very unpleasant and his division might suffer heavy casualties. Lumsden agreed with him; he asked if I would personally speak to the divisional commander on the telephone. I did so at once and discovered to my horror that he himself was some 16,000 yards (nearly ten miles) behind his leading armoured brigades. I spoke to him in no uncertain voice, and ordered him to go forward at once and take charge of his battle; he was to fight his way out and lead his division from in front and not from behind.[42]

Admirable firmness but the real problem was that Monty's plan was not, at this stage, working. Both Custance and Gatehouse were correct in not wishing to see their formations decimated to no purpose. They were not faint-hearted merely pragmatic. Of course, this would simply not do for the Army Commander:

> ... there would be no departure from the plan. I kept Lumsden behind when the others had left and spoke very plainly to him. I said I was determined that the armoured divisions would get out of the minefield area and into the open where they could manoeuvre; any wavering or lack of firmness now would be fatal; if he himself, or the commander 10th Armoured Division, was not 'for it', then I would appoint others who were.[43]

By 04.20 hrs Lumsden, doubtless still smarting, instructed that 24th Armoured Brigade must attain its goal and that the 8th had to have one of its regiments moving forwards to maintain contact with 9th Armoured on its left. Initially, it appeared that two regiments from 24th Armoured were on 'Pierson' by the time dawn broke on the 25th though this was probably inspired more by optimism than reality, but all three regiments of 8th Armoured had filtered through the single cleared lane past the mines. 9th Brigade and the New Zealand Divisional Cavalry, in the teeth of fierce bombardment, had moved perhaps half way to their objectives. Here they were stalled by a hail of rounds from dug-in tanks and guns perhaps 1,000 yards distant. Currie now sought permission from Freyberg to retire and replenish before attacking but his request was denied. Custance, as he moved west, was coming under an intensive and increasing enemy fire. The bare ground offered no suitable features for taking hull-down positions so he fell back to the eastern slope of the ridge. By now, with the New Zealanders' 5th Brigade in situ and the fresh battalions of lorried infantry crowding in, the locality was becoming rather congested:

> One of my recollections is about our divisional coppers. The Military Police manned the entrances to the gaps in the enemy minefields throughout the early days of our

attack. It was a lonely job, not without its dangers from odd shells and mines going up. I was most impressed by their fortitude and I passed up and down to have a word.[44]

In 13 Corps' sector to the south, renewed efforts to force the passage of the dense 'February' minefield, despite the immense courage of both sappers and infantry to clear the lanes, were not ultimately successful. The soldiers of 131st Brigade succeeded in passing through but could get no further such was the weight of enemy fire. Despite the storm of fire, sappers, mostly with the patient prodding of bayonets, cleared two lanes. The tanks, from 22nd Armoured Brigade, rumbled forward under bright moonlight and a deluge of iron, losing thirty-one vehicles. Neither they nor the infantry could do any more.

After over twenty-four hours fighting, Montgomery had to take stock and consider his next move. The opening phase had gone partly according to plan, though at no inconsiderable cost. The infantry of 30 Corps had done all that was humanly possible and had succeeded in the majority of instances in securing their objectives. In so doing they had overcome enemy minefields, strongly held outposts and strongpoints. They had killed large numbers of the Axis defenders and taken more as prisoners. The artillery had performed outstandingly. But the fact remained that though there was a break-in there was no break-out. Much more would need to be done.

> I remember my husband telling me of the first night of the battle of El Alamein, the deadly silence when they were waiting to attack, how he looked at a small photo of me, saying goodbye, thinking this is the end. Of a young lad beside him, scared, how he hung on to my husband. The night was still black, then it seemed as though the heavens opened, the barrage of the guns. At another time they were dug in, in a trench, and he and this young man were just looking over the top, and then my husband said, 'I can see the whites of the German eyes' and he kept telling this ginger lad to keep his head down. Then he just put his head up again and they got him between the eyes.[45]

Dawn on 25 October and the situation was effectively one of stalemate.

10
Second El Alamein: 'Crumbling'

Were you there when the guns rained destruction

To smash the mailed gauntlet of might.

When the barrage broke in a sheet of flame

Which rent the dark portieres of night;

When a breach was made in the minefields

That armour might enter the race.

And the portals of Hell needs must tremble

As eighty-eights answered apace?

El Alamein Tapestry

If Montgomery was now clear what he wished 30 Corps to achieve in the north, there remained the question of how to proceed in the south where 13 Corps' attempt the night before had failed. Harding had ordered his engineering officer Lieutenant-Colonel Withers to continue gapping, even though this would have to be accomplished in broad daylight. Withers understandably considered this tantamount to suicide. Leading his men personally, the colonel found enemy fire so intense at the northern gap only he and one other officer in two tanks attempted to move through. This bold attempt was successful despite both tanks being hit and served to prove that the way was largely clear of mines but that it was the ferocious accuracy of enemy fire which rendered the lanes impassable. The hapless infantry still pinned down could not hope to move until dark. 22nd Armoured (Roberts) was ordered to remain stalled between the two minefields to provide some measure of support.

Horrocks was minded to call off the effort but was left with only two viable options for further offensive action. He could either throw in his last reserve 132nd Brigade, and attempt to batter his way through once again or shift the axis of attack towards the western flank of Munassib. This was at least clear of mines and he could use 50th Division (Nichols) with 4th Light Armoured Brigade (Roddick). Though Horrocks had to make do with talking to de Guingand, as the Army Commander was closeted with Alexander who had arrived for a situation report, the chief of staff was later able to confirm Monty's agreement that the second option was indeed preferable.

During the night attack by 13 Corps on 23/24 October, differences of opinion on map-reading led to the infantry and sappers embarking on different routes which left enemy strongpoints intact. Axis artillery added to the crescendo of fire deluging the lanes. The Germans were adept at laying down smoke around the exits so that, as the British tanks emerged they were perfectly silhouetted. Riding into this storm of fire, the armour would halt to seek and engage. Stationary, the tanks made even more perfect targets. AP and tracer hurtled across the ground like swarms of angry bees. Tanks trying to manoeuvre fell foul of un-cleared mines.

The solid-shot shells of the 88s coming at you were a white streak. So was that of the Russian 7.62, but the 5cm PAK shell glowed red like tracer. Not that you really registered it consciously. By the time you had seen it, the shell had flashed past. The 88 travelled at thousands of feet per second – it was just a flash and a bang if it hit. The intelligence bulletins put out by Eighth Army said that tank crews tended to claim falsely that they had been fired on by 88s. None of us was in any doubt when we were under fire that it was 88s we were up against. Being hit was a nightmare experience. The Grants and the early Shermans ran on high-powered aircraft fuel. It was dangerous stuff – highly inflammable. A white hot shell entering into the vehicle turned it into a sort of fire-bomb. You see all our vehicles carried extra tanks on the outside of the turret. It would almost be true to say that when they were hit the American tanks blew up ... They were horrifying sights.[1]

Battering forward through 'February' had little to recommend it and, in all likelihood, would only result in further and unacceptable casualties. In the event, that night's attack put in by 69th Brigade (Cooke-Ellis) did not achieve concrete results. It was in fact a failure, a rather costly failure and, with this, offensive moves in the south ground to an unsatisfactory halt. Little had been gained though enemy tanks in the south had been pinned there and 7th Armoured was pulled back behind the minefields. 44th Division (Hughes), which had sustained heavy loss, took responsibility for the sector south of Munassib, bolstered by the Free French.

> I rode up to the start line on the back of a tank ... along a desert track that had a double bend in it where it passed through two low hills. There were the splattered remains of men, blown at the rock face, where some poor devils had been too near a shell burst. In the open there was a truck 'brewing' up and it was in our path, highlighting each movement of ours to the enemy ... Whoever laid out that minefield knew what he was doing. He had straddled a ridge with it so that to cross it you became a sitting duck on the skyline. A mortar bomb fell on our Bren gun and one of my friends, a corporal, lost part of the top of his skull. I put on a shell dressing and tied it under his chin like a bonnet. It must have been about that time that a metal fragment went through my hip, escaping through the left buttock, but I felt nothing at the time. I half rose, ready to dash forward, when I felt a frightful searing pain in my leg, or rather two pains, one when the bullet went in at the front and one when it emerged at the back. This bullet fell out of my hose [sock] top when I was being cleaned up at the dressing station.[2]

'Ming the Merciless' in the northern sector, had already appreciated the tactical significance of rising ground to his immediate north leading to Point 29 which, providing panoramic observation, was of significance to both sides. Initial probing had confirmed that, from its present positions, 2/48th Battalion could attain the ridge without traversing any minefields. Fortuitously, on the evening of 25 October, an enemy patrol had been netted and the haul included a unit commander, complete with maps and a willingness to share. His revelations confirmed the location of two battalions of German 125th Regiment from 164th Division. Whithead's 26th Brigade had only 2/48th and 2/24th available for the planned attack but 40th RTR with its forty lumbering Valentines would be accompanying.

Fire support was provided by the mass of divisional artillery beefed by two regiments each of field and medium guns. Some 14,508 rounds from the 25-pounders went over with a further 1,066 of 5.5-inch shells. Though their relief (2/17th) was delayed by the barrage, 2/48th moved forward on schedule and advanced 1,000 yards to take their objectives. From here, 2/24th would continue to advance but, with commendable élan, the lead company of the first battalion dashed the final bound to assail Point 29 which, after a sharp fight, was secured. Matters went less favourably for the second battalion which ran into stiffer opposition. The barrage moved away into the distance as losses mounted. No real progress beyond the first 800 yards could be made and the battalion commander decided to consolidate and dig in. The unfortunate result of this was that the successful charge pushed out only a narrow salient. Nonetheless, the key objective had been taken as had numerous prisoners. Private P. E. Gratwick won a posthumous VC during the course of this hard fighting.

While the Australians were attacking in the north, the intention had been that 24th Armoured Brigade would remain in place west of Miteiriya Ridge during the night. At dawn, it should move up with 2nd Armoured Brigade, motoring south of Kidney Ridge. This eminence was to have been secured by 7th Motor Brigade at the time Morshead was attacking north. Confusion reigned over the exact positioning of those Axis strongpoints still holding out and which were due to be mopped up by Wimberley's highlanders and this obfuscated 1st Armoured Division's role overall. Finally, it was decided that Briggs' main function would be to support the attacking infantry and assisting Fisher's brigade in making progress. The latter's attempts to get onto Kidney Ridge proved quite costly, opposed by Italian tanks from Littorio Division. Meanwhile Kenchington, whose briefing with Briggs had got rather muddled, had endured a day of sporadic shelling. When the divisional commander and subordinate did finally meet, Briggs ordered 24th Brigade out of its exposed positions west of Miteiriya Ridge. The net result was that the brigade retraced its route as far back as Springbok Road, then moved via Star track to join up with Briggs, 'their third [night] without sleep'.

A jeep came speeding down the line of stationary tanks – the Colonel – shouting for everyone to start up and get ready to move. I noticed that the roar of the engine woke those members of the crew who had been snatching forty winks inside. Looking down into the fighting chamber, I could see fairly well in the red glow of the radio pilot light. The gunner was easing his long legs and settling himself more comfortably in his seat, while the operator with his feet on my bottom seat was dozing fitfully with his head on his chest. Seeing me climb in and adjust my headphones, they looked enquiringly at me and when I nodded, there was a general air of wakefulness. We lurched forward and entered the passage in our own minefield and I spoke on the intercom and reminded the driver to keep to the right and close to the green lights. The operator who had been watching the outside world through his periscope suddenly spoke, 'Looks like Regent Street.'[3]

For 51st Division, that night's tasks comprised attacks by 1st Gordons on 'Aberdeen'; 5th Black Watch against 'Stirling' and 7th Argylls on 'Nairn'. Some doubt as to exact locations lingered. Part of 'D' Company 1st Gordons was already on or around the objective. The rest of the company, after some tribulations, reached their comrades while B Company, too far south, were shot up by Axis troops who had converted burnt out Allied tanks into temporary, ad hoc bunkers. 'Aberdeen' was not reduced. 5th Black Watch easily overran 'Stirling' but 7th Argylls suffered grievous loss before securing 'Nairn'. Wimberley, at 04.20 hrs, suggested that the night's gains might facilitate a move south by 1st Armoured Division, bypassing 'Aberdeen' still in Axis hands. Leese passed this intelligence on to Lumsden who preferred the more cautious option of offering support to the infantry. It was proposed that Fisher move up to cover 9th Division's left flank but even this limited manoeuvre proved abortive.

As ever the Axis forces were resolute in mounting local counter-attacks. Hans Schilling saw plenty of action during these days. A number of his comrades had previously served in the French Foreign Legion and while these old sweats proved somewhat difficult to control, one, a leather-faced ex-legionnaire from Hamburg named Otto Kindereith, used to spend a lot of time serving punishment. In battle, however, such truculent veterans swiftly proved their worth:

> I watched an attack go in one day during the El Alamein battle and Kindereith was the one in an attack. The captain got out of the trench first and everyone followed him but he was shot as soon as he started running. There was nothing we could do where we were but Otto Kindereith was closer and he just walked out with an MG34 firing it over his arm. Everyone gave him all the cover they could while he stooped down and picked up the captain and brought him back to the trench.[4]

By late afternoon on 25 October the Desert Fox was back in command and the unfortunate Stumme had suffered a fatal coronary; the hero's return was a pronounced fillip for his hard-pressed forces. He was concerned over the scale of his casualties even though the Allies had, thus far, failed to break through. In the north these had been particularly heavy where Allied superiority in artillery and aircraft had battered both Trente and 164th Divisions. Both had lost heavily in men and guns. His Axis armour had to be carefully preserved. Outnumbered and short of fuel, wastage could not be made good. Daylight on the 26th revealed the extent of Australian gains in the north and the relative weakness of Axis dispositions. 15th Panzer was flung into a counter-attack, supported by Italian XX Corps and battered 164th Division.

British intelligence officers, like Sir Edward Boulton, experienced difficulties with the enigmatic coding adopted by some senior officers:

> I was in constant communication with General Lumsden requesting news and giving commands which I had the greatest difficulty in trying to pass on, and with Corps HQ who wanted to know what Lumsden was doing and saying and what was happening. Like many ex-cavalry officers he never used codes but gave orders in parables to confuse the enemy and often ourselves [Lumsden was idiosyncratic with his home-made ciphers]. The first command was entirely phrased in terms of an eighteenth century battle, the history of which I did not know, and though I assumed what he meant I was unable to reach any of our ops staff ... the second command was simpler as it was all about tarts walking down a street and being picked up by one brigadier or another, identified by Christian names.[5]

Thus far, actions by 13 Corps had kept 21st Panzer/Ariete moored in the south. Rommel had now to decide if he should send these formations to shore up the situation in the north. This was a critical decision. It was questionable if he would have sufficient reserves of fuel to send them back again. By nightfall the Axis tanks were on the move, leaving only elements of Ariete in the south. At the same time, 90th Light Division was to shift the bulk of its formations from El Daba to south of Sidi El Rahman and move Trieste Division from Fuka to fill the void. This was a gamble, for Monty's 7th Armoured Division in the south had not moved. Rommel was forced to shunt his resources like a chess player seeking to anticipate his opponent's next move, in the knowledge a single slip could result in checkmate.

Sir Edward Boulton again:

In the meantime, many of our tank personnel had perished during the first night in the minefields and enemy gunfire, including Colonel Eadie and Bill Lewisham (heir to Lord Dartmouth) in the Staffordshire Yeomanry amongst many others; the flies were so numerous and enormous it was almost impossible to eat and we lived for the week mainly on Benzedrine tablets and without a wink of sleep.[6]

In the north, 30 Corps had achieved most of its final objectives but the costs had been high and there were no immediate reinforcements available for either New Zealanders or South Africans. 13 Corps could do no more at present, having failed to make any serious impression in the south and 10 Corps was not yet free of mines and obstacles that would permit tanks to range freely. Captured papers suggested the Axis strategy was simply to wear down any attacks through robust defence rather than committing the precious panzers to a counter-stroke. This was clearly working. In fact Montgomery did not perhaps realise how grave Rommel's supply situation had become and how pessimistic he was.

By noon on 26 October, Montgomery had re-considered his position and issued fresh instructions, echoing his prevailing caution. The Highlanders were to continue mopping up and the Australians would make a further effort during the night of the 28th. 10 Corps would have a role in securing 30 Corps gains but would further be expected to advance west and north-west of Kidney Ridge. In the south, 13 Corps was not immediately expected to undertake further offensive operations, keeping 7th Armoured Division intact remained the priority. With his habitual patience Monty planned to redistribute units between 13 and 30 Corps and draw into reserves some of those formations which had been heavily engaged: the New Zealanders with 9th Armoured Brigade, 10th and possibly 7th Armoured Divisions. Allied losses in armour amounted to some 300 tanks though many could be repaired and 900 remained fit for action.

Keith Douglas again recounts the full nastiness of battle first hand:

The men with me were walking along bent double as though searching the ground. I said to them, 'It's no good ducking down. If you're going to be hit you'll be hit; run across the open ground. Run.' They began to trot reluctantly, and I ran ahead. Presently I saw two men crawling on the ground, wriggling forward very slowly in a kind of embrace. [The reason for this soon became obvious] As I came up to them I recognised one of them as Robin, the RHA Observation officer whose aid I had been asking earlier in the day: I recognised first his fleece-lined suede waistcoat and polished brass shoulder titles and then his face, strained and tired with pain. His left foot was smashed to pulp mingled with the remainder of a boot. But as I spoke to Robin saying, 'Have you got a tourniquet, Robin?' and he answered apologetically, 'I'm afraid I haven't ...' I looked at the second man. Only his clothes distinguished him as a human being, and they were badly charred. His face had gone: in place of it was a huge yellow vegetable. The eyes blinked in it, eyes without lashes, and a grotesque huge mouth dribbled and moaned like a child exhausted with crying.[7]

Montgomery's orders to Lumsden provided that 7th Motor Brigade should put in an attack that night. The corps artillery, with support from that of 30 Corps, would lay down a barrage. Kidney Ridge was so named as it is said to resemble the shape of a kidney bean. This was about all that was agreed and there were differing opinions as to its exact location or even 'whether it was a ridge at all'. It appeared to lie across from the extreme-right flank of Wimberley's Division. Roughly a mile north-west and the same distance south were two enemy positions labelled 'Woodcock and 'Snipe'. It was decided these should be eliminated but there was uncertainty as to exactly where they might be found. The plan for 26 October was that 2nd KRRC was to aim for 'Woodcock' while 2nd Rifle Brigade marched on 'Snipe'. Once the infantry had attained their objectives, leaving their start lines at 23.00 hrs, then at dawn on the 27th 2nd Armoured Brigade would deploy north of the former position and 24th Armoured Brigade would move to the south of the latter. The dispute as to geography between Highlanders and tankers had been resolved in favour of the infantry, 'a bitter pill for desert veterans to swallow'.

During the afternoon of 26th October the corps and divisional commanders arrived and a plot was hatched whereby two battalions were to attack respectively two features to be known as 'Snipe' and 'Woodcock' that night, following an attack by units of the Highland Division. At this conference numbers of officers were gathered on the 'sheltered' side of a Churchill tank when a passing sergeant of the Royal Corps of Signals let out the most weird and realistic noise of AP shot travelling at speed. Everybody wondered what on earth had happened and they burst out laughing![8]

Snipe

In a fog of dust-blanketed dark, 2nd KRRC advanced from their start lines, moving along Moon track though without any moonlight. The dispute as to what lay where hindered any effective barrage and the battalion, which also ran into opposition, progressed slowly to the extent that, by dawn's creeping light, they were still short and south of their objective. The battalion commander judged the ground here untenable and therefore withdrew to a more suitable position, about 1,000 yards north of the ridge and the same distance short of 'Woodcock'. To the south of 2nd KRRC, 2nd Rifle Brigade encountered similar difficulties; the pall of dust obscured start line and objective alike, compounded by the fact the guns were pounding away to the north.

Their commanding officer, Lieutenant-Colonel V. B. 'Vic' Turner decided to march toward the sound of the guns and lightning flashes of exploding rounds, swinging around and continuing for two relatively uneventful miles. The motor platoons advanced on foot, shielded by a screen of carriers. Having reached what they presumed was their objective, they dug in. This was no easy matter in the stony terrain, as Sergeant Longstaff recalls:

> We started to dig in, but it was rock. I found some old German army mortar bomb boxes, which I filled with rocks to build a sangar in front of my men. Then we put some boxes over the top of us so that the overhead shrapnel bursts wouldn't come down like rain and chop us up. A shell doesn't have to explode underground – if it explodes above, it creates even more casualties, because it's coming down like an umbrella. My lads were well trained on this.[9]

> The following morning there was a certain amount of controversy with regard to our position, the 'Jocks' having placed 'Stirling' and 'Aberdeen' in places with which we did not agree. I was sent over to one of these battalions on our left to find out (a) where they thought they were, and (b) if they could assist us in any way. The 'Jocks' were right in their map-reading.[10]

Attaining the objective was the signal for the support units to move forward, sixteen 6-pounders of 'S' company and eleven more from 239 Battery 76th Anti-Tank Regiment RA. Due to circumstances the medical team was prevented from following. Bad ground disabled a number of vehicles and only thirteen of the battalion guns and six of the RA got through but bringing vital ammunition for the MGs and much-needed water. In such confusion, the artillery officer from 2nd RHA was mislaid, a vital presence, one that would soon be 'sorely missed'. A posse of carriers had investigated rising ground south-west of the battalion. Here they blundered into an Italian operational base with a German unit clearly in sight. Undisturbed by these impudent intruders, the Axis columns began a leisurely drive westwards at dawn only to be raked by British guns; fourteen 'kills' were claimed.

> I went in as a Bren gunner with a foot platoon, loaded with spare mags and hand grenades. There was no number two on the Bren. The other lads were carrying spare mags. Our objective was about 2,000 to 3,000 yards ahead. The Bren carriers were forward of us. We were on our start line at about 23.00 hrs: there wasn't much moon, and we stood waiting. As we waited for the word to advance, the thoughts of how and what's going to happen went through my mind: we were all the same, nerves taut, parched lips and throat. Then suddenly we were off, with the artillery giving covering fire and all hell was let loose.[11]

With battalion HQ sited in an old German dugout and in the centre of a rough oval-shaped perimeter, 'A' company with ten guns had the north-east quadrant, 'C' company with four of the 6-pounders held the west and 'B' with a further six guns the south-east. Meanwhile, 24th Armoured Brigade had been slow in getting underway. Uncertainty compounded by exhaustion and the swirling pall of cloying dust meant lead units were not motoring forward until 07.30 hrs. Somewhat unhelpfully, their first contact was with Turner's men whom they commenced shelling! It appears that the British tanks may have mistaken some hulks near the riflemen's trenches as 'live' enemy armour.

Having been appraised of their error, both they and the rifles were soon hotly engaged as two dozen or so Axis tanks were observed forming up on the higher ground south-west. 47th Royal Tanks were the lead formation and swiftly saw their number reduced as the battle hotted up. Six vehicles were knocked out in rapid succession. Despite gallant attempts the British armour could make no headway and were withdrawn behind higher ground in rear, half a mile distant from and east of the infantry. Both Italian and German tanks attacked, over a dozen of the former and twice as many of the latter, who were seeking out 24th Armoured Brigade. These were engaged and eight knocked out. The riflemen were holding on but reduced to four guns per company area and low on ammunition.

The redoubtable Longstaff, with his platoon, was hotly engaged:

Our position was called 'Woodcock' and the next one to us was called 'Snipe'. It was in that position two days after our first attack, that my battalion knocked out 14 tanks in the major attacks – it was the most tanks knocked out by any battalion of the British army ever – a record. But that record was only to last two days, because the 2nd Battalion, the Rifle Brigade, under Colonel Vic Turner, who received the VC, became immortal over the battle of Snipe. They knocked out 90 odd vehicles and tanks.[12]

As the Axis tanks withdrew, their guns took up the crescendo, deluging the exposed position. Then the enemy tanks tried again, nine Italian vehicles sweeping in from the south. Sergeant Calistan commanded the only gun which could bear upon these swift-moving targets and he found himself with the battalion commander as loader with Lieutenant Toms as No. 1. Calistan coolly held his fire, directed by Turner and destroyed six of the enemy in quick succession. Less than a handful of live shells remained. Toms dashed to his jeep, and revved back loaded up and with bullets humming around like angry bees as the three surviving Italians stormed ahead, regardless of their losses. The jeep was hit and burst into flames while the two officers battled to save its vital cargo. Turner was seriously wounded and, despite his best efforts, prevailed upon to take cover. Calistan then calmly disposed of the surviving enemy. He was the only man unwounded of the three.

About five in the evening another counter-attack came in. By the sound there wasn't so much fire coming from our anti-tank guns. Whether they had been knocked out or were just short of ammunition, we didn't know. We found out after it was a combination of both. Again, the remaining anti-tank guns did a wonderful job. Round about this time I glanced behind me, and to the right rear was a Panzer III. I told the lads to keep their heads down. This was our lot. Out front there was quite a movement of vehicles, but our thoughts were on the enemy tank at our rear. We knew that there was a 6-pdr anti-tank gun to our right and facing the front, but there was no firing from it. Presuming the crew were knocked out or were out of ammo, if one of us were to crawl to it, perhaps we could have a go at the panzer. We did a John Wayne, raising a tin hat above our slit trench. We did this and the tank gave it a burst from his MG. It would have been suicide for any of us to get out and have a go. All of a sudden there was an explosion over our position. We all thought that his was the tank firing at us with his 75. Deeper we crouched in our position. Then there was a pall of smoke and the smell of burning rubber. We looked over the edge of our trench … the panzer was burning.[13]

While the riflemen's battle raged, the exact whereabouts of their comrades in 2nd KRRC remained unclear and it was late morning before the Queen's Bays made contact. 2nd Armoured had moved forward that morning initially believing opposition to be weak. They were soon disabused. Axis forces were gearing up for a counter-stroke and 21st Panzer were about to be committed. Point 33, which was the true location of 'Woodcock', remained in German hands with 2nd Armoured strung out in a south-westerly line falling just short of the east flank of Kidney Ridge. 'Kills' claimed included a dozen German, two Italian tanks and four 88s. By 13.30 hrs the Queen's Bays were ordered against Point 33, beefed by a trio of heavier Churchill tanks. This attack failed; one of the Churchills was disabled by enemy fire, the others by mechanical difficulties and the survivors withdrew. 10th Hussars were engaged in a sharp fight, claiming three enemy tanks destroyed but, for a couple of hours, relative calm descended.

After reporting to HQ, a visit was paid to one of companies of the 'Woodcock' battalion with whom we had a troop; in addition the 'Deacons' [this mounted a 6-pounder on an AEC Matador truck] had been put into action to their left rear; having suffered some casualties, they were withdrawn, having achieved nothing except capturing a few Boche who had remained hidden underground.[14]

Rommel was not idle. Having brought 21st Panzer into the ring he planned a significant blow towards Kidney Ridge supported by the remnant of 15th Panzer, Littorio and elements of Ariete. In the north, 90th Light Division with cover from Ju87s was to strike at the Australians. It was not until 16.00 hrs that the attack developed; forming up had again been hindered by the persistent attentions of Desert Air Force. As the Axis armour rolled forwards, attempting to pass south of 'Woodcock', Fisher's tanks delivered a 'murderous fire'. They then engaged 10th Hussars, obligingly offering the riflemen a most convenient target for their 6-pounders.

Over the ridge they trundled, a tight bunch of a dozen first coming into my view and showing black against the skyline but too far away from us to be able to do much about it. They stopped at about 3,000 yards and two or three K4s [PzKw Mark IV] began to shell the infantry lying around the tanks. All the while we watched them closely through binoculars and, holding our fire, hoped that they would grow bolder and move in closer. This they refused to do, but one of two K3s skirmishing around the others suddenly came within reach of Shermans on our right and in a couple of minutes one of them was smoking furiously and the crew racing for cover, while the other tanks lumbered off up the ridge out of range.[15]

Between them the two British units likely accounted for twenty enemy tanks, though the mass advancing from the south continued to rain shells on 2nd Rifles battered positions. The counter-stroke had been seen off and Rommel was on the point of despair:

It was later learnt that a determined attack had been launched by enemy tanks on the 'Snipe' battalion. A very fine show was put up by the A/T guns of that unit and thirty-seven tanks were destroyed. Part of one of our batteries had the honour of taking part in this action, but had a minor role as all the 'plum' positions were occupied by infantry guns.[16]

Having fought magnificently the riflemen rather hoped they might now be relieved. That was the intention but neither carriers nor men appeared. The wounded had been evacuated and remaining survivors later withdrew by companies. By 23.15 hrs battalion HQ had pulled back. This was fortuitous as Allied shelling had stirred up a hornet's nest in the adjacent Axis operational base with the occupants, thus rudely evicted, seeking a new home in the 'Snipe' position. Even if the riflemen's final tally of seventy-six enemy armoured vehicles destroyed veered towards the optimistic a later, objective, assessment still counted thirty-seven; a formidable score.

John Longstaff was still holding on:

Through a dust storm, Bill Stanbridge the quartermaster, brought up his 30 hundredweights with rations for the whole of B Company – all in sacks full of bully beef and biscuits and the luxury of a few tins of sardines. He had gallons of petrol and boxes of ammunition, including sticky bombs and extra mines. I was horrified the next morning to see that I had about 200–300 gallons of petrol about ten feet away from me, bags of bloody mines. We had to crawl out and disperse this stuff, knowing very well that if one shell had hit the petrol or the mines, bits of us would be floating around the desert.[17]

As the exhausted survivors limped back, they could do so with immense pride for theirs had been a stunning feat of arms:

As it was we'd suffered a hell of a lot of casualties – our machine gunners had suffered in particular. I had one vehicle for the whole of the company and we put the wounded on it. They got back all right ... As we were marching or walking through, tired, lacking in sleep, and hungry but proud, with our rifles slung over our shoulders, we were stopped by a redcap at one of the points. 'Who are you, Sergeant?' 'My name is Longstaff, Sergeant: Rifle Brigade. He looked, and he was smart, this redcap. He shouted out to the gunners, 'It's the RBs.' The gunners cheered and even now I cry. The redcap saluted every one of my lads – every one. I don't like bloody coppers, but that one redcap to me personified the best that the military police had ever had in the desert.[18]

Lee's 133rd Lorried Infantry Brigade had been instructed to advance with all three battalions (2nd, 4th and 5th Royal Sussex with a detached company of the Royal Northumberland Fusiliers). Of these, 4th Royal Sussex got off to a very bad start, a 'blue on blue' firefight with 1st Gordons assaulting 'Aberdeen'. Another company came to grief attacking a strongly held post. Having advanced two miles and taken a haul of prisoners while also knocking out several guns, the survivors found themselves exposed in unforgiving and unyielding terrain, out of touch with any and all of their comrades. Far worse was to follow when Axis armour found them after dawn, overwhelming their guns and corralling the 300-odd survivors; around 60 had become casualties. The remainder of the brigade fared better: 2nd Battalion reached Kidney Ridge but were held by heavy and costly fire while 5th Battalion lay further east, also intact but having suffered losses. As the 4th Battalion were dying, the tanks of 9th Lancers and the Bays, which had moved forward, were ordered to stay as they were and then fall back, ample time for breakfast. Fisher's motor battalion, the Yorkshire Dragoons, further north had also been badly mauled. As Michael Carver observes: 'This naturally led to considerable bitterness and recrimination.'[19]

'Crumbling' Continues

At his morning conference held at 08.00 hrs on 28 October with Leese, Lumsden and their respective staffs Montgomery intimated he did not intend any further offensive action in the area of Kidney Ridge. The line 'Woodcock' – 'Snipe' would become a defended zone held by 10th Armoured Division and then handed over to 30 Corps while 1st Armoured Division was to be withdrawn. Morshead would be attacking in the north that night and 10 Corps had to be ready to exploit from the southern flank. Freyberg's New Zealanders would be used in the north to follow the hoped-for success of the Australians with the attached armoured brigade deploying, as Freyberg had himself suggested, to secure the open, southerly flank of the division. As the Aussies were going in that night, the 28th, 6th New Zealand Brigade would move into their old positions during the next. On the night following the move, that of 30/31 October, the Kiwis would attack in turn. Freyberg's brigades were weakened by attrition and losses, thus he would take under command successive British brigades which would be detached for this purpose – 151st Brigade (50th Division), 152nd (51st Highland Division), 131st (44th Division) and perhaps, if needed, the Greeks. Priority for replacement machines would be given to 9th Armoured Brigade.

The Reverend Charles W. K. Potts had exchanged his dog collar for an infantryman's rifle and pack, determined to do his bit in a more muscular vein:

> The inferno that was the great battle of Alamein. The appalling din of guns firing and of shells bursting, the grim sights of mangled men and twisted corpses, the nauseating smell that was a mixture of sulphur and rotting human flesh, the mental strain from sleeplessness and responsibility, the fear of breaking down in front of the men; all these became everyday things.[20]

Morshead's task was considerable – to enlarge the salient won at Point 29 and to win ground sufficient to afford a firm base for the reinforced New Zealand Division's further big push along the coast. The Australians would move north-east, crossing the railway line to reach the road. Attacking units would then swing south-east using the road and rail highways to work around behind enemy units holding the tip of the salient. An intense artillery bombardment heralded this assault but, as the objective of each of the three brigades differed, this was of necessity a most complex programme. The fury of the guns was sufficient for the Panzerarmee battle report to dub this 'the heaviest artillery fire which had so far been experienced'.[21] At 22.00 hrs, the three Australian brigades moved up. Windeyer's 20th had 40th RTR in support. His 2/17th Battalion held point 29 and they, with 2/15th Battalion, were to push northwards for two miles then, sending in 2/13th Battalion, make a further bound 2,000 yards east. The tanks would deploy between the first two battalions to fight off any Axis armour. Despite some notable difficulties including an unexpected, lethally booby-trapped minefield and Axis shelling, the attack progressed well and the brigade had, by midnight, secured its objectives.

The former reverend was more than doing his bit, targeting apparently lifeless enemy hulks with the intention of demolishing any that still harboured hostile intent with a 'sticky' bomb:

Before I reached the nearest tank I put down the suitcase. I had already primed the bombs. I went forward now with only one bomb in my right hand, and my revolver in my left hand. It amused me to think that I would be a very poor revolver shot left-handed – not that I was much good with my right hand ... We had not expected to find any snipers in the nearest tanks, but I had a look round just the same. I banged on the door of the first tank. 'Excuse me,' I said with a rather feeble attempt to be witty, 'but is there a sniper in there?'[22]

This accomplished, 26th Brigade (Whitehead) was to secure a not inconsiderable area between the extreme northern tip of the penetration and an expanse of barren salt marsh, east of the road, itself east of the railway tracks. A major obstacle lay in the strongpoint known as Thompson's Post. 2/23rd battalion was to secure the main road some way north-east of 2/13th Battalion. Thompson's Post remained the objective of 2/24th. The third battalion, 2/23rd was to dash forward in carriers and riding on the hulls of their supporting Valentines from 46th RTR. Just attaining the start line proved both difficult and hazardous, due to complex manoeuvring and omnipresent dust clouds. It was 23.40 hrs before they moved forward and immediately encountered difficulties in locating gaps in the Allied minefield.

Barely 600 yards beyond this they ran into Axis mines and sustained fire. Men leapt from tanks as tracer zipped through the moonless night. Confusion swiftly ensued as the battalion commander led forward those men he could collect and, though some may have penetrated as far as the railway line, they were pushed back. The Valentines did attempt to provide support but they themselves suffered heavy loss. 24th Brigade (Godfrey) was already placed east of the railway and was tasked to advance to the north-west and effect a junction with 26th Brigade. The prevailing chaos led Morshead to the inevitable decision, taken at 04.50 hrs, that the attack could not proceed further.

Reverend Potts' assault on Axis derelicts proceeded, without response, till a final trio of vehicles stood some distance away. These looked more ominous and a comrade offered to draw fire with his Bren carrier:

> I agreed. These last three tanks were some distance forward of the others. Bill set out while I walked forward, keeping a little to his left. He opened fire with his Bren from the carrier, then ran around the nearest tank and came back towards me. His carrier was not much more than about fifty yards away from me when there was a loud report and the carriers was lost in a black cloud of dust and smoke. The men within escaped though all had severe burns; 'Are you alright?' I asked. But then I could see that all was not well. All three of them were badly burned and I saw that they were in great pain.[23]

Morshead's assault had not achieved its final objectives, though the butcher's bill had been relatively light. It had inflicted losses on II/125th Panzer Grenadier Regiment and eliminated an Italian Bersaglieri Regiment. A half-hearted counter-attack towards Point 29 next morning failed to develop. For Rommel, there was no good news. He heard, on the 29th that another tanker, the *Luisiano* had been sunk. With the Axis fuel crisis biting deep, Rommel was considering how he might break off and withdraw. This would be a most difficult extrication, given how his forces were so fully committed and getting his infantry away intact seemed nigh on impossible. Montgomery, knowing the Axis to be desperately stretched, decided to shift the direction of his next blow further south.

An Axis assessment from 28 October provides an entirely pragmatic view:

Today's fighting, again with very heavy artillery and air support and of a most bitter nature, cost both sides heavily in men and equipment. The enemy lost 37 tanks, bringing the total since 23rd [October] to 293. 510 prisoners have been taken to date. Our own missing now totalled 1,994 Germans and 1,660 Italians. According to reports most of our prisoners were wounded. The number of available tanks had dropped further, in particular, the hitherto intact 21PzDiv had considerable losses.[24]

Now, Freyberg was to attack on the night of 31 October/1 November, with Point 29 as his right pivot and across a frontage of some 4,000 yards. During the preceding night, Morshead's weary Australians were to seek to finish that which they had earlier begun and achieve all final objectives. 26th Brigade would thrust north-east to seize ground thus straddling both road and railway. Phase two of their attack would involve advancing along the line of the tracks, eliminating Axis outposts and reaching the rear of the enemy in the tip of the Salient. The reduction of Thompson's Post was to constitute a final objective, though a single battalion would attempt to strike directly for the coast. Potts, desperate to get his wounded mates out of danger, offered to bring up a second carrier but the enemy fire was too accurate:

Then I saw one of our tanks, about two hundred yards away to the left rear. It was well ahead of all our other tanks. I ran to it for help to get Bill and his crew to safety. Anxiety lent me wings and I ran like a hare. I have a vague recollection of machine-gun bullets shooting up spurts of dust round my feet as I ran. I do not know if the Germans were aiming at my legs, which are thin enough to make a very poor target even if they were stationary.[25]

Repeated and sustained sorties pounded Axis positions during daylight hours. Rising to the attack at 22.00 hrs, 2/32nd Battalion gained its objectives. At 01.00 hrs on 1 November 2/24th and 2/48th Battalions rose for the next bound. Initially both made progress down the length of the track but cohesion was lost and casualties were sustained. Both then fell back towards the ground won by the first wave. This reverse denied any chance of success for the proposed third wave but the fourth was not dependent. At 04.25 hrs 2/3rd Pioneer Battalion moved into the attack but met with no more success and withdrew behind the man-made shelter of the line. Again, there was no final success, though some 500 prisoners had been bagged.

Even though the Australians had failed to reach all of their objectives, the tactical situation was critical from Rommel's perspective. A remnant of 125th Panzer Grenadiers was cut off but initial moves by 361st Panzer Grenadiers were seen off by Allied artillery. Rommel now had to draw on his slender reserves to form an armoured battlegroup from 21st Panzer which put in an attack along the railway line at 13.00 hrs. 2/32nd Battalion with 40th RTR fought a savage fight which was renewed around 16.00 hrs. The slow and under-gunned Valentines suffered badly in the exchanges of fire and twenty-one were knocked out before the survivors were permitted to withdraw. Next morning battle was again joined with much hard fighting. Both sides took and gave ground but the Australians clung to their hard-won gains. Rommel was at least successful in reaching 125th Panzer Grenadiers.

Charles Potts, racing to aid his badly burned comrades, found the British tank already disabled, having lost a track:

> It was beginning to get dark. I ran back to where I had left Bill and the others. Again I drew the enemy fire. I reached the place but I could not see them. I wondered frantically if I had lost my sense of direction.[26]

Throughout the fighting remained bitter and contested, the Axis gave ground grudgingly and after extracting the maximum price; once dispossessed they stormed back with sustained counter-attacks. Sergeant Longstaff, having survived the earlier fight now found himself once more in the thick:

> Then there was the second part of the battle of Alamein. I got my reinforcements – although the battalion was not ever again to be up to strength. We were to take up the positions held by two battalions – the Norfolks and the Durham Light Infantry. Those lads had been through hell far more than we'd been through, no mistake about that. They'd tried to break through but they'd suffered badly.[27]

John Longstaff was fortunate insofar as it was A rather than B Company who bore the main brunt and sustained heavy losses: 'We in B Company could do nothing except drop on the ground where we were and try and give covering fire.'[28] Worse was to follow – a friendly fire incident or 'blue on blue' in the modern vernacular:

So, when we went in again, another bastard accident took place. An order was given for one of our platoons to attack a machine gun. They attacked it – but it was one of our own machine-gunners. Half my bloody platoon was killed in that one bloody battle by my own mates. Then we had to withdraw. I followed the moon for direction, with Johnny Judd badly wounded and another lad called Latchmere, who was supposed to have played football for Spurs, also badly wounded with four or five machine gun bullets through his guts. Johnny was never to fight again. We deposited them at the first aid station and we goes back.[29]

There was still no sign of break-through. Rommel was stretched but not bursting. It is impossible, however, to overstate the advantages which accrued to the Allies through control of the skies and havoc wrought by Desert Air Force. Though armoured formations might be relatively safe, movement of soft-skinned and supply vehicles behind Axis lines during this critical 'dogfight' phase was continually interdicted by attack from the air. Nor should the corrosive effect on morale be overlooked, as Montgomery himself observed:

> The moral effect of air action is very great and out of all proportion to the material damage inflicted. In reverse direction, the sight and sound of our own air forces operating against the enemy have an equally satisfactory effect on our own troops.[30]

The damage inflicted upon Axis shipping was steadily increasing the pressure on Rommel's jugular. On 1 November two more Italian ships, *Tripolino* and *Ostia*, laden with fuel and ammunition were sunk. As Kesselring was trying to fly in fuel stocks from Crete, Maleme airfield, site of the Axis landings in May 1941, was also bombed.

As 8 November, the date fixed for the 'Torch' landings approached, Churchill needed a decision in the Western Desert. Much has been said about the 'long screwdriver' applied by Whitehall to the desert campaigns, usually to detrimental effect. Tradition in the British army is for the local commander, while he receives his general orders from his superiors, to be permitted discretion as to how he puts these into effect. This convention was not one which appealed to the Prime Minister. When frustrated by Montgomery's brusque intransigence, he was apt to remind Brooke of the shortcomings of 'Your Monty'. In Montgomery, Churchill had finally discovered a will and egotism to match his own. Churchill found Monty's bland briefing from 28

October, detailing his proposed re-grouping disquieting. Monty, as ever, was brimful of confidence:

> It was fairly clear to me that there had been consternation in Whitehall when I began to draw divisions into reserve on the 27th and 28th October, when I was getting ready for the final blow. Casey had been sent up to find out what was going on: Whitehall thought I was giving up, when in point of fact I was just about to win … I told him all about my plans and that I was certain of success; and de Guingand spoke to him very bluntly and told him to tell Whitehall not to bellyache. I never heard what signal was sent to London after the visit and was too busy with SUPERCHARGE to bother about it; anyway I was certain the CIGS would know what I was up to.[31]

Montgomery was indeed busy drafting the final orders for what he intended as the knock-out blow. He fully understood the strategic requirements:

> I knew that Operation TORCH, mounted from England, was to land in the Casablanca-Oran area on the 8th November. We must defeat the enemy, and break up his army, in time to be of real help to TORCH. Quite apart from wanting to get to Tripoli first! But more immediately, the timing was affected by the need to get the Martuba airfields so as to assist by giving air cover to the last possible convoy to Malta, which was short of food and almost out of aviation fuel; the convoy was to leave Alexandria about the middle of November.[32]

He then went on to assess the tactical position at El Alamein and the manner in which he intended to deliver his next major assault:

> I decided on the night of 30th/31st October the 9th Australian Division would attack strongly northwards to reach the sea; this would keep the enemy looking northwards. Then on the next night, 31st October/1st November, I would blow a deep hole in the enemy front just to the north of the original corridor; this hole would be made by 2nd New Zealand Division which would be reinforced by the 9th Armoured brigade and two infantry brigades; the operation would be under the command of 30 Corps. Through the gap I would pass 10 Corps with its armoured divisions … We already had the necessary divisions in reserve and they had been resting and refitting … What in fact, I proposed to do was to deliver a hard blow with the right, and follow it the next night with a knock-out blow with the left. The operation was christened SUPERCHARGE.[33]

11
Second El Alamein: 'Supercharge'

Were you there when the desert lay silent
And they counted the cost that was paid
To ransom a world and its freedom
Mid the sand dunes and the graves?
Well, this was the arras of battle.
The weft and warp of our strife.
With bonds that were forged forever
From the broken threads of life.

El Alamein Tapestry

I spent the morning [30 October] writing out my directive for SUPERCHARGE. I
always wrote such orders myself, and never let the staff do it. This was the master plan
and only the master could write it. The staff of course has much detailed work to do
after such a directive is issued. This procedure was well understood in the Eighth Army
(and later because of experience in the Mediterranean, in 21 Army Group).

Operation SUPERCHARGE will take place on night of 31st Oct/1st Nov. The
operation is designed to:

(a). Destroy the enemy armoured forces.

(b) Force the enemy to fight in the open, and thus make him use petrol by constant and
continuous movement.

(c) Get astride the enemy supply route, and prevent movement of supply services.

(d) Force the enemy from his forward landing grounds and aerodromes.

(e) Bring about the disintegration of the whole enemy army by a combination of (a),
(b), (c), and (d).

We know from all sources of intelligence that the enemy is in a bad way, and his
situation is critical. The continued offensive operations of Eighth Army and the R.A.F.

have reduced him to such a state that a hard blow now will complete his overthrow. The first stage in the blow is the operation being staged by the 9th Australian Division tonight on the Northern Flank; success in this operation will have excellent repercussions for SUPERCHARGE.

SUPERCHARGE itself, tomorrow night 31st October/1st November, will be the second blow and a staggering one, and one from which I do not consider he will be able to recover.[1]

Thus Monty defined the crushing offensive which was to finally break the deadlock and knock the Axis 'for six'. He makes it quite plain that doubts from subordinates, Lumsden being clearly 'in the frame' here, will not be tolerated. As ever, the army commander radiates optimism and purpose. All that has occurred and is about to happen is part of a plan, he is in control. He did, however, quite quickly decide to modify this basic plan:

It was clear to me that the stage management problems in connection with SUPERCHARGE were such that if I launched on this night it might fail. I therefore decided to postpone it for 24 hours to deliver the blow on the night 1st/2nd November. This delay would help the enemy. To offset this I extended the depth of penetration for a further 2,000 yards, making 6,000 yards in all – the whole under a very strong barrage. I should add that there were doubts in very high places about SUPERCHARGE, and whisperings about what would happen if it failed; these doubts I did not share and I made that quite clear to everyone.[2]

Monty was aware that his enemies were not necessarily all on the other side of the wire and mounting frustration in Whitehall would explode if decisive results were not soon achieved.

On 1 November what was hoped to form the final crushing blow that would indeed hit the Axis for six was unleashed:

At 1 a.m. SUPERCHARGE began and the attack went in on a front of 4,000 yards to a depth of 6,000 yards. It was a success and we were all but out into the open desert. By dusk we had taken 1,500 prisoners.[3]

In the first wave would be the two infantry brigades attached to NZ division and each would be backed by a regiment of Valentine tanks. Following behind, 9th Armoured Brigade with its three tank regiments would make the final bound of 2,000 yards to eliminate the enemy gun line along or by the Rahman track. 10th Corps would follow 9th Armoured with 1st Armoured Division hungry to debouch into the open and seek out Axis tanks. Though Monty had intended to begin on 31 October, Freyberg had prevailed upon his to delay for twenty-four hours to allow his exhausted troops some measure of respite and permitting the necessary re-deployments to take place. On 1 November, 01.05 hrs would be the appointed hour when the massed guns would speak. Despite the strain and tension of continuous fighting, 8th Army retained its cherished sense of humour:

> One of the funniest incidents I recall was as follows: Early one morning after the start I saw one of our burly Aussie gunners walk over to his gun position's 'Thunder Box'. Having settled himself he began to read last month's *Sydney Times* no doubt, when Jerry started his morning hate. A round fell some two hundred yards behind him. Without further ado he shouted a correction: 'Up four hundred, one round gunfire'. Almost immediately a shell whizzed overhead and landed two hundred yards ahead. With complete composure, having got his bracket, he called out: 'Down two hundred, five rounds gunfire.' You can guess the rest. He was blown off his thunder box and sailed through the air with the greatest of ease.[4]

As ever during this battle, Desert Air Force was in the vanguard. At 21.15 hrs, Allied bombers plastered Tel el Aqqaqir, Sidi abd el Rahman and Ghazal Station. Some spectacular and satisfying explosions rocked the night skies and damage to DAK signals capacity was palpable. The RN made some demonstrations along the coast and 13 Corps, though much denuded, was still charged with ensuring the enemy believed there was some offensive activity in the south. As waiting infantry crouched under the storm of steel hurtling overhead, they experienced that particular tightening of the stomach and dry-mouthed anticipation:

> Whilst awaiting the order to move forward, we all lay down on the desert with safety catches on and bayonets fixed. Suddenly, we were all on our feet and moving forward. As far as could be seen, to both left and right of us, men were advancing with their rifles in the port position, their bayonets glinting in the pale moonlight. Full moon had been days ago so the night was quite dark … As we advanced the feeling of pride and exhilaration was unmistakeable.[5]

On the left, 152nd Brigade from 51st Highland Division would advance across a frontage of some 2,000 yards with, on the right, 151st Brigade from 50th Northumbrian Division covering a similar distance. 8th and 50th RTR rumbled behind with just under forty infantry tanks apiece. The left flank of the penetration would be entrusted to 28th Maori Battalion with 133rd Lorried Infantry Brigade securing the right shoulder. Infantry surged forward:

> There were reddish coloured explosions ahead of us and bullets, both tracer and otherwise coming our way. I remember seeing forms sink to the ground, but our orders were to keep going and not to stop for wounded or dying. Later we passed slit trenches with forms slouched over them facing in our direction ... Above all the din, the sound of the pipes could clearly be heard, and even an Englishman can feel proud to belong to a Scottish regiment when he hears the shrill warlike sound of a pipe tune above the racket all around him. [Despite some scattered opposition the attackers made ground rapidly.] Our objective was about two miles ahead of us, and all too soon we were upon it. Before we reached it we met Germans and Italians coming towards us with their hands in the air, and I aired my schoolboy German telling them which way to go. The Italians were terrified and kept yelling out, 'Madre' – it was a very cold night and we were only wearing our KD shirts and shorts, yet we were all in a sweat.[6]

Kiwi sappers had gapped the mines, and battalion vehicles were soon moving up unimpeded, residual pockets of resistance eliminated and prisoners taken. As ever, there was a blood price to be paid for all such gains:

> What is wrong with my arm? I look down at my middle where it feels to be. It is not there. It is lying twisted up above my head. God! It is knocked off. No. It is still joined and only as I lift it down and lay it across my chest do I feel the agony of it; the sand is stained with blood in the moonlight.[7]

Such viscerally poetic writing was echoed by the war reporter Godfrey Talbot:

> Up in front where the shells were crashing red, the noise was a diabolical mixture, with the crackling of small arms fire and the bursting of mortar bombs. Flares went up and lit all the sandy, scrubby, hummocky ground; they burnt very bright and made

you feel somehow naked. There was the crisscross of tracer fire and rocket like bursts, through it all sometimes you heard the drone of aircraft.[8]

His recollection of armour moving up is particularly haunting:

When we saw the armour moving up it was an almost ghostly sight. Tank engines roared and tracks squealed as the columns moved forward. Black, noisy shapes in the night, each tank creating a choking fog of dust as it moved through the sand; you could hardly see them in these clouds until they were nearly on top of you. And so we saw these strange dramatic glimpses of the armed might of the Eighth Army moving into battle.[9]

Prior to 'Supercharge' Montgomery had ensured 9th Armoured Brigade was restored to full strength. Moving up from base areas at 20.00 hrs, familiar fog and dust soon cloaked the approaches. Enemy shell fire, though random, scored some hits among the lorried infantry and A/T guns. A significant number of vehicles fell by the wayside through an unhappy mix of breakdown and confusion. Zero hour for Currie's tanks was 05.45 hrs but this was, upon request, delayed by thirty minutes to allow some sorting out. There was thus only around a further half hour of sheltering darkness left before the armoured regiments surged past the infantry and towards the Rahman track, supporting barrage pounding ahead. On the right, 3rd Hussars and Royal Wiltshire Yeomanry made good ground but, as they came within range of the guns lining the track, found themselves hotly engaged. To their left, the Warwickshire Yeomanry had it rather worse and losses began to mount as the enemy gun line flamed and barked. At this point 9th Armoured was under command of the New Zealanders, though by 09.00 hrs authority would pass to 1st Armoured Division. As more tanks from the division came up survivors from the battered regiments grouped to fight on the right.

As you know, we should have attacked in the darkness; instead we went in at dawn. That half-hour's delay cost us dear. We were like so many targets in a shooting gallery. At one time during the attack, the dawn wind came up and blew the sand away. It seemed to me that there was a half-circle of guns firing at us, and not just a single line of guns but row after row of them. And they all seemed to be firing at once.[10]

As a gap was prised in the enemy line, two of Monty's armoured car regiments, the light horse of a desert campaign, sought to ease themselves through and break out into the open, there to wreak whatever mischief they could. At Tel el Aqqaqir Royal Dragoons found their passage still barred but infiltrated south of there to speed west, seeking targets of opportunity:

> We left our location and passed through the minefields in single file. No shot was fired at us. The only impediment to our progress occurred when the first car ran into an 88-mm gun pit filled with German dead. One or two more cars, including three petrol replenishing lorries, got stuck in slit trenches, but most of them pulled out when dawn broke and fought their way up to us. The enemy was too astounded to do anything as we came through, or else the Italian section thought we were Germans, and the German section thought we were Italians. They waved swastika flags at us with vigour and we replied with achtung and anything else we could think of which, with an answering wave, would get us through their lines.[11]

It had been hoped that the attack by the Kiwi Division would bring on the seemingly inevitable counter-attacks and that 1st Armoured Division, with remnants of 9th Armoured Brigade, would be well placed to deal a significant blow against any move from either north or west. Consequently, 2nd Armoured Brigade was intended to deploy some two miles north-west of Tel el Aqqaqir where 8th Brigade was to assemble and 7th Motor Brigade took station between the two. By 07.00 hrs, 2nd Armoured was moving up towards the embattled 9th, sappers leading the way. Blanketing dust and cloying, oily smoke swirled in perfect confusion. Enemy tanks and guns began to exact their toll. Just over three hours later, 8th Armoured was advancing, tasked to continue south-west but they too were brought to a standstill by intense fire.

Taking part in the assault was 7th Rifle Brigade; Sergeant D. A. Main recalled details:

> In the early evening of 1 November we were told that the 7th Motor Brigade would attack at midnight to force a gap for our tanks. When darkness fell I tossed up with my particular friend Sergeant Brine to decide who would split the watch until midnight. I won and slept first. Meanwhile we had sent out a patrol which could only hear enemy rations being distributed and we were unaware whether the enemy positions were Italian or German.[12]

As they moved off, bayonets fixed, Main's platoon was behind the two leading. Initially all was calm but some fifty yards short of the enemy, all hell broke loose and men began to drop in the face of deadly accurate, sustained Axis fire:

> Above the noise of the explosions I heard the company commander, Major Trappes-Lomax, shout: 'Up the Rifle Brigade! Charge!' Trappes-Lomax disappeared through a hail of tracer bullets. I felt he couldn't go in by himself and I gave the order to charge. I went through the enfilade fire and I couldn't understand how I had not been hit. It was like daylight with the flares and mortar explosions. Sergeant Brine had run straight into a German machine-gun. He was hit all over and before he died he asked to be placed facing the enemy.[13]

Deployment was not following the plan as intended, but Rommel's tanks were being drawn into the fight and worn down by grinding attrition. It was at close quarters and savage:

> Even in daylight you couldn't see the guns until they fired, and then if they missed you had to get them with your first shot or you were dead. There was no mercy shown to crews – tank crews or gun crews. We shot them up as they ran – they did the same to us when we baled out. It wasn't such a gentleman's war.[14]

For 'war without hate' this was anything but gentlemanly. It was bloody attrition:

> There was for me no excitement in the charge. I'd seen it all before, and after a certain time you look round the faces of your mates and you realize with a shock how few of the original mob are left. Then you know it's only a matter of time before you get yours. All I wanted to do was to get across that bloody ground and through the guns. As I passed one position – the gunners were prostrate, I think with fear – I saw the gun couldn't be swung round very easily. They were only good for 'action front' – well they had a little bit of a traverse, about 15 degrees either side of a zero line, I should think; so once we were past them they couldn't really shoot us up the arse.[15]

If the fog of war assisted the Axis, daylight brought opportunities for Desert Air Force. Enemy vehicles, massing west of the Rahman track, were deluged with 163 tons of bombs. As the bombers delivered their deadly payloads, Allied fighters, mainly Hurricanes, were providing close support above the lines of British tanks. Despite the odds Luftwaffe sorties twice attempted to intermeddle, firstly twelve Ju87s then forty more, with fighters, met each time by Hurricanes and seen off, both sides losing two fighters each. For German infantrymen like Hans Schilling the dwindling of vital supplies was utterly disheartening:

Supplies were our main problem. Before we left Alamein, during the battle after the retreat, we kept waiting for supplies to get through. The British had our lifeline throttled. We used to wonder how the British had so many submarines and planes to sink our ships. We especially needed petrol – there was constant rationing and any unauthorised use of a vehicle was heavily punished. El Alamein was a hell.[16]

Oddly enough, there were patches of calm in all that frightening fury, and there were jeeps racing about, organizing something or other I suppose. The infantry didn't like us [tanks]. First of all we attracted shell-fire, and many 'overs' usually pitched onto them. I felt sorry for them just sitting there in all that shelling without being able to hit back – it couldn't have been nice.[17]

As 9th Armoured's depleted tanks battled their way forward, a murderous attrition between armour and guns, von Vaerst then put in a strong counter-attack, committing both panzer divisions, which hurled themselves at the threatened shoulders of the thin salient 9th Armoured had butted into the gun line. The desert floor was soon littered with smouldering and flaming hulks of destroyed tanks, gun barrels twisted and pointing accusingly. Majestic and aloof, Allied bombers droned overhead, seeking fresh targets.

Rommel Decides to Disengage

By 20.15 hrs on 2 November von Thoma had given his commander-in-chief a bleakly realistic assessment of Panzerarmee Afrika's position:

No breakthrough had occurred; the Axis line was holding.

Nonetheless he was out-numbered and out-gunned, subject to continual air attack.

By the 3rd he would be lucky to have more than 35 'runners' among his tanks and infantry strength was severely eroded.

His A/T guns had been significantly reduced in number.

He had no reserves.

It was therefore inevitable the 8th Army should at some point, and soon, break-through.

It was therefore time to withdraw.

Rommel concurred. British attacks were, as he felt, both ponderous and predictable, therefore a planned withdrawal, at this juncture, was feasible and might yet be carried through without further and fatal losses. New positions at Fuka had already been scouted and Ariete Division would now move to Tel el Aqqaqir to bolster Italian XX Corps while XXI Corps retreated on their right flank. Under cover of night, Italian X Corps would disengage and slip around behind sheltering mine marshes between El Taqa and west of Bab el Qattara. From there to Quatani minefield would be held by Ramcke's *fallschirmjager*. As the amount of ground to be covered was nowhere greater than ten miles, it was proposed to execute these manoeuvres on the night of 3 November while the mobile units, Italian XX Corps, the panzers of both armoured divisions, 90th Light and 19th Flak Divisions, would form a rearguard screen.

Antennae quivering with finesse and informed of enemy intentions via Ultra, the shift was already understood: 'There were indications the enemy was about to withdraw; he was almost finished.'[18] Montgomery saw the decisive moment as being at hand. What remained of 9th Armoured Brigade clung to the northern shoulder as 1st Armoured Division's two brigades deployed to attempt to hold on around Tel el Aqqaqir (8th) and ground to the north-west (2nd). The north flank of the salient was held by 151st Brigade (Durhams) while the Highlanders occupied the southern 'wall', armour facing west. The Allies had not yet taken all of their original objectives – the ridge of el Aqqaqir was not completely secured nor had the full 'Skinflint' bound been achieved. Nonetheless, a decisive armoured clash was underway. As the days of 'balaklavering' were now distant, British tanks, dug in, awaited the panzers. When these failed to make headway Axis guns took up the gauntlet flinging down a fearful curtain of fire. For British infantry this was a most unpleasant time:

> We were up the sharp end with a vengeance. I'd never seen any shelling like that before ... the worst I'd seen, and every time it died down the tanks would roll forward again to our slit trench line and fire their guns. Then they would pull back and Jerry would send some stuff back, all of which fell in our area. The battalion's anti-tank guns had it very bad; for a long time they were out in the open and unprotected.[19]

Monty could sense the very fulcrum of battle had been reached.

He was well supplied with intelligence via Ultra decrypts and his superiority both on the ground and in the air was substantial. On the evening of 2 November, 152nd Brigade with 2nd Seaforths and 50th RTR was to capture 'Skinflint' while, a little later, 5th Royal Sussex from 133rd Lorried Infantry Brigade was to assault 'Snipe'. Both attacks would go in under cover of a heavy barrage. In each instance the infantry secured their objectives and a respectable haul of Italian prisoners from Trieste. With these strongpoints eliminated the prime obstacle to a westerly break out was the Axis gun line along Rahman track. Lumsden now, in the late evening, proposed to deploy his infantry (7th Motor Brigade) in a bid to seize a two mile stretch of ground north-east of Tel el Aqqaqir. Once they were on their objectives, 2nd and 8th Armoured Brigades would advance for three and a half miles westwards. This would enable 7th Armoured Division, early on 3 November, to leapfrog 1st Armoured and drive toward Ghazal Station.

Keith Douglas, while a member of that charmed circle of writers based in the Delta, was very much up at the sharp end. At one point a foot patrol, led by an experienced corporal, not disposed to show over-regard for tank officers, requested assistance. They had identified Axis snipers using burnt out hulks as cover – 'them Jerry derelicts over there' – and requested the armour flush them out: "I should have thought you could run over the buggers with this," he said patting the tank ...' Douglas's troop commander gave a cautious thumbs up to the co-operation and the target area was hosed with MG fire, at least till the weapon jammed:

> Evan cleared and re-cocked it. It jammed again. A furious argument followed; even maintaining that the trouble was due to my not passing the belt of ammunition over the six-pounder and helping it out of the box: I pointed out that the belt was free on my side.[20]

A rather unseemly slanging match followed, tempers frayed by the stress of battle. The MG now had to be stripped while the troop commander advised he was going back to the NAAFI for lemonade and buns. Douglas was momentarily distracted by the corpse of a Libyan soldier sprawled in the indifference of death while his fuming gunner was obliged to continuing fretting over his weapon:

We got the biscuit tin off the back of the tank and mounted the gun on it loose, on the top of the turret: from this eminence, as we advanced again, Evan sprayed earth and air impartially, burning his fingers on the barrel casing, his temper more furious every minute.[21]

Presently an infantry officer joined the tankers, replete with primed grenades: 'Very good of you to help us out old boy.' The British were now closing in upon the hulks:

A few yards from the left of the tank, two German soldiers were climbing out of a pit, grinning sheepishly as though they had been caught out in a game of hide and seek. In their pit lay a Spandau machine-gun with its perforated jacket. So much, I thought with relief, for the machine gun nest. But men now arose all round us. We were in a maze of pits. Evan flung down the Besa machine-gun, cried impatiently, 'Lend us your revolver, sir,' and snatching it from my hand, dismounted. He rushed up and down calling 'Out of it, come out of it, you bastards' etc. The infantry officer and I joined in this chorus, and rushed from trench to trench; I picked up a rifle from one of the trenches and aimed it threateningly, although I soon discovered that the safety-catch was stuck and it would not fire; the figures of soldiers continued to arise from the earth as though dragon's teeth had been sown there.[22]

More and more Germans were now virtually queuing to throw in the towel, the British gathering their captives like shepherds with the enormous dog-like tank lumbering after. This activity was now beginning to attract the unwelcome attentions of Axis guns:

As the main body of prisoners was marched away under an infantry guard, the high explosive began to land closer to us. I did not feel inclined to attack the further position single-handed so I moved the tank back and tacked it on to the column of prisoners. The mortar stopped firing at us, and some of the infantry climbed on to the tank to ride back. I reported over the air that we had taken some prisoners.[23]

Douglas's CO was hugely impressed by this burgeoning bag of prisoners and instructed the officer to ensure the PoWs were sent back to the brigade commander for interrogation, so he would get the credit for this:

This was unfortunately more than my conscience would stand. I felt that all the work had been done by Evan and the infantry officer and said so. This was a bad thing to say to Piccadilly Jim [the colonel] because it showed him that I did not agree with him about snatching little gobbets of glory for the regiment wherever possible. The infantry were in another brigade, as Piccadilly Jim knew. Evan said: 'You were a bloody fool to say that sir; you've as good as thrown away an MC.'[24]

To add insult to injury the tankers found their infantry passengers had repaid them by appropriating some choice items of loot:

We were shocked to find that the infantry had stolen all our German binoculars while enjoying our hospitality as passengers on the tank. We all bitterly reproached them and I regretted ever having wished to give them extra credit. We had left, however, a large stack of machine guns and rifles, which we dumped. Three Luger pistols which we kept; these are beautiful weapons, though with a mechanism too delicate for use in sandy country.[25]

The planned attack by 7th Motor Brigade was an expensive failure, born from a catalogue of errors. Orders arrived late, intelligence was lacking and gathering dusk frustrated any recce. Guns were ready and plentiful but devoid of a meaningful programme. Zero hour was fixed for 01.15 hrs but the three battalions seem to have got off badly from the start, running into an alert, well-prepared enemy and could achieve little. Further muddles arose as 10th Corps HQ became convinced 2nd KRRC was on Point 44 at Tel el Aqqaqir. Acting on this incorrect and rather pious assessment, 4/6th South African Armoured Car Regiment dashed forward and came to grief. During the hours of darkness Desert Air Force continued with business as usual. Enemy transport clustered around Ghazal Station was pounded and Maleme airfield on Crete received a further pasting.

For the British tanks, tasks were for 2nd Armoured Brigade to bolster 2nd KRRC, allowing 8th Armoured Brigade to exploit south-west. Axis guns and tanks dug in along the Rahman track frustrated efforts by the former brigade while more guns, mainly 88s held up the latter. During the course of that afternoon the Notts Yeomanry attempted charge the line 'balaklavering' with no more success than previously. Though some vehicles may have reached the line of the track, net result was more losses. However, 3 November brought intimations from the Australians in the north and 13 Corps to the south that the enemy was or appeared to be withdrawing. As the morning wore on, 1st Armoured Division also appeared to be pushing forward against weakening resistance:

> On 3rd November one of the troop commanders and No 1 of the battery working with the armoured brigade had the satisfaction of capturing an Italian tank; they walked up to it with revolvers, knocked on the front door, and the crew came out and surrendered.[26]

When writing to his 'Dearest Lu' the same day, Rommel was singularly pessimistic:

> The battle is going very heavily against us. We're simply being crushed by the enemy weight. I've made an attempt to salvage part of the army. I wonder if it will succeed. At night I lie open eyed, racking my brains for a way out of this plight for my poor troops ... We are facing very difficult days, perhaps the most difficult that a man can undergo. The dead are lucky, it's all over for them. I think of you constantly with heartfelt love and gratitude. Perhaps all will be well and we shall see each other again.[27]

Sensing that the dam was about to burst, Montgomery imposed two further operational tasks upon the infantry of 51st Division. That afternoon, at 16.45 hrs they would attempt to seize a span of the Rahman track west of 'Skinflint'. Later, under cover of darkness, they would strike south, aiming at Tel el Aqqaqir and a portion of track lying south. These moves would, it was hoped, finally allowed the South Africans to get their cars out into the open and join in the merry havoc Royal Dragoons were enthusiastically creating. Monty had already deduced that Rommel might attempt to form a fresh line on suitable ground either at Fuka or perhaps Matruh. Once these attacks achieved their objectives 10th Corps would seek to break out north towards the coast. Freyberg, his division beefed up accordingly, would march west in a move to flank the Fuka position from the southern approaches. He might then have to prepare for a further advance towards Matruh, 10th Corps detaching one division to hold ground gained at Fuka.

Hitler Intervenes

Rommel was indeed now seeking to disengage. At this crucial juncture, Montgomery found he had an unexpected ally in the person of the Führer himself. Adolf Hitler ordered Rommel to hold his ground 'not to yield a step'.[28] Mussolini, in the unlikely event Rommel would take notice, sent a similar order through Cavallero. Sick at heart Rommel read the order out over the telephone to von Thoma, who was understandably outraged. Both he and his army commander understood that such an order spelt nothing but destruction. Though phrased in suitably flowery terms the Führer's direct order was crystal clear:

> To Field Marshal Rommel ... It is with trusting confidence in your leadership and the courage of the German-Italian troops under your command that the German people and I are following the heroic struggle in Egypt. In the situation in which you find yourself there can be no other thought but to stand fast, yield not a yard of ground and throw every gun and every man into the battle. Considerable air force reinforcements are being sent to C in C south [Kesselring]. The Duce and the Comando Supremo are also making the utmost efforts to send you the means to continue the fight. Your enemy, despite his superiority, must also be at the end of his strength. It would not be the first time in history that a strong will has triumphed over the bigger battalions; as to your troops, you can show them no other road than that to victory or death.[29]

This was, for Rommel, a bitter blow and yet, who would dare defy Hitler? Such heroic prose which ignored every tactical and strategic reality, promising reinforcements that did not exist, amounted to little more than insult. The only remedy was in compromise which might give the appearance of compliance yet also provide a means of partial escape. 90th Light, Italian X and XXI Corps must hold their ground but von Thoma was permitted to withdraw the remnants of his panzers six miles west of Tel el Aqqaqir with Italian XX Corps. Ariete, coming up from the south, would deploy on von Thoma's right flank. Darkness would provide the cloak and Rommel's reply to the Führer stressed the crippling losses already sustained. Having let that sink in he requested, early on 4 November, permission for a withdrawal as far as Fuka. He might yet salvage something in spite of Hitler's best efforts.

At 2 a.m. I directed two hard punches at the 'hinges' of the final break out area where
the enemy was trying to stop us widening the gap which we had blown; that finished
the battle.[30]

Montgomery, on the evening of 3 November, was firmly and rightly
convinced Rommel was seeking to break off. The Australians had
penetrated further along the coast in the north and found Thompson's
Post abandoned. The Allied commander now ordered Wimberley's
Highlanders to mount three lunges. At 17.45 hrs 5/7th Gordon
Highlanders, supported by tanks from 8th RTR would aim to seize a
section of the track some two miles south of Point 44. Some hours later,
beneath the cloak of night, 5th Indian Brigade was to make a further
bound of two miles. Early on the morning of 4 November at 06.15 hrs,
7th Argylls would attempt to seize the elusive prize of Point 44 itself.
The Gordons' attack began with a misapprehension and concluded in
tragedy. 1st Armoured Division, quite wrongly, assumed 8th Brigade
had passed to the west of the current objective and that mere mopping
up remained.

Thus it was deemed that air and artillery support were, in
such an instance, redundant. Nothing more than a blanket of
smoke would be needed and the infantry could ride comfortably
on RTR tanks. The tankers had doubts but these were brushed
aside. In fact, as the attackers soon discovered, the enemy were
still in possession and in no mood to be easily dispossessed. Tanks
were destroyed and efforts to redirect the bombardment became
confused, a confusion assisted by breakdown in radio contact. Men
were lost and Valentines knocked out with the infantry forced to
dig in, under fire from a presumed non-existent enemy, well short
of their objective.

Brigadier Russell, commanding 5th Indian Brigade, experienced
frustrations of a different nature. His difficulties in forming up meant
he had to seek an hour's delay in igniting the barrage, now back to
02.30 hrs. He also decided to switch operational roles for two of
his battalions. Despite these significant glitches the overall attack,
once launched, proved entirely successful, Axis withdrawal having
commenced leaving only stragglers for the net. The story of the Argyll's
attack was similar; opposition melted, though some shells were still
falling. Soon, as dawn's lightning finger illuminated the ground, the

armoured cars were away, racing like hounds over open desert:

> It was full daylight and, getting among the soft transport vehicles, our work of
> destruction began. In the first quarter of an hour the two squadrons destroyed 40
> lorries, simply by putting a bullet through the petrol tank and setting a match to the
> leak. The crews of lorries which had got bogged in the breakthrough, transferred
> themselves to German vehicles holding petrol. Spare men climbed aboard Italian
> vehicles mounted with Breda guns, and on we pushed Germans panicked from their
> lorries into slit trenches. We had no time to take prisoners. We just took their weapons
> and told them to start walking east. Only those who refused were shot; few refused.[31]

More sedate, the tanks of 22nd Armoured Brigade were also moving
forward, at last in open ground. The infantry were still unimpressed at
the sight: 'They flew pennants. I did not know these little flags had any
meaning. I thought they were typical of the bullshit bravado of tank
mobs.'[32] Some, however, witnessing the beginnings of the developing
tank battle between 7th Armoured Division and Italian XX Corps, were
caught by the imagery of warships, majestic on the ocean of the sands:

> The tanks – there seemed thousands of them – looked like a whole fleet of little boats
> on the sea. Miles away, to the left of me, there was a great dark cloud where there
> was a great 'stonk' going on. There were little shiny specks dodging about. I could see
> flashes where there were guns firing.[33]

This action heralded the demise of Ariete Division. In the north, as the
Australians probed along the coast, it was a very similar story. Desert
Air Force had already picked up the scent and had chased retreating
columns throughout the dark, Wellingtons pouncing between El Daba
and the sea where targets clustered invitingly. Tell-tale columns of
smoke and bright flaring bursts of explosions offered resonant witness
to the enemy's flight as stores were abandoned and burnt. For Hans
Schilling and his surviving comrades, the retreat was exhausting and
dispiriting – beaten they might be but were not yet defeated:

> On the way back, near the Egyptian border, we found a cache of petrol through a
> simple accident. One of our men had gone for a walk with a shovel and when he
> dug his hole he found these cans. It was a British petrol dump and everyone worked
> all night to dig it up. But these were only drops in the bucket. We kept losing our

equipment, leaving our vehicles behind – setting fire to them or shooting the tyres out. From this time we wondered just how far back we would have to go. We knew we could still lick the other side, but not until someone turned the tap on for us. We were told they were preparing the Mareth line for us already. But we went on and on, through Tripoli for the last time, and there was nothing at the Mareth Line inside Tunisia, nothing behind it.[34]

For Rommel, the scale of this defeat was enormous. Assessments differ, but the Axis had lost something in the order of 30,000 prisoners, two thirds Italian and perhaps as many as 20,000 dead and wounded. Most of his Italian formations had been decimated and such transport as could be found reserved for German survivors. Out of nearly 250 tanks DAK could barely field three dozen and though the Italians had more runners these were inferior and no match for Shermans:

The Italian divisions in the south, in front of 13 Corps, had nothing to do except surrender; they could not escape as the Germans had taken all their transport. I directed Horrocks to collect them in, and devoted my attention to the pursuit of Rommel's forces which were streaming westwards.[35]

Well might the marching soldiers have lamented, many would never see Rome or Naples, Milan or Bologna again:

Captain, captain of the guard
Summon the buglers all,
Make them stand in the barrack square
And sound the demob call.

Driver, driver of the truck,
Start your engine off,
We're in a hurry to get home;
Of war we've had enough.

Oh driver, driver of the bus,
Run through the streets of Rome;
Make her go like a racing car,
We're hurrying to get home.

Italian marching song

One remark from my diary at the time is significant. 'We are throwing stones at the Italians and they are running away.' There was no doubt that the enemy, at last, was in retreat.[36]

Can you wonder that, the battle having lasted some twelve days and ended in complete victory, I keep saying that he [Montgomery] was in a class by himself as an army commander.[37]

The Price of Victory

Such a victory, resounding as it was had been dearly bought, Allied losses were heavy in all arms:

2,350 officers and men killed.

8,950 wounded.

2,260 missing.

Some 500 tanks damaged, say half of which could be repaired.

111 guns of all types destroyed.

97 aircraft of all types lost (as against say 84 Axis), though the Allies had flown a vastly greater number of sorties at nearly 12,000, six times the Axis total.

For the weary soldiers still sweating it out in the 'Blue', victory, however sweet, did not alter life's daily realities beneath relentless desert skies. Private Crimp serving in 7th Armoured found:

The desert, omnipresent, so saturates consciousness that it makes the mind as sterile as itself … Nothing in the landscape to rest or distract the eye; nothing to hear but roaring truck engines; and nothing to smell but carbon exhaust fumes and the reek of petrol. Even food tastes insipid, because of the heat, which stultifies appetite. The sexual urge, with nothing to stir it, is completely dormant … The most trivial actions, such as cleaning the sand off weapons, making a fire or brew, or, when you're lying down by the truck, moving position into a patch of shade … seem utterly not worthwhile and require a tremendous effort to perform … Then, of course, there are the flies. Lord Almighty, that such pests should ever have been created! … At the moment of writing there are five crawling over my hands and I'm spitting as many away from my mouth.[38]

Montgomery subsequently divided the fighting at El Alamein into three distinct phases.

First, the break-in, which he defines as a struggle for tactical advantage. He felt that this was successful, though the record might tend to question.

Secondly, the crumbling or dogfight phase, aimed at 'crippling the enemy's strength'. This did succeed; a nasty, vicious attrition that told heavily in favour of the Allies. This was as much due to the fact Rommel squandered his precious resources in set piece counter-attacks in unfavourable conditions. Allied success was mainly due to Axis inability to learn from past mistakes and a propensity to fling men and vehicles into a maelstrom where the Allied held vital trumps in air and artillery superiority.

Finally, the break-out which Monty saw as successful as it was aimed at the weakest link in the crumbling Axis chain, the juncture between Italian and German units. Rommel had taken the gamble of drawing his remaining strength into the northern sector where he was misled into thinking the final blow would be directed.[39]

> If your enemy stands to fight and is decisively defeated in the ensuing battle, everything is added unto you. Rommel's doom was sounded at Alam Halfa; as Von Mellenthin said, it was the turning point of the desert war. After that, he was smashed in battle at El Alamein. He had never been beaten before though he had often had to 'nip back to get more petrol'. Now he had been decisively defeated. The doom of the Axis forces in Africa was certain – provided we made no more mistakes.[40]

Monty was not shy in attributing the victory to his own strategic genius. In this he may have been prone to overlook that much of the strategic planning had been done previously by others such as Auchinleck, Dorman-Smith, Gott and Ramsden. These are not mentioned. Nonetheless, even his most constant critics must concede that Montgomery brought to 8th Army cohesion, a simplicity and directness of approach that had been lacking. He restored confidence:

> Generals who become depressed when things are not going well, who lack the 'drive' to get things done, and who lack the resolution, the robust mentality and the moral courage to see their plan through to the end – are useless. They are, in fact, worse than useless – they are a menace – since any sign of wavering or hesitation has immediate repercussions down the scale when the issue hangs in the balance.[41]

General Carver puts it rather more succinctly:

It may have been expensive and unromantic but it made certain of victory, and the certainly of victory at that time was all important: 8th Army had the resources to stand such a battle, while the Panzerarmee had not and Montgomery had the determination, will power and ruthlessness to see such a battle through.[42]

Subsequent writers, most notably perhaps, Niall Barr, have offered a more objective assessment, though the critical development in the fighting skills of British arms during the period before and during the El Alamein offensive is acknowledged by all. A key component in final victory is perceived as the re-concentration of artillery which 'dominated the Alamein battle'. Too often the guns had been distributed in penny packets without the impact and delivery of a detailed programme which brought a telling weight of firepower to bear. The Royal Engineers too, had broken the stalemate of the minefields by perfecting gapping techniques. While the clearing of mines had remained hazardous it had been accomplished, with loss and confusion in some cases but generally the clearance work had been a superlative example of planning, technique, courage and resourcefulness in action.

As the hounds were unleashed, Robert Crisp and his comrades bounded after the survivors of 90th Light struggling along the coastal ribbon:

The most exciting moment of the battle was when we first cut the coast road in an effort to head off the 90th Light Division. Long columns of Italian and German transport were still swarming along the road westward. My tank was first onto the road, being in the recce squadron. It really came as a tremendous surprise to the enemy when they heard the rattle of our machine guns ... They put in one attack only with about twenty tanks, but of these only two managed to break through, the rest were destroyed. We collected a tremendous bag of prisoners, tanks, lorries and transport of all kinds.[43]

John Strawson is of the opinion that the last word on the battle should be left to General Carver, a most distinguished student of the campaign. I believe him to be entirely correct:

To the infantryman in the attack or sitting it out day after day in his slit trench in the front line; to the tank crew grinding forward in the dark and dust among the mines, or trying to edge forward by day towards the ridge from which the anti-tank guns were firing; to the sapper clearing the mines, the anti-tank gunners and, to a lesser extent, the other gunners, it frequently seemed a chaotic and ghastly muddle. The area of the salient east of Kidney Ridge was the worst of all. The whole place was knee deep in dust. Nobody knew where anybody or anything was, where minefields started or ended. There was always somebody firing at something and usually somebody being fired at, but who and what it was and why was generally a mystery. To try and find out led from one false clue to another: the information one gleaned would probably be wrong anyway.[44]

The battle was won but could the rout be transformed into *Götterdämmerung?*

O, Lord, our only Master
Our victories were Yours,
Pray keep us now and after
May peace be assured.
Look up you sons of Glory,
The Crusader flags unfurled;
Remember our true story;
'We fought to free the world'.
So hoist our Banner highly,
Our cause shall not be lost;
For we were the proud Eighth Army,
Our emblem was the cross.

Eighth Army hymn

12
The Long Pursuit

The Battle of El Alamein may be said to have ended at dawn on 4th November, with the enemy breaking away and the British setting out to catch him ... Seldom can a communiqué have been more welcome to the Allies, nor, indeed, to the free world at large, than the announcement from Cairo on 4th November that the Axis forces were in full retreat ... Mr. Churchill has praised the whole achievement as one which will always make a glorious page in British military annals, and observes that 'It marked in fact the turning of the "Hinge of Fate"'.[1]

My ultimate objective was Tripoli; this had always been considered the objective of Eighth Army. But unfortunately the operations to get there had become known as the 'Benghazi Handicap' – as one officer expressed it to me: 'We used to go up to Benghazi for Christmas and return to Egypt early in the New Year'.[2]

A great deal has been written about the pursuit after Alamein, much of it critical. Prominent among critics was Rommel himself: 'The British command continued to observe its usual caution and showed little evidence of ability to make resolute decisions.'[3] In part this is unfair. The victory at El Alamein represented a further, and this time final, swing of the pendulum. Captain Smedley was one of the hounds:

As we pushed ahead, the Italians were surrendering in their thousands. We just said 'March east – march back to Cairo'. We left the mopping up to be done by those behind us. Eventually, when the thing came to a grinding halt in our area, we spent about a week going out in patrols finding pockets of wretched Italians. Their officers or the Germans had pinched all their transport. Some were starving and had no water. I remember getting sixteen Italians on my armoured car, hanging on like grim death. They were absolutely delighted the war was over, they weren't very enthusiastic, to put it bluntly. They were conscripts – Mussolini had called them up. I think half those poor devils didn't want to fight at all; it was the Germans who put up most of the tough resistance.[4]

The Final Swing

As the problems engendered by the 'pendulum' effect were by now well understood, there had been close and detailed planning undertaken between 8th Army and GHQ. Given the importance and sensitivities inevitably occurring, a single designated staff section from GHQ under Brigadier Surtees, the DQMG, was allocated for liaison and proved highly effective. Victory in the North African Campaign was to be won as much by patient staff work and logistical capacity as offensives in the field. Indeed without this, no such triumphs could possibly have been achieved. The desert railway was a key element in the overall strategy of supply. A series of railheads would be developed along the north flank of the advance. The distance from Alamein to Tobruk was some 335 miles. Water was key to running the railroad and an order for US-built diesel locomotives which ran on comparatively little was providentially delivered in October 1942.

Corporal Peter Taylor, a rifleman from the same battalion as John Longstaff, also witnessed the Axis rout:

It was about the 12th day of Alamein when the enemy really started to go. The desert was littered with Alpine boots and rucksacks with a cover which was made with the hide of a deer or elk or something – hair-covered rucksacks. We found out afterwards that this Alpine regiment had been hurriedly sent from Italy across to Tripoli and whistled down to the battlefield almost before they could pause for breath. All their Alpine boots had been hung on the outside of their packs. They had been put straight into the front line to hold positions. This stuff was all over the place – the dross of an army, if you like – tins and cans and bullets and guns and rifles, boots, packs, hats – a hundred and one things everywhere: burnt out vehicles and tanks – and a few graves, though not many.[5]

Road repairs were an obvious priority as the need to commission ports would have to keep pace with the advance. Initially the smaller harbours of Matruh, Sollum and Bardia would be pressed into early service. Tobruk, despite the terrible damage wrought by continuous bombing was able, within a week of its capture (19 November), to receive a daily tonnage of supply which was nearly double that of initial estimates. Benghazi, which fell a day later, represented a great technical problem as, having no natural harbour, man-made works were easily slighted. Work began immediately and in earnest with supply commencing as early as 26 November. Impressive as this was, the speed of the advance was such that progress could only be sustained by impressive labours of the transport companies. These largely unsung and outwardly unglamorous formations provided the arteries through which supply and replenishment could pass. Without this circulatory system, the body that was 8th Army would have quickly ground to a dead halt.

Corporal Taylor again:

> Everything had been thought of – that was why the spirit was so good. After years of being pushed around by the Axis forces, at last we were holding our own and doing a bit better than holding our own. We were actually beating them. Everybody could see we were beating them. It wasn't because they were short of weapons – they had almost as much as we had – but we had a little bit of the edge with the Sherman and the anti-tank guns; we had a bit of the edge.[6]

Any enemy airfield was a keenly sought prize. Some were degraded by vehicles, others slighted by the foe but Desert Air Force had a set drill to meet such challenges. After an initial recce, engineers, sappers and a construction crew would move in to assess the damage and commence necessary repairs. The RAF Regiment would provide ground troops to secure the perimeter. Following on was the initial technical team from the squadron assigned, then fliers and their machines. This process was slick and efficient but, until equipment and supplies could be flown in, the transport required added to the existing congestion on the over-taxed roads.

Some Allied officers appear to have got rather carried away, as Sergeant H. E. M. Russell also serving in Intelligence could confirm:

> I was interrogating a few German prisoners; the locality was on the edge of an enemy minefield. Some apoplectic top-brass type appeared on the scene and became obsessed with the notion that my interrogees knew a way through the minefield. They protested that they did not, that they were not engineers, and had only recently in the hectic troop movements moved into that sector.

The officer became shrilly insistent and Russell reminded him of rules under the Geneva Convention. This did not go down well:

> The top-brass was adamant ... and almost exploded – we were in the middle of a battle and he might lose men. Just as we were about to begin this idiotic business, imperilling them and me, news flashed over the blower that some armoured cars had found a way through. Both the Jerries and I were profoundly relieved at this providential intervention.[7]

When, on 4 November, it became clear, as Monty had predicted, that the long-awaited and hard-won breakthrough had been achieved, the tempo shifted from grinding attrition to fluid warfare spread across a vast canvas, not unlike the late summer and early autumn of 1914 on the Western Front in reverse. Freyberg had, under his hand, two additional lorry-borne infantry brigades, 9th Armoured and 6th Light Armoured Brigades. His instructions were to push steadily westwards, over the desert tracks for sixty miles, passing through Sidi Ibeid, which would place him on the Fuka Escarpment. 10th Corps was to swing around west of Sidi Abd el Rahman to scoop up Axis forces trapped in the pocket thereby created.

Sergeant Russell again:

> The fourth of November; on this day an incident occurred which for me has remained unforgettable. Our 4th Light Armoured Brigade pressed on harassing the enemy in his retreat. Towards the end of the afternoon the Brigade HQ stopped and brewed up our tea and prepared a meal. While thus engaged a cloud of dust was observed over the brow of a distant hill – a quiver of apprehension. Was it a mobile enemy column coming in to attack? As the picture focussed, we saw that it was a long column of hundreds of prisoners being marched to the cage. They approached and our men gazed at the sight in a sort of stilled amazement; suddenly someone started to cheer.[8]

All Allied forces now committed to the chase were themselves battered and depleted by the hard-fought battle; no obvious reserves remained. One plan had been to breathe life and substance into shadow 8th Armoured Division (Gairdner) and create a fresh, independent striking force. To bring this up to strength, however, could only have been achieved by denuding other formations and Monty swiftly discounted the notion. The task of completing the destruction of DAK and 90th

Light would be left to 10th Corps and the Kiwis. It was here in the north that the final maelstrom would be orchestrated. In the south, Axis infantry, deprived of means of escape, 'would wither away or be captured'.[9] Monty's message to 8th Army, timed at 08.15 hrs 4 November was, as ever, upbeat. He reminded his troops of the hard fighting they had endured and that the hour of final victory was at hand: 'The enemy is in our power and he is just about to crack.'[10]

The Chase

The campaign was now one of extreme rapidity.

Desert Air Force was already straining at the leash, as tensed as hawks for the kill. That the Allies continued to enjoy near-total air superiority was providential for progress on the ground was severely hampered by a vast build-up of traffic, congesting the minefield gaps. This giant, motley scrum of vehicles would have presented a perfect target had the Axis been able to take advantage. Freyberg was hamstrung in his efforts due to the wide dispersion of his formations. 4th Light Armoured all the way back on Springbok track did not commence its advance until daybreak on the 4th. By mid-morning they were no further west than Tel el Aqqaqir, so thick was the press with 10 Corps units also struggling westwards. It was 14.00 hrs before 9th Armoured, following on, began to move; 6th New Zealand Infantry Brigade were at a similar pass. By the fading of the light, lead elements of the division were some fourteen miles south of El Daba. Freyberg entertained hopes he could kick-start the advance at 23.00 hrs. As the author of the OH rather drily observed: 'This hope was not realised.'

Congestion hampered the efforts of 10th Corps, the diversion of guns to support the attack by 5th Indian Brigade and a cloying skein of early morning mist had exacerbated these difficulties. By around 09.30 hrs lead elements of 2nd Armoured Brigade were sparring with 21st Panzer. 7th Armoured Division got underway about the same time and took on the remnant of Ariete which, high odds notwithstanding, fought gallantly until almost completely destroyed. Lumsden ordered Gatehouse to lead 8th Armoured Brigade around to the south-west, avoid the melee and pass round behind the enemy formations. Rommel was aware that, to save his army, he must be permitted to fall back to

Fuka. He telegraphed Hitler at 11.15 hrs, stating the situation was now critical: 'We cannot expect any new German forces. Added to this the Italian troops have no more fighting value because of the enemy's great superiority on the ground and in the air ...' Hitler replied tersely later that evening: '... I have caused the Duce to be informed of my views; in the circumstances ... I consent to your decision.'[11]

Again the Führer obliged Montgomery with his truculence. By the time consent was received the Axis position had deteriorated rapidly. The panzers, already depleted, were ripe for shaking, and von Thoma, leading with his forward units, was captured. Trooper Lindsay of 10th Hussars was present:

Heat haze in the desert, even in November, was enough to distort vision, and this is perhaps the reason why the captain and I did not see a large, immobile shape about 200 yards in front of us. For all I know it may have been camouflaged as well. Anyway, neither of us saw that it was a Panzer III until there was a sudden flash, followed immediately by a crashing explosion. A 50mm armour-piercing shell had torn through one side of our Dingo and had passed out through the other side. The solid shot had passed between Captain Singer's head and mine, without injuring either of us. I reversed the Dingo very quickly ...[12]

Having alerted British armour, the Hussars had the satisfaction of seeing the enemy tank 'brew up'. There appeared to be only one survivor who was waving a white flag:

We drove towards the upright figure, and I could see that he was holding his pistol upside down, that is by the barrel and he had a white handkerchief in his left hand ... I could see that there were rank badges on his lapels and on his shoulder straps. He had a very large pair of binoculars round his neck. The German walked forward, then stopped, saluted Captain Singer and handed over his pistol. Both officers then shook hands.[13]

For trooper Lindsay, spoils included the general's fine binoculars.

The inevitable hiatus caused by the loss of so dynamic a field commander caused further difficulties. Nonetheless, the retreat was got underway. Formations in the south, Italian X and XXI Corps with Ramcke's paratroops, would move immediately while forces remaining in the north fell back in good order, 90th Light on the coast road, DAK in the centre and Italian XX Corps on the right, further south. Unhampered by the rampant congestion which had delayed the Allied pursuit, these mobile formations gained the level, high ground atop Fuka escarpment. This feature stands east of the main coastal escarpment, running north/south before, some miles south of the coast road, it bends eastwards and eventually merges into the flat. In his approach march Freyberg was aiming not to ascend by the road but across the desert, keeping south of Alam el Qassim.

Due to the prevailing confusion and spread of his forces the 23.00 hrs deadline proved infeasible and he delayed zero hour till 05.30 hrs. At this point DAK was retreating along a similar axis to that of the New Zealanders' pursuit, experiencing similar difficulties. There was a gap of seven or eight miles between the main bodies and both were aiming to reach the higher ground. Meanwhile 8th Armoured Brigade, attempting their wide, flanking sweep, could make little headway in the enveloping darkness and paused to await any fitful moonlight. Between El Daba and Fuka a solid mass of Axis transport crowded the road, a most inviting prospect but Freyberg could not promise to attain his objectives before 10.00 hrs. 1st Armoured Division was ordered to converge on El Daba; 7th Armoured Division was to interdict the highway between there and Galal. The latter was also the objective for 10th Armoured. Desert Air Force continued their nightly ministrations without respite, inflicting considerable damage on Axis soft-skinned transport. The Royal Navy too was active, ensuring the sea offered no alternative escape.

Through the whole of the desert campaigns, the Royal Navy had acted as 8th Army's right-flank guard; George Blundell served in a series of executive roles aboard HMS *Kent*:

> The most exciting and awe-inspiring incident was when one of our fighters chased four Eyeties down our port side at a good height. Shortly afterwards we witnessed three planes go down. Two were like great flaming rockets hurtling in to the sea. They came down great red glows with a vast tail of black smoke and smashed themselves into the sea – a terrible sight.[14]

Making up for lack of progress during the night, 8th Armoured Brigade dashed the thirty miles to Galal in four hours. This involved some brisk rearguard skirmishing. An Italian column was met and dealt with and the charge continued for a further nine miles, driving along both highway and railways towards Fuka. Freyberg had a less fulfilling morning. His advance was slower than anticipated. Lead units, though they covered some thirty miles of ground, ran into both panzer rearguards and un-gapped mines. Shells now began falling and the laborious task of clearance consumed a full three hours. By dusk only two formations, 4th Light Armoured and 5th NZ Infantry Brigades, had crossed the mine-marsh. DAK thus reached the plateau ahead of the hounds, but their situation remained serious, disorganized and thinly spread. As a stand was deemed reckless, Rommel gave the orders for a further withdrawal under cover of night.

[5 November] moving forward rapidly, sitting on top of the ACV and greatly elated. Some distant dust-clouds were said to be the Germans getting away. There was the cheering sight of the 'Air Umbrella' – Bostons in formations of eighteen. The Colonel said it's the end of the Germans in Africa; I did not believe him.[15]

Montgomery too, sensed the need for haste. Victory had been won but this could still turn to ashes if Rommel escaped annihilation. The Desert Fox was never more dangerous or brilliant than when his back was against the wall. His soldiers were defeated but were far from beaten. Monty urged more haste upon Lumsden, setting as the armour's objective the area of Derna-Tmimi-El Mechili. 5 November had netted rather meagre gains, stragglers had been rounded up but the bulk of the fleeing enemy had got clear. As preliminary moves, 7th Armoured was to divert towards aerodromes at Sidi Haneish and Quasaba while 1st Armoured Division whose lead units (2nd Armoured Brigade) were already some miles west of El Daba, was to embark upon a wide flanking movement which would place it in position to then advance upon Matruh. In executing these orders 7th Armoured Division was constrained to turn south-west to avoid entanglement with the New Zealanders but ran into further mines and finally halted twenty miles short of its objective. 1st Armoured Division fared little better, supply vehicles became lost; lack of fuel caused some elements literally to run dry, overworked tank engines swallowing vast quantities of gasoline. Those who had fuel pressed on at a lively pace but increasingly progress stalled as tanks ran dry, 'everyone fuming'.[16]

Despite the frustrations, the overall management of the campaign had attained new heights of efficiency as Corporal Taylor noted:

> The casualty evacuation and withdrawal of people of ours who were killed was incredible. The wounded were got away extremely quickly in jeeps and little armoured cars with stretchers built on to the back of them – strap him down and whoosh – off. They have an orderly sitting on the back to see the chap didn't get bounced about. The medical evacuation was heartening because people had been told, 'If you get wounded, you'll be whipped away straightaway.' We'd never had this sort of thing before.[17]

For the transport companies it was not only the speed of the advance but difficulties of ground and movement which impeded replenishment. As dusk was falling on 5 November a supply convoy moved westwards to make contact with the divisional 'B' echelon. By now the tracks were horribly churned and deeply rutted. Soft sand and a maze of old trenches added further pitfalls, unseen until encountered in the inky darkness. Rain, sluicing down in monsoon like torrents, added further miseries. Net result was that the going became increasingly difficult for wheeled transport. Tanks could move relatively unimpeded but only if they had fuel in their tanks – no fuel, no pursuit. 5 November had also been a disappointing day for Desert Air Force, the very speed of pursuit made close coordination increasingly difficult. That degree of intimate liaison which had obtained during the battle could not therefore be as easily sustained.

For Rommel this was fortuitous. Luftwaffe squadrons were in exceedingly poor shape and promised reinforcements were still nowhere in sight. Rommel by this time was doubtless rather cynical over such bland assurances. Allied difficulties gave the Desert Fox his opening for a further planned withdrawal westwards. During the hours of darkness on 5/6 November he pulled 90th Light back towards Matruh, 21st Panzer to Quasaba and the remainder into the vicinity of 'Charing Cross'. Desert Air Force was by no means idle. These moves were harassed by both fighters and bombers but deteriorating weather conditions and the inevitable confusion over retreating foe and advancing friend limited sorties. Despite these difficulties of supply Freyberg's division resumed its advance on the morning of 6 November, pushing on towards Sidi Haneish with 9th Armoured Brigade leading. Fuka itself, the escarpment and several Axis airfields fell to 8th Armoured Brigade. Rain, in great muddied torrents, was becoming a real problem, soaked and exhausted prisoners were rounded up in penny packets, though 133rd Lorried Infantry Brigade at Galal captured 1,000 more.

With the creeping light of grey, rain-lashed dawn 22nd Armoured Brigade ground on towards Quasaba. Its advance was blocked by elements of Voss Reconnaissance Group and tanks of 21st Panzer, also afflicted by chronic fuel shortage. As the waves of rain lashed the battlefield with biblical fury the leviathans clashed, crash and flame of gunfire stabbing through the gloom. Before the remnants broke off, German losses steadily mounted and sixteen tanks and a quantity of guns were claimed. Though activity in the air was muted, US bombers hammered Tobruk and then Benghazi, sinking more vital tankers. So rapid was the pace of the advance that 8th Army was outpacing some of its air support.

Dawn on 7 November found 90th Light and 21st Panzer at Matruh with the remainder of the Axis forces centred on 'Charing Cross'. Rain had lashed the sodden ground into a churned frenzy of cloying mud to the extent that even tracked vehicles, those which had fuel, could move only on the road. 10 Corps was still tasked to reach Matruh, the New Zealanders Sidi Barrani and 7th Armoured Division, Sollum. Despite poor flying conditions there was some action in the air. Luftwaffe transports attempted to fly fuel up to the front line, Ju87s attempted to bomb 1st Armoured while Allied fighters shot up Axis vehicles along the coast road. 10th Armoured Division, with fuel to move dispatched 8th Armoured Brigade to seize that portion of highway lying between Fuka and Matruh resulting in contact with German stop lines just east of the objective. Anti-tank guns from 90th Light halted the British tanks and conducted a skilful rearguard action, breaking off after dark so that cautious patrols sent out at first light on 8 November found the ground bare.

While this great *chevauchée* was unrolling, rear echelons continued as before, including the hard-pressed medical services. Ronald Joynes was a volunteer orderly and witnessed the shameful treatment of wounded Italian native auxiliaries, Libyans, at the hands of some Egyptians:

> We saw examples of man's inhumanity to man. Some of the Egyptian orderlies were
> dreadfully uncaring towards those poor Libyans, even though it was sensible to send

them to Egyptian hospitals because they spoke Arabic. There I saw an orderly ... who deliberately picked up a Libyan with a broken arm by his broken arm.[18]

Rommel was still intent upon a further withdrawal. His tactics were to form a fresh block at Sidi Barrani permitting the rump of his forces to filter through the narrow passes at Halayfa ('Hellfire Pass') and Sollum. Without reference to Rommel, Cavallero and Bastico decided that a stand should be made on the axis of Mersa Brega–El Agheila–Marada and that substantial reinforcements would be fed in. These would comprise two infantry divisions, the Spezia and Young Fascists with an armoured division (Centauro). Panzerarmee could be further replenished with German tanks and guns from Italy. To facilitate this process of rebuilding, Rommel would need to hold current ground for at least a week. The German Field Marshal was understandably furious at being sidelined in a war that he was conducting, remaining adamant in his dealings with Comando Supremo that his army was in no state to fight a major engagement. Hitler, on 22 November, finally weighed in on his ally's side and issued another order to hold the El Agheila position to the last man. Rommel privately and correctly concluded 'they [Comando Supremo and OKW] did not see things as they were, indeed they did not want to'.

In the south, Allied 13 Corps had begun its advance against sporadic opposition. A rearguard offered spirited resistance south of Jebel Kalakh but slipped away under cover of darkness. Some 6,000 prisoners were eventually mopped up but Ramcke's paratroopers with the rump of Folgore showed their mettle in a sharp fight and, though they lost some prisoners, withdrew in good order. These *fallschirmjager* were still very much an elite and undefeated. Ramcke and his survivors, roughly battalion strength, rejoined the main Axis forces on the 7th. By 14 November the total 'bag' of captured Axis prisoners, the bulk of whom were Italian, had topped 17,000.

As the long pursuit unfolded, the daily business of support services continued. Captain Pleydel was much taken with the evils of social disease:

I am glad to say, I had no cases of VD. My lectures on first aid, splints etc were interspersed with lectures on unwise sex, and the effects of VD. I laid it on so thick that two men fainted during one lecture. We were standing up, in the sand and thump, thump down they went – reproachful glances in my direction.[19]

It was not Montgomery's intention to allow his enemy respite. Before dark on 9 November Rommel's forces had been cleared from Sidi Barrani and Freyberg was marching on Sollum as 7th Armoured Division, in another wide, flanking arc pivoting upon Fort Capuzzo and Sidi Azeiz. Twenty-four hours later and 4th Light Armoured was at the approaches to Halfaya Pass. Kippenburger's infantry scaled the heights with commendable élan taking some 600 Italian defenders prisoner. Now replenished 22nd Armoured, also on 10 November, reached El Beida. Egyptian soil would soon be clear and the fall of Hellfire Pass spurred the Axis retreat. Montgomery had already ordered a temporary halt on the line of Bardia – Capuzzo – Sidi Azeiz, to allow for supply to catch up. The pursuit in the interim would be continued by armoured cars.

Though Montgomery could have been, and was, criticised for the apparently ponderous nature of the pursuit, he was well aware of the mettle of his opponent and did not intend to hand him the opportunity for a counter-stroke. The pendulum had swung too often before and if Monty was systematic, even cautious in his advance to El Agheila it remained his steadfast intention to deal the Axis so severe a blow that their ruin in North Africa would be assured. By 12 November the hounds were coursing west of Tobruk, scene of such great heights and profound depths of Allied hopes, which was entered the day after. On the 14th Lumsden detailed four flying columns, each with specific tactical objectives:

Column (a) 12th Lancers was to seize the vital airfields at Martuba, which it accomplished next day (finding the aerodrome flooded and unserviceable), then press on to take the aerodrome at Derna. The former, Monty had identified as a key objective to provide air cover for Malta-bound convoys.

Column (b) HQ 4th Light Armoured Brigade, to assist in the capture of Martuba then press on towards Benghazi. The main component of each of the columns was armoured cars though this one had a troop of Grants with it. All possessed units of field, anti-tank and flak guns.

Columns (c) (The 11th Hussars) and (d) (The Royal Dragoons) were to take Msus airfield, then beat up any enemy still standing between Benghazi and Antelat. Taking enemy airfields enabled fighter squadrons to begin operating from new forward bases but neither day bombers nor fighter bombers were able to operate as effectively partly from a dearth of targets and partly from difficulties in getting supplies of bombs so far up.

Renewed worries over fuel supply hampered the Axis; 90th Light and Italian XX Corps came to a forced halt outside Barce, the former's rearguard just avoiding 4th Light Armoured. Next day, 16 November, the rains returned, water-laden winds whipping the dust to a consistency of glue, no one moved, no one could. On 17 November, as the tempest ameliorated, Monty, realizing the Panzerarmee was hamstrung by want of fuel, again urged Lumsden to sweep in from the south and force the enemy into a pocket. Bad weather and supply problems severely hampered 10 Corps and Rommel came to regard 18 November as the most critical day of the retreat. The flying columns heading west were constantly sparring with Axis rearguards. Sergeant Robert Hill, serving with 1/6 QRR found himself in a murderous skirmish as he led a recce patrol towards the outskirts of battered Benghazi:

> I was in the lead Bren-gun carrier. As we advanced everything was so quiet it seemed unnatural. Then all of a sudden artillery opened up. The second carrier was hit, so we picked up the crew, one of whom was wounded. We carried on advancing at a faster speed and found out where the enemy were. In doing so we came to a wadi and as we got to the lips we spotted an enemy machine-gun nest. The corporal alongside me popped a hand grenade into the nest, getting rid of that one. We turned to our left flank and carried along the lip of the wadi and wiped out four more machine-gun positions and captured four prisoners before returning to our lines; the chap who was wounded died on the way back.[20]

Hill was awarded a well-merited MM for this action. By the 20th the British again entered Benghazi, another dot on the map 8th Army had cause to recall. Finally, during the night of 23/24 November Rommel was able to deploy his survivors in the Mersa Brega–El Agheila area. He had not escaped unscathed, far from it, but the Panzerarmee was still in the field and still capable.

Despite problems of exploiting and supplying newly captured forward air bases, Desert Air Force maintained the upper hand, beating up remaining Axis fields and preventing the diminishing power of the fuel-starved Luftwaffe from interfering with 8th Army ground operations. By a bold initiative Coningham succeeded in establishing 'Landing ground 125' 100 miles or so north-west of Jarabub. Essential equipment, personnel and stores were flown in and the place made operational in exemplary time. By 13 November, Hurricanes from the strip were shooting up Axis traffic on the road between Benghazi and El Agheila. This impudent hideaway sprang more surprises over the next few days, even though it was largely devoid of any anti-aircraft cover. After several satisfying and productive days during which time much useful harm had been done, the planes withdrew. This was the flyer's equivalent of a deep commando raid and remarkably successful. During the latter stages of the Axis retreat to El Agheila Desert Air Force sorties continued to exact a toll on enemy shipping. Within a week three more tankers and large supply vessels were sunk or effectively destroyed.

The End of the Race

At Rastenburg on 28 November, Rommel attempted to reason with Hitler. In this he was singularly unsuccessful and was subjected to a near-hysterical diatribe which ignored all of the uncomfortable realities the Field Marshal had vainly attempted to introduce. The Führer was not minded to countenance a further withdrawal – the El Agheila position must be held at all costs, that Rommel lacked the means to do so and, in the attempt would invite the total disaster he had so skilfully avoided thus far, did not feature in the discussion. Monty could not possibly have asked for more.

El Agheila, nonetheless, had bad memories for 8th Army; too much blood and materiel had been expended there. Montgomery could sense British units were not looking forward to more desperate fighting with the bloodshed of Alamein still fresh. He had fixed upon Tripoli as his immediate strategic goal and its attainment would require the reduction of the El Agheila line and the secondary, rearward position at Buerat. Rommel had determined upon a policy of nominal acquiescence to Hitler's raving, masking a series of further staged withdrawals. In the circumstances, as might be expected, he was quite right and, as early as 6 December, had begun to dispatch his marching formations further west.

Montgomery had, in his usual careful manner, made detailed preparations for a renewed offensive on 15 December but sensing the hare was poised for flight sent in the hounds on the 11th instead. His intention was to engage the enemy frontally, on the coast, with 51st Highland Division while Freyberg executed a wide flanking move to the south which would strike home against the Axis forces on 14 December. But the Desert Fox was too canny. The initial Allied probing confirmed his suspicion that a major assault was imminent and he pulled back forthwith. The New Zealanders made a desperate dash to close the jaws of the trap but, hamstrung by supply difficulties, failed to net more than some 450 prisoners. The bulk of Rommel's forces with his guns and armour slipped clear.

As ever the Panzerarmee conducted its retreat with skill and some panache. A series of rearguard actions were fought as the Axis forces set up a number of temporary stop lines, employing mines, booby-traps, anti-tank guns and ditches. On 15 December the lead elements of 8th Armoured Brigade fought a brisk engagement and inflicted some loss but like a will o' the wisp Rommel avoided encirclement. The New Zealanders battled bravely on, nearly trapping a rearguard unit at Wadi Matratin, some sixty miles west of El Agheila. Confusion and onset of darkness allowed the Germans to escape, dynamiting bridges and culverts as they went, sowing a liberal, lethal crop of mines to mark their passage, a bitter harvest for the pursuing Allies. The chase continued with a further clash at Nofilia on the evening of 16 December. Here the Kiwis, with 4th Light Armoured Brigade, came up against elements of 15th Panzer. The redoubtable Kippenberger deployed his brigade for a mad and daring dash, charging forward in their vehicles till obliged by bad ground and the weight of enemy fire to dismount. A brave attempt but again frustrated by a strong defence which slipped away in darkness.

This was hard fighting, deadly and relentless but Montgomery's longer game was working, the road to Tripoli stretched invitingly ahead. Almost the 'Msus Stakes' in reverse as 8th Army charged westwards, great columns of men and vehicles moving under clouds of dust and churned sand. Presently, the nature of the terrain began to shift as the Allies entered the fertile coastal belt Il Duce was trying so hard to deny them, his North African empire coming rapidly unstuck. On 23 January 1943 11th Hussars, one of the formations which had first 'bounced' the Italians in 1940, entered the deserted streets of Tripoli. The place was as silent as the grave, defeat closing in like a mantle of despair. The funereal atmosphere was shattered when one begrimed wag stuck his head from the turret and shouted 'Taxi!'[21] The pendulum had swung for the final time.

From Alamein to Tunis,

Forward did we go;

The proudest of all armies –

Thro' Italy and o'er the Po.

O'er Desert sands and mountains,

The sea and in the air,

Ever onward marching,

Thrusting everywhere.

So hoist our Banner highly,

Our cause shall not be lost;

For we were the proud Eighth Army,

Our emblem was the cross.

Eighth Army hymn

Tunisian Campaign

Churchill, at last, after seemingly endless frustration and heartache had what he desired, a major strategic breakthrough. Rommel was not finally beaten, nor was the Axis presence in North Africa immediately expunged as much hard fighting remained, for the Desert Fox nothing but the bitter dregs of defeat. All of his restless brilliance could not now stem the rot and none knew this better than he. During the course of Rommel's unsatisfying interview with Hitler he had been advised, in florid terms, that: 'The Afrika Korps no longer matters.'[22]

Nearly three weeks earlier, on 8 November, a joint Anglo-American fleet had made several landings on the coast of French North Africa. The long-heralded liberation of Vichy provinces had begun. The Allies came ashore at Algiers, Oran and Casablanca. If Eisenhower, as C in C, was expecting a rapturous welcome he was sadly deluded. The French in fact resisted, treating the landings more as a hostile invasion than liberation. Memories of the sinking of French ships and the fight for Syria rankled. Even the presence of the Americans, who might be expected to be less tainted than the British, did not prevent stiff fighting. Admiral Darlan, who commanded all Vichy forces, was a rabid anglophobe and had to be bribed with residual power as 'supreme civil authority'. This angered supporters of De Gaulle and the Free French who regarded the admiral with loathing. Compromises were needed as speed was of the essence. The Axis had to be caught and crushed between a swift advance from the west with Montgomery closing in from the east.

Prior to the slogging match that would become the Tunisian campaign SAS/LRDG had performed superbly in harrying the Axis retreat, like terriers snapping at the slinking fox. Despite their successes Montgomery was not an admirer of Special Forces. An initial meeting between the general and Colonel David Stirling, commanding his SAS desperadoes, did not go altogether well:

'What makes you think Stirling [asked Monty] that these men [volunteers Stirling requested] will fight better under your command than under mine. And, anyway, they won't be ready for the battle ...' I [John Hackett] couldn't resist saying, 'Well they may not be trained in time for the next battle but they will be trained for the one after that and the battles to follow.' ... This was too much for Monty. He hammered the map at Alamein and said, 'There will be no other battle in Africa. This is going to be the last battle. My mandate is to destroy Rommel, and I propose to destroy him,' he said, tapping the Alamein position, 'just here.' ... David, who was never well known for his obsequiousness, said: 'Oh yes General, but the last general told us something like that, and the one before him too.' We didn't get any recruits you won't be surprised to hear.[23]

Despite the mounting odds, Axis reinforcements were arriving in Tunisia and an active defence was underway. The country was mountainous and winter rains barely a month away. General Anderson, commanding British 1st Army, made good progress, despite renewed activity from the Luftwaffe. Rommel continued to fall back, ignoring all and any pleas to make a stand. By the end of November, Anderson's forces appeared to be closing in upon Tunis but deteriorating weather imposed its own check. Anderson's planned swoop down from the hills was met with determined resistance, the formidable Tiger (PzKw VI) making its first appearance. Fighting hard and utilising interior lines the German defenders could not be budged. Allied losses were mounting steadily and the Axis forces were able to mount a series of sharp, local counter-attacks. Then the rains began to fall in earnest

turning ground into quagmire, bogging men and vehicles in a viscous
sea of impotent misery. Tunis was not about to fall and Eisenhower
wisely decided to suspend further major operations.

On 15 February 1943, 8th Army moved against Rommel's positions
at Beurat. Hopelessly outnumbered and outgunned, Panzerarmee
could only continue with a further withdrawal. A major conference
was held at Casablanca where Eisenhower revealed his intentions
for a further offensive in Tunisia, though Brooke felt such a move
unwise. The potentially contentious question of who should exercise
overall command once 1st and 8th Armies were united was settled in
favour of Eisenhower, with Alexander as his subordinate and Tedder
having direction of all Allied aircraft. De Gaulle had been persuaded
or browbeaten into a makeshift accommodation with General Giraud.
Rommel had retired behind the relative security of the Mareth Line
which afforded him a respite and the opportunity of striking a fresh
blow in the west.

As ever, the Desert Fox chose an ambitious and risky strategy while
his fellow officers, Von Arnim, commanding 5th Panzerarmee in North
Tunisia and, equally predictably, Kesselring favoured a less perilous
course. The result was an inevitable compromise. The Germans made
initial gains. The Americans, facing these battle-hardened desert
veterans, were caught off-guard and suffered losses but the offensive
soon began to run out of steam. Von Arnim had severe doubts and
these translated into lukewarm support. Rommel's assault on the
Kasserine Pass, spectacular and rapid, ran into a thin screen of Allied
guns and stalled. With resources depleted and the Allies recovering, the
attack was abandoned.

Alexander was frankly appalled by the unprepared state of his
American allies but the crisis in the western sector had passed. Rommel
was ordered to launch a blow in the east, despite his misgivings,
exacerbated by failing health. This attack, hurled at 8th Army positions
at Medenine in early March, ran into a well-prepared and concealed
gun line; both tanks and infantry were badly shot up as they struggled
to come to grips. Rommel's last attack was a total failure. He left
North Africa for a final attempt to talk sense into Hitler but the Führer
still was not listening. The Desert Fox had seen the last of North Africa,
placed on mandatory sick leave. Von Arnim was left to oversee the final
Götterdämmerung.

Despite heavy losses incurred at Medenine, von Arnim felt he could continue to hold the Mareth Line, still formidable and with both flanks secure. The line was, however, less solid than the Germans might have hoped. Indefatigable as ever, LRDG had found practicable gaps through which Montgomery proposed to send a powerful force comprising Freyberg's Kiwis, bolstered by armour. As the New Zealanders executed their dashing left hook, 30 Corps would batter down the front door and break through from east to north. This frontal attack ran into stiff opposition and a series of difficulties. The bridgehead, so dearly won, was nearly lost when adverse weather intervened on the Axis' side. The DLI hung on fiercely as the panzers stormed their makeshift positions calling on the Durham men to surrender. The Durhams declined the offer and clung on grimly till finally relieved. As more British tanks appeared the Germans sought to disengage and retreat westwards. Again DAK managed, by dint of resilient rearguard actions and rapid manoeuvre, to escape the closing net but 8th Army had still notched up another important victory.

Relentlessly, the Allies tightened the vice. General Patton, with the US 2nd Corps, displayed his customary bullish energy. Von Arnim was threatened with encirclement. The Italian General Messe commanded a strongly posted Axis line which was to be assaulted using both 1st and 8th Armies. Montgomery was to punch though at Gabes Gap to break out onto the coastal plain where his superior armour would deploy to best advantage. Ghurkas led the assault in a classic night attack to secure vital high ground but 51st Division ran into heavy fire, losing many casualties and the Germans again avoided encirclement. Finally, Indian soldiers from 8th Army shook hands with Americans from Patton's 2nd Corps. By 10 April Sfax had fallen and Sousse two days later.

It was during the afternoon of 7 May that elements of 6th and 7th Armoured penetrated the streets of Tunis. As John Strawson points out the 11th Hussars had been one of the first units to begin 'biffing' the Italians prior to Compass in 1940. Alan Moorehead witnessed this climatic scene:

> They roared past German airfields, workshops, petrol and ammunition dumps and
> gun positions. They did not stop to take prisoners – things had gone far beyond that. If
> a comet had rushed down that road, it could scarcely have made a greater impression.

The Germans were now entirely dazed; wherever they looked, British tanks seemed to be hurtling past.[24]

Despite these expanding triumphs, Alexander had decided the final blow must fall further north and thus be delivered by 1st Army, though 8th Army was to assault the remaining Axis bastion at Enfidaville. This was essentially a sideshow. In part this was due to recognition that the Enfidaville position was an extremely strong one. Nonetheless, the orders were subsequently modified, perhaps in consequence of matters in the north proving more strenuous than anticipated. Several army commanders had grave doubts over the attack on the Enfidaville defences, fearing the price paid in casualties would be exorbitant. Montgomery, as ever, was aggressive and fully confident. Hans Schilling was among the defenders:

At this time we held a terrific position, near Enfidaville, a perfect defending line and very secure. There was a long gradual slope in front of us and an abrupt steep fall behind us, about sixty or eighty metres. We were dug in just behind the top of this ridge, out of sight of the enemy in front of us. The French attacked us twice, coming up the slope screaming with their officers behind urging them on. We cut them down [Schilling records that there 'were no holds barred' fighting the French as the majority of their troops were Black Africans]. The last attack was put in by the British. There was a fantastic artillery bombardment this time to soften us up. They didn't appreciate the situation we were in – the shells whistled five or ten metres over our heads and exploded harmlessly down below us, so nothing happened to us. We could sit there with our backs against the top of the ridge and throw stick grenades over, and they just rolled down. We were on the back side out of view and safe from the British artillery. Then, when we looked over the top, we let them have it with everything, machine guns, machine pistols, carbines, grenades. It lasted for about half an hour and then it all died away.[25]

In the third week of April, fighting in this sector reached an intensity and fury easily the equal of the worst which had gone before. Men scrambled, fought and died on scarred and rock-strewn slopes, pounded by artillery and small arms, a soldier's battle of rifle and bayonet. As this attack stalled, similar difficulties were experienced in the north, where Axis formations bitterly contested each foot of mountainous ground. Montgomery, not to be denied a victor's crown, renewed his attack on 25 April. Both sides fought with great skill and valour, losses again were high, every inch of ground contested. The result was a temporary stalemate. Jemadar Dewan Singh serving in 5th Indian Infantry Brigade experienced this murderous contact first hand:

> I was challenged in a foreign language. I felt it was not the British language or I would have recognised it. To make quite sure I crept up and found myself looking into the face of a German. I recognised him by his helmet. He was fumbling with his weapon so I cut off his head with my khukri. Another appeared from a slit trench and I cut him down also. I was able to do the same to two others, but one made a great deal of noise, which raised the alarm. I had a cut at a fifth but I am afraid I only wounded him. Yet perhaps the wound was severe, for I struck him between the neck and the shoulder.

Singh fought it out with an increasing number of Germans and was eventually beaten to the ground with a plethora of wounds. His platoon was by now coming up and showering the Axis with grenades allowing him to sham. In the confusion he made good his escape, nearly being shot by his own:

> Not recognising me, I heard one of my platoon call, 'Here comes the enemy, shoot him!' I bade them not to do so. They recognised my voice and let me come in … My hands being cut about and bloody, and having lost my khukri, I had to ask one of my platoon to take my pistol out of my holster and put it in my hand; I then took command of my platoon again.[26]

For veterans like Hans Schilling, fighting in such close proximity to Italian allies was a novel experience:

> When I got to Tunisia we fought close to the Italians for the first time. One night we heard a great uproar in the line beside us, it was Italian soldiers. They were going to make their night time meal from a couple of goats they had procured from somewhere. The goats got loose and the noise we heard was the sound of all the Italian soldiers chasing after them. In the end they were caught and a great cheer rose up. The goats were butchered and this was their meal. We Germans watched a few Italian officers and NCOs looking on and not helping – they had already eaten. Good food they kept for themselves. I do not think anyone could blame the Italian soldiers for their behaviour. We Germans did not regard them as disciplined soldiers, but they were given very little and their officers looked after themselves first.[27]

On 6 May, Alexander planned a final, overwhelming blow in the north. To add irresistible weight to Anderson's assault, two veteran 8th Army units, 4th Indian and 7th Armoured Divisions, would be detached in support, together with 201st Guards Brigade. Thus, two units which had endured the whole gruelling campaigns in the Western Desert, including the original 'Desert Rats' would take part in what promised to be the last battle. Von Arnim knew the plight of his exhausted survivors, some 135,000 Germans and nearer 200,000 Italians, was desperate. Despite the odds Axis defenders continued to fight long and hard as the onslaught began. After intensive bombardment and a successful break-in, dusk found the leading British units some fifteen miles from Tunis. Next morning British armour and armoured cars rolled into the city. On 12 May von Armin and General Messe each formally surrendered their commands. At 14.15 hrs on the 13th Churchill finally received the telegram from Alexander he had waited so long to read:

> Sir, it is my duty to report that the Tunisian campaign is over. All enemy resistance has ceased. We are masters of the North African shores.

The final message from Afrika Korps to OKH was less exultant:

> Ammunition shot off. Arms and equipment destroyed; in accordance with orders received DAK has fought itself to the conclusion where it can fight no more; the German Afrika Korps must rise again.[28]

It was utter defeat but without shame, the Afrika Korps had fought with steadfast courage and honour throughout. No man who had fought with Rommel in the desert need fear disdain. Alan Moorehead again:

> On May 10th I set off up the Peninsula through Hammam Lif to see one of the most grotesque and awesome spectacles that can have occurred in this war – an entire German army laying down its arms.[29]

For Hans Schilling this was a bitter pill. He and his comrades had fought doggedly:

We were still on those hills [Enfidaville] when the fighting stopped on 12 May. We saw the British coming up and further over the Italians were running out with big embraces. The war was over for us. We smashed our weapons and threw them away ... It was a strange thing walking up to someone you had been shooting at a few minutes before ...[30]

The War in the Desert was over but the bones of some 22,000 British and Imperial soldiers would remain: 'For most of them there is a grave in the sand ... only a mound of sand that the wind will soon soften and gently erase.'[31] Countess Ranfurly, now in Cairo, noted in her diary entry for 16 May: 'Last week all Axis forces in Tunisia surrendered. The struggle for North Africa is ended. It will not be long now before we invade Hitler's fortress, Europe.'[32]

Though the Desert Campaign had been won, the wider global conflict still raged. Many of the hard and bitter tactical lessons had to be learnt over again on very different battlefields. British armies toiled through the endless mud and sleet of the Italian campaign, battling the seemingly endless stop lines thrown up by Kesselring's troops in a country seemingly created for defence. Others landed in north-west Europe on D-Day and after to finally liberate the Continent. Victory was still a long way distant in the spring of 1943 but the era of continuous defeat was over and the men of 8th Army became the stuff of legend. El Alamein was indeed the final swing of the pendulum.

If you can keep your kit, when all around you
Are losing theirs and blaming it on you;
If you can scrounge a gag when all refuse you,
But make allowance for their doubtful view;
If you can wait, and not be tired of waiting,
Or, being pushed, let no man push you back,
Or, being detailed, waste no time debating
But force a British grin and hump your pack;
If you can drink, and not make drink your master,
And leave the thinking to your N.C.O.,
If you can meet with dear old Lady Astor
And treat her just as though you didn't know –
If you can bear to see your rations twisted
Into the weird concoction known as stew;

If neither knees nor face are ever blistered,

And neither flies nor fleas can worry you;

If you can face the other fellow's chinnings

And turn deaf ears to their unleashed abuse;

If you can force your heart and nerve and sinew

To serve on guard when you should be relieved,

And swear like hell with all the breath that's in you,

With all the curses ever man conceived;

If you can walk with blondes and keep your virtue,

Or ride in trams and keep your pay book safe;

If needle stabs and castor oil don't hurt you,

And rough angora shirts don't even chafe;

If you can fill a sandbag every minute,

Dream that your trench is Lana Turner's flat –

Yours is the blue my son, and all that's in it.

And what is more, you are a DESERT RAT.

R. F. Marriott (*Crusader* No. 37, 11 January 1943)

Chronology

1938
September – General Percy Hobart forms the Mobile Division (later 7th Armoured Div.) in Egypt.

1939
3 September – Britain declares war on Germany.

1940
11 June – Italy declares War on Britain; 11th Hussars involved in initial border skirmishes.

11 August – Italians invade British Somaliland.

19 August – British withdraw fully from Somaliland.

13 September – Italians invade Egypt and occupy Sollum.

17 September – Italians occupy Sidi Barrani.

20 September – British open the Takoradi aircraft reinforcement route through West Africa to Egypt.

12 November – OKH issues the order to create a force to support the Italians in N. Africa.

8 December – Wavell launches Operation 'Compass' under the command of General O'Connor.

11 December – Sidi Barrani recaptured; British counter-offensive proceeds with less difficulty than anticipated.

17 December – Sollum recaptured.

1941
5 January – British enter Bardia.

22 January – Australians enter Tobruk.

29 January – British re-invade Somaliland.

30 January – British enter Derna.

5–7 February – British defeat Italians in Battle of Beda Fomm.

25 February – British complete re-conquest of Somaliland.

27 February – Initial skirmishes with Afrika Korps.

5 March – First British troops withdrawn from theatre to be deployed in Greece.

24 March – Panzerarmee takes El Agheila.

31 March – Rommel attacks Mersa Brega.

3 April – Germans occupy Benghazi.

7 April – Generals O'Connor and Neame captured. Germans occupy Derna.

10 April – Tobruk besieged, Rommel bypasses garrison to press eastwards.

13 April – Tobruk surrounded, Bardia falls.

14 April – Axis assaults on Tobruk defences repulsed.

28 April – Germans occupy Sollum.

May/June – British intervention in Iraq (effectively subdued by 1 June).

5–12 May – 'Tiger' convoy brings much needed armour across Mediterranean.

15 May – British launch Operation 'Brevity'.

16 May – British complete conquest of Ethiopia.

20 May–1 June – Germans launch Operation 'Mercury' to take Crete, Allied survivors evacuated by RN.

June/July – British open campaign against Vichy French in Syria.

15 June – British launch Operation 'Battleaxe'.

22 June – Barbarossa begins.

1 July – Auchinleck replaces Wavell.

25 July–8 August – British intervention in Persia.

14/15 September – Rommel launches raid on Sofadi.

18 November – British launch Operation 'Crusader'.

19 November – British enter Sidi Rezegh.

21 November – Sortie by Tobruk garrison to effect link with forces around Sidi Rezegh.

23 November – Germans fare better in confused tank battles.

24 November – Rommel makes a dash across Egyptian border.

26 November – Auchinleck takes over direct command of 8th Army from General Ritchie.

30 November – Rommel tries to sever the corridor between British forces from Tobruk and Sidi Rezegh.

6–8 December – Massed battles around and south of Sidi Rezegh.

10 December – British relieve Tobruk.

13–17 December – Rommel's series of counter-attacks are eventually beaten off.

19–24 December – British occupy Derna (19th), Mechili (19th), Barce (23rd), Benghazi (24th).

1942
January

2 January – British re-capture Bardia.

6–8 January – Rommel's offensive from Agedabia is beaten back.

12 January – British occupy Sollum.

17 January – British regain the Halfaya Pass.

21 January – Axis offensive pre-empts Operation 'Acrobat' – British forces worsted and forced into retreat.

23 January – Germans re-take Agedabia.

February

2 February – British occupy Gazala Line and lay plans for offensive – Operation 'Buckshot'.

4 February – Axis re-capture Derna.

May

26 May – Axis offensive against the Gazala Line.

June

2 June – Axis besiege Free French forces at Bir Hakim on southern flank of Gazala Line.

3 June – General Ritchie's attempted riposte founders, 150th Brigade destroyed.

10 June – Free French ordered to abandon Bir Hakim.

12/13 June – Major tank battle ranges around 'Knightsbridge' position.

14–17 June – British withdrawal to Egyptian border.

18–21 June – Axis pressure on Tobruk which falls followed by Bardia.

24 June – Axis forces enter Egypt.

25 June – Auchinleck assumes personal command of 8th Army.

27/28 June – Axis forces successful in Battle of Mersa Matruh.

July

2/3 July – First Battle of El Alamein begins.

4 July – 8th Army launches counter-attacks.

10 July – Australian gains from Italians.

26 July – Further British attacks held off.

26 July – Official end of the battle – a limited British victory.

August

18 August – Alexander replaces Auchinleck as C in C Middle East and Montgomery is appointed to 8th Army following the death of General Gott.

31 August – New Axis offensive opens; the Battle of Alam Halfa.

September

3–7 September – Unsuccessful attack by NZ division in Alam el Halfa area, battle ends as a limited British defensive victory.

October

1 October – 8th Army stages attack in the Deir el Munassib sector.

23/24 October – Second Battle of El Alamein opens after initial bombardment – the 'Break-in' phase.

24/25 October – the 'Crumbling' phase.

26–28 October – the 'Counter' phase.

29/30 October – Stalemate.

November

1/2 November – 'Supercharge'.

3–7 November – Break-out and pursuit by 8th Army.

8 November – Allied landings in French North Africa – Operation 'Torch'.

1943

14–25 February – Axis offensives from Sidi Bou Zid to Kasserine, initially successful but finally repulsed.

6 March – Further Axis offensive – Battle of Medenine.
20–27 March – 8th Army breaks through Mareth Line.
23 March – US forces defeat Axis at Battle of El Guettar.
6 April – 8th Army defeats Axis at Battle of Wadi Akarit.
13 May – Remaining Axis forces surrender at Tunis; end of the Desert War.

What did I see in the desert today,
Where the frantic lizard runs?
The song of death was shouted forth
As the gunners manned the guns.
The men who'd pledged for Motherland
Their freedom and their lives,
Swore as they sweated in the smoke
To man the Twenty-fives

L. Challoner

Dramatis Personae

Allied Commanders

Alexander, Field Marshal Harold, Rupert, Leofric, George 1st Earl of Tunis KG, OM, GCB, GCMG, CSI, DSO, MC, PC 1891–1969.

An old Harrovian, son of the 4th Earl of Caledon, Alexander was commissioned into the Irish Guards and served with distinction in the trenches, twice wounded and winning both the MC and DSO in 1916, becoming the youngest lieutenant-colonel in the British Army. Rather oddly, in the aftermath of the Great War, he led the Baltic German Landeswehr in their successful bid to see off Soviet aggression. In 1940 he was commanding I Corps of the BEF at Dunkirk, just after Montgomery was appointed to lead II Corps. In February 1942 he was dispatched to Burma as GOC, where he supported Slim and 14th Army while dealing with the anglophobe US 'Vinegar Joe' Stillwell, a most difficult character. He was due to lead 1st Army for the 'Torch' landings but Alanbrooke nominated him to replace Auchinleck as GOC Middle East Command.

He presided over the successful conclusion of the Desert War and led 15th Army Group in Sicily and then onto the Italian Peninsula. He had hoped to command the ground forces for 'Overlord' but Alanbrooke considered Montgomery more suited. Monty himself was, with characteristic rudeness, more scathing: 'The higher art of war is quite beyond him.' If he was not a field commander of the first rank he possessed charisma and a flair for diplomacy. Unlike Montgomery, he commanded an entire theatre, remaining popular with both British and US senior officers. Eisenhower would have preferred him for 'Overlord'.

Auchinleck, Field Marshal Sir Claude, John, Eyre GCB, GCIE, CSI, DSO, OBE 1884–1981 ('the Auk').

An Ulster Scot from Fermanagh, his father was a soldier and Auchinleck served initially in the Indian Army, commanding 62nd Punjab regiment. In the First World War he saw hard service in Mesopotamia, the Middle East and Suez. He created a reputation for bravery, integrity and a deep concern for the welfare of the men under his command. In 1940 he inherited the poisoned chalice of the doomed Franco-British command in Norway. He then commanded V Corps before being appointed as GOC of Southern Command. His subordinate was Bernard Montgomery, who now had V Corps. The two men did not bond, as Montgomery recorded, 'I cannot recall that we ever agreed on anything.'

In December 1940 he was appointed as C in C of the Indian Army and intervened in the Iraq crisis in the following spring. In July he succeeded Wavell to Middle East Command. After his subsequent removal and replacement by Alexander he declined the newly hived off Persia and Iraq Command, remaining 'on the shelf' for a period. Reinstated as C in C of the Indian Army, he indefatigably supported Slim and 14th Army, earning unstinted praise from the latter. His subsequent involvement in Partition was less cordial and he disagreed with Mountbatten. In 1947 he resigned and retired, his integrity unblemished. His declining years were spent in North Africa and he died at Marrakesh. A somewhat reserved character, he was nevertheless loved by his men and respected by most of his peers. His contribution to victory in the Desert War has been steadily reassessed as time passes. The 'Auk' remains a revered figure.

Brooke, Alan, Francis 1st Viscount Alanbrooke KG, GCB, GCVO, DSO 1883–1963.

After Dunkirk, Alanbrooke became, in December 1941, CIGS. His philosophy was to maintain pressure on Axis forces in North Africa and then Italy. He opposed the US headlong rush towards opening a Second Front and supported Montgomery despite the latter's frequent clashes with Eisenhower and often impossible behaviour. He was also able to deal with Churchill's mercurial temperament and relentless interference with the military conduct of the war.

Campbell, Major-General John ('Jock'), Charles VC, DSO & Bar 1884–1942.

Campbell was a native of Thurso, an accomplished horseman, who served with the RHA. In 1940 he was a lieutenant-colonel commanding the artillery of 7th Armoured's Support Group. He was an exponent of all-arms flying columns, 'Jock' columns as they became known. He won his VC in November 1941 for a spirited defence of Sidi Rezegh airfield. In February 1942 he was promoted to lead XIII corps only to be killed in a minor traffic accident barely three weeks later.

Cunningham, Sir Alan, Gordon GCMG, KCB, DSO, MC 1887–1983.

Born a Dubliner, brother of Admiral Lord Cunningham of Hyndhope, he served in the RHA during the First World War. He later commanded British forces who successfully stormed Italian-held territories in East Africa, taking over 50,000 prisoners and removing the Axis presence. He was subsequently appointed to command 8th Army in August 1941 but he proved less effective against DAK and hesitancy led to his swift removal, spending the rest of the war in non-combat positions.

Dorman-Smith, Brigadier Eric 1895–1969 ('Chink').

Dorman-Smith was a controversial character who, when he fell out with the military establishment post-war, celticised his name to Dorman O'Gowan and became associated with an IRA campaign during the 1950s. Opinions among his contemporaries varied. Sir Basil Liddell Hart regarded him very highly, Montgomery did not. He was unquestionably a most capable staff officer who briefly held the rank of Major-General. Born in Cavan in Ireland he was Commandant of the Middle East Staff College, served under O'Connor and was Chief of Staff to Auchinleck, losing his position when the Auk was sacked. He served afterwards as a brigadier in Italy where he continued to be controversial.

Freyberg, Bernard, Cyril 1st Baron Freyberg VC, GCMG, KBE, DSO & 3 Bars 1889–1963.

Born in England, his parents moved to New Zealand where Freyberg trained and then practised as a dentist. He joined the TA and then secured a commission in RND Hood Battalion. He had an extremely active battlefield career in the First World War, suffering a host of wounds and winning a VC on the Somme. Freyberg was an outstanding leader of men, utterly fearless and a lion in battle. Churchill favoured him, during the inter-war years. Churchill bid him 'strip his shirt and show his scars' – which were legion. He was probably the youngest general in the British army. He was appointed in the Second World War to command the 2nd New Zealand Expeditionary force and 2nd NZ division.

Wavell gave him command in Crete, a thankless task and one which was perhaps beyond his capacity. Controversy remains over his handling of Ultra intelligence. Given German superiority and total command of the air it is perhaps difficult to see how anyone could have done better, though his political masters in Auckland were not best pleased. At divisional level he was a highly competent and energetic tactician, serving through North Africa and Italy and on good terms with Montgomery. After the war he was appointed Governor-General of New Zealand. He died when one of his old war wounds finally ruptured.

Gott, Lieutenant-General William, Henry, Ewart CB, CBE, DSO & Bar, MC 1897–1942 ('Strafer').

Having served with distinction in the KRRC with the BEF 'Strafer' Gott (so-named in the First World War after *Gott strafe England*) was stationed in Egypt in 1939 commanding 1st Battalion KRRC. A series of rapid promotions followed for this blunt, soldierly figure. By early 1942 he had risen to lead XIII Corps. Some observers have suggested he was thus promoted beyond his capacity: 'It has not been unknown for a commander to pass from disaster to disaster, but it is quite without precedent for any commander to pass from promotion to promotion as a reward for a succession of disasters.' Nonetheless, Gott was firm favourite to succeed to full command of 8th Army following Auchinleck's eclipse. He was, however, killed following an attack on the plane in which he had been travelling, thus making way for Montgomery.

Guingand, Major-General Sir Francis, Wilfred de ('Freddy') KBE, CB, DSO 1900–79.

Educated at Ampleforth and Sandhurst, Freddie de Guingand joined the Middlesex regiment in 1919 and served, during the inter-war years for some time as a secondee to the King's African Rifles (1926–31). Latterly he held appointments at Camberley Staff College and as Military Assistant to the Secretary of State for War before becoming Director of Military Intelligence Middle East. From the time Montgomery succeeded Auchinleck, de Guingand acted as his chief of staff, a post wherein he combined zeal and ability with that flair for diplomacy so noticeably absent in his commander.

Horrocks, Sir Brian Gwynne KCB, KBE, DSO, MC 1895–1985.

Something of an all-rounder, Horrocks competed in the 1924 Paris Olympics and latterly enjoyed a second career as a broadcaster. He also spent fourteen years as Black Rod for the House of Lords. His academic record was undistinguished and he was lucky to be commissioned into the Middlesex Regiment. His company was surrounded at Armentieres in October 1914 and he was captured, ill-used and maltreated by the Germans. He learnt Russian and was deployed during the abortive intervention in the Russian Civil War, before serving for a time in Ireland. In 1940 he served under Montgomery and by 1942 commanded 9th Armoured. He next took over X Corps from Lumsden (see below) and fought with distinction throughout the Tunisian campaign before being badly injured in a bombing raid on Bizerte. He recovered from his wounds in time to lead XXX Corps in Normandy and during 'Market Garden'.

Leese, Lieutenant-General Sir Oliver, William, Hargreaves 3rd Baronet KCB, CBE, DSO 1884–1978.

An old Etonian and Coldstreamer, Leese was wounded three times on the Somme and commanded 20th Guards Brigade in France during 1940. By 1941, in the desert, he was leading 15th Scottish Div. and then commanded XXX Corps. He went on to lead 8th Army in Italy, and was sent to Burma in 1944 as C in C Allied Land Forces South-East Asia. This appointment proved unsuccessful and he was eventually removed. Outside the army he was a renowned expert on cacti.

Lumsden, Lieutenant-General Herbert CB, DSO, MC 1897–1945.

Having studied at Eton Lumsden joined the TA before being commissioned into the RHA as a FOO in which capacity he won an MC in the First World War. An expert horseman he competed in several

Grand Nationals, despite a height disadvantage (he was a tall man, over six foot). He commanded the 12th Royal Lancers with some dash during the retreat to Dunkirk. In the desert he led 1st Armoured and his sometimes difficult personality was considered a factor in the defeat at Gazala. At El Alamein he commanded X Corps and had a strained relationship with Montgomery who felt he was tardy in the pursuit of DAK after the 'Break-Out' phase of the battle. He was consequently removed from command. He was appointed to VIII Corps in the UK before being sent as Churchill's representative to MacArthur in the Far East. On 6 January 1945 he had the misfortune to be on board USS *New Mexico* when the ship was struck by a kamikaze and Lumsden was among the dead.

Montgomery, Bernard, Law 1st Viscount of Alamein KG, GCB, DSO, PC 1887–1976 ('Monty').

Born in London into a rather impoverished Anglo-Irish clerical family, the future Field Marshal did not have a happy childhood. His mother was some years younger than his father and shamefully neglected her children. The family spent time in Tasmania when his father was appointed to the see. Though Montgomery senior inherited an estate in Ireland this was significantly encumbered and the family lived in straitened circumstances. Montgomery later failed to attend his mother's funeral being 'too busy'. He subsequently blamed this unfortunate beginning for a bullying temperament.

Montgomery was commissioned into the Royal Warwickshire Regiment in 1908 and saw service on the Western Front where, in 1914, he was severely wounded by a sniper's bullet (to the extent his grave was dug in anticipation). Having recovered fully he served under General Hubert Plumer in IX Corps of 2nd Army. During the lean inter-war years, when the army shrank dramatically, he held appointments on the Rhine and in Ireland where, forthright as ever, he fearlessly argued that allowing the Irish Nationalists self-determination was the only satisfactory route as the country could only be subdued by a degree of harshness inconceivable in Britain. He held appointments at the Staff College, Camberley and went on to command 9th Infantry Brigade.

He married Elizabeth Carver to whom he was devoted and had a son, David. Tragically Elizabeth died following an infection from an insect bite in 1937. Montgomery was inconsolable and threw himself more obsessively than ever into his work which remained the anodyne for his deep loss. It was suggested that he also harboured suppressed homosexual tendencies.

In 1939 he had severe doubts as to Britain's preparedness for war, a view vindicated by the BEF's performance in France. After Dunkirk, where he served with some distinction, he did not endear himself by blunt criticism of his superiors. His frustrations often emerged as downright rudeness. Tact and diplomacy were not among his qualities. In July 1940 he was appointed as deputy-commander V Corps where he soon fell out with Auchinleck and relations between the two men were never cordial. His ideas on the welfare of his troops, which were to earn him a huge following, often alarmed his exasperated superiors. A notion that army brothels ('horizontal refreshment') should be provided, was not untypical of his approach. He consistently failed to see why his bulldozer approach might ruffle feathers and he was not of a disposition that fostered compromise.

His undeniable successes in the Desert War made him the inevitable choice for command of Allied Land Forces for 'Overlord' under Eisenhower. Monty was quickly and bitterly at odds with Air Marshal Tedder, a feud that continued after the war. His plans for the Normandy breakout were much criticised at the time. The tactical solution proved elusive and costly though in strategic terms the plan finally succeeded and led to the savage denouement of the Falaise Pocket. Operation Market Garden was a failure though Montgomery, who would never admit to errors, disingenuously claimed it was a '90% success'. Throughout his relations with Eisenhower, who displayed admirable and unending patience, and the Americans were strained. His arrogance and conceit, allied to an obsessive flair for publicity, alienated more than a few. He was beloved by many but despised by some. He showed a genuine and enduring care for his men, meticulous in planning and training, cautious with their lives. His attitude towards subordinates was dismissive, bordering on cruel and he showed a hearty contempt for superiors.

His career after the war as CIGS was curtailed due to his inability to deal effectively with others in peacetime. His hubris soared and his often bizarre opinions on subjects as diverse as apartheid and Chinese Communism were increasingly out of step in changing times. His memoirs were vituperative and further alienated contemporaries, particularly Auchinleck who came in for a waspish savaging. He became, in his declining years, both an anachronism and an institution. Monty, for all his failings, produced victory from defeat. His image is that of the British army of the Second World War coming of age and going on to victory after victory till the final capitulation of Nazi Germany.

O'Connor, General Richard, Nugent KT, GCB, DSO & Bar, MC, ADC 1889–1981.

Born in India, O'Connor served with the 2nd Battalion Cameronians and remained involved with his old regiment for the rest of his life. He served mainly in signals and was awarded his MC in 1915, followed by a DSO. In the inter-war period he served under J. F. C. Fuller, then on the North-West Frontier and Palestine. At Mersa Matruh in 1939 he commanded 7th Div. facing the Italian 10th Army. He achieved outstanding success leading Operation 'Compass'. On 6 April 1941 in confused conditions, he and General Sir Philip Neame were taken prisoner by a German patrol near Martuba.

For two and a half years O'Connor remained captive in Italy, despite a daring series of attempted escapes. His chance finally came with the collapse of Italy in 1943 and he and Neame finally made good their deliverance. He went on to command VIII Corps in Normandy for the break-out battles around Caen. Subsequently, after 'Market Garden' he was removed from command of his corps, allegedly as Monty found him insufficiently robust in dealing with his American counterparts.

Ritchie, General Sir Neil, Methuen GBE, KCB, DSO, MC 1897–1983.

Ritchie was commissioned, like Wavell, into the Black Watch in 1910, winning his MC in Mesopotamia. He held a succession of staff appointments under Wavell, Alanbrooke and Auchinleck, all of whom regarded him highly. The latter gave him temporary command of 8th Army but his appointment lasted six, often very difficult, months. His handling of the fighting at Gazala and afterwards highlighted shortcomings and Auchinleck relieved him of command in June 1942, though he went on to lead XII Corps on D-Day.

Wavell, Sir Archibald 1st Earl Wavell GCB, GCSI, GCIE, CMG, MC, PC 1883–1950.

Wavell spent his formative years in India, studied at Winchester and Sandhurst, following his father into an army career and being commissioned into the Black Watch. He served in the South African War, in Russia as an observer and then through the First World War, losing an eye at 2nd Ypres in 1915. He served in a succession of staff roles and in GSO1 appointments during the inter-war years. In 1937 he was promoted GOC British forces in Palestine and Trans-Jordan. His appointment to GOC Middle East came in August 1939.

He successfully directed British forces to rout the Italians in Operation 'Compass', netting 130,000 prisoners. When he was replaced by Auchinleck he was sent to India where he commanded the hopefully named 'ABDA' (American-British-Dutch-Australian) forces attempting to stem the seemingly inexorable advance of the Japanese. In January 1943, he was replaced by the Auk, becoming Governor-General of India in September (he had been made a Field Marshal in January 1943). He stayed in office till superseded by Mountbatten in 1947. His own son followed him into the Black Watch but was later killed in Kenya. Wavell was much respected by his contemporaries with the notable exception of Winston Churchill who had little time for him. Wavell was reserved in manner and not accustomed to resisting the Prime Minister's bellicosity and constant interference. He rightly opposed the Greek adventure but failed to be more resolute; Churchill chose to assign blame to him for this and the subsequent Cretan debacle.

Sir Basil Liddell-Hart 1895–1970.

A leading strategic thinker of the inter-war years and respected military historian whose ideas were linked to those of Major-General J. F. C. ('Boney') Fuller (1878–1966) and General Percy 'Hobo' Hobart (1885–1957).

Arthur William Tedder, 1st Baron Tedder of Glenguin GCB 1890–1967.

Tedder served as Deputy-Supreme Commander under Eisenhower and campaigned relentlessly against Montgomery. This animosity persisted even when Monty was CIGS after the war.

Axis Commanders
Armin, General Hans-Jurgen von 1889–1962.

A Prussian of military stock from Silesia, he served on both the Eastern and Western Fronts in the First World War. He began the Second World War under Guderian during Barbarossa where he sustained serious wounds, commanding 39th Panzer till November 1942. Transferred to Tunisia he served initially under Rommel and succeeded him as C in C of Army Group Africa, surrendering in May 1943.

Bastico, General Ettore 1876–1972.

A native of Bologna he held commands in Ethiopia and the Spanish Civil War, and latterly as Governor of the Dodecanese. His command in North Africa was diminished with Cavallero's appointment and, after the loss of Libya, became largely meaningless. He was nonetheless made a Marshal.

Bayerlein, General Fritz 1899–1970.

A Bavarian who fought in the infantry on the Western Front where he won his Iron Cross, he served under Guderian in Poland. At Alam Halfa in the Desert War he took over command from Nehring when the latter was wounded. He was himself subsequently invalided home but went on to fight both in Normandy and the Ardennes. He was part-Jewish.

Cavallero, Marshal Ugo 1880–1943.

A Piedmontese, who rose rapidly up the command ladder during the First World War and displayed great strategic insight contributing to a number of Italian victories, he commanded in East Africa in 1938 and went on to serve in Greece and Albania. His appointment in North Africa was obfuscated by his poor relationship with the volatile Rommel. Latterly, he was embroiled in the Italian collapse of 1943. For a while he was favoured by the Germans but became hopelessly compromised and preferred suicide.

Gariboldi, General Italo 1879–1970.

He commanded 30th Infantry Division in Ethiopia and then 5th Army on the Italo-French border in North Africa. In March 1941 he was appointed to replace Graziani but was subsequently removed due to his poor relationship with Rommel.

Graziani, Marshal Rodolfo Marchese di Neghelli 1882–1955.

Youngest colonel in the Italian army during the First World War, he commanded Italian forces in Libya in the 1920s, where his uncompromising policies earned him the unfortunate sobriquet of 'Butcher of Libya'. He served with equal ruthlessness in Ethiopia – 'The Duce will have Ethiopia with or without the Ethiopians'. After his predecessor Balbo died in a 'friendly-fire' incident in 1940 he was appointed as C in C North Africa. The destruction of 10th Army during Wavell's offensive compelled his resignation. After the war he was condemned to nineteen years' gaol for war crimes but served only a few months before being released.

Guderian, General Heinz 'Schneller Heinz' 1888–1955.

Guderian is regarded as father of the Third Reich doctrine on armoured warfare and one of the most influential German officers, though never given his Field Marshal's baton. His influence on the tactics of armoured warfare and blitzkrieg was profound and he is credited as the architect of victory against France in 1940.

Kesselring, Field Marshal Albert 'Smiling Albert' 1885–1960.

A Luftwaffe Generalfeldmarschall and C in C Mediterranean Theatre, where he was technically subordinate to the Italians and Rommel's command was a separate entity. He made strenuous efforts to maintain supplies to the Afrika Korps though he disagreed with Rommel's strategy, after the fall of Tobruk, of advancing into Egypt while Malta still held out. Hitler, in this instance, favoured Rommel. Kesselring went on to maintain a skilled and stubborn defence of Italy as the Allies clawed their way up the Peninsula.

Messe, General Giovanni 1883–1968.

Having served in Libya then through the First World War, Messe was instrumental in the development of elite infantry formations, 'Arditi'. Latterly he served in Ethiopia and Albania, coming to North Africa as C in C in January 1943. He was careful to placate his nominal deputy Rommel. He was promoted Marshal just in time to surrender Axis forces in May 1943.

Nehring, General Walther 1892–1983.

He commanded the DAK from May 1942 having served an apprenticeship under Guderian. He was badly wounded in an air raid during the Battle of Alam Halfa but recovered sufficiently to command German forces in Tunisia during November/December 1942. He later fought on the Eastern Front.

Ravenstein, General Johann von 1889–1962.

Descended from a line of soldiers, one of whom was an aide to Blucher at Waterloo, he served with distinction of the Western Front in the First World War winning both the Iron Cross and the Pour le Merite ('Blue Max'). He worked in industry under Weimar but rejoined the ranks in 1934, serving in Poland and France where he added the Knight's Cross to his honours. In April 1941 he was promoted to Major-General, commanding 21st Panzer and that October was again promoted to Lieutenant-General. He was captured at Capuzzo a month later by the New Zealanders.

Rommel, Field Marshal Erwin Johannes Eugen 'The Desert Fox' 1891–1944.

Born in Wurttemburg, the legendary general showed early promise as an engineer and, throughout his life, displayed an amazing grasp of technology. He joined the 124th Wurttemburg Regiment in 1910, to his family's dismay and went on to serve with distinction in France, Romania and Italy during the First World War, winning the Iron Cross and Blue Max. After the war he remained in uniform, a colonel in 1938. An early convert was Goebbels whose influence, combined with Rommel's own natural flair for showmanship, contributed to the lustre attaching to his laurels after 1940. Influence gained him command of 7th Panzer despite a lack of armoured experience and the misgivings of some of his superiors. He displayed, in the battle for France, his trademark energy, dash, fire and utter ruthlessness, though this was always tempered by chivalry.

He threw back the British counter-attack at Arras and drove his men and machines relentlessly, earning them the sobriquet of the 'Ghost' division. Latterly, and to his fellow-commander's chagrin, 5th Panzer was placed under his command and his swift marches sealed the fate of elements of French 1st Army. His camera was always to hand despite the pressure and he never missed a 'photo opportunity' – adding the Knight's Cross to his honours. He moved to command 5th Light Division then 21st and 15th Panzer in North

Africa where his legend thrived. After the defeat, such a reverse rather diminished his image of invincibility, and he languished in the backwaters of the Balkans (Army Group E) and then Northern Italy (Army Group B).

With Kesselring's appointment he was moved to Normandy, where his driving energy strove to transform the defences studding the Normandy beaches. In the height of the subsequent battle, on 17 July 1944, he was severely wounded when his car was strafed. By now his charisma had waned and he was implicated, on extremely tenuous grounds, in the July Plot against Hitler. This alleged association led to his being offered the disgrace of a trial, with the consequent persecution of his family or taking his own life. For Rommel, a devoted husband and father, there could be only one course. Ironically this distanced him from the Nazi regime he had so assiduously served and preserved his post-war image.

While capable of inspiring great loyalty, he could equally alienate many fellow officers, particularly subordinates whom he drove hard and relentlessly. His relations with the Italians were scarcely cordial. He was bold to the point of recklessness, leading from the front, unsparing of his personal resources, heedless of danger. Valour and dynamism are admirable but may be misplaced. As a tactician few would disagree that he was brilliant, able to understand every nuance of battle and respond with the swiftness of genius. His competence as a strategist was less assured. Some would aver his appreciation of the strategic position in North Africa was blinkered and he allowed his flashes of tactical lightning to divert attention from an untenable position. In North Africa he was continually hindered by lack of motor transport in a campaign fought over vast distances, served by ports that were too small at the end of a long logistics trail across unfriendly waters. He was hamstrung by what has been described, perhaps unfairly as 'useless Italian ballast'. His genius for the armoured thrust was unexcelled yet such unrestrained boldness constantly exposed his forces to disaster through logistical failure.

Sir David Hunt, an intelligence officer on Alexander's staff, described his talents: '… his real gift was for commanding an armoured regiment, perhaps a division and that his absolute ceiling was an armoured corps'. Many thousands of 8th Army veterans who experienced the Desert Fox at first hand might have been less dismissive.

Stumme, General Georg von 1886–1942.

As a Lieutenant-General in 1939 he commanded 2nd Light Division in Poland then went on to lead 40 Corps in the Balkans. In Russia he served under von Bock's command but came under a cloud due to security lapses. Sentenced by court martial, he was rehabilitated due to von Bock's influence. During Rommel's critical absence in the opening hours of Second El Alamein he commanded the Panzerarmee but succumbed to heart failure at a critical moment.

Thoma, Lieutenant-General Willhelm Ritter 1891–1948.

A native of Dachau, he fought on both fronts during the Second World War and was captured in 1918. He later fought in Spain and then Poland. Promotion followed rapidly and he commanded 17th Panzer during 'Barbarossa'. He briefly replaced Nehring when the latter was wounded and then, very briefly, on the death of Stumme on 24 October 1942 before Rommel returned. On 4 November he was again captured and sent as a PoW to England where he was an important German officer in various camps and much respected, despite having a leg amputated in 1945. He died of a heart attack three years after the war's end.

> What did I see in the desert today,
> Besides the rocks and the sand?
> I saw the squadrons in the sky of bomber and fighter command.
> I heard the thunder of their work,
> I saw their lightning stroke,
> And far across the skyline came the rolling clouds of smoke.
> Whilst incoherent in their rage
> The chattering Bredas spoke
>
> L. Challoner

Notes

Introductory: 'The Blue'
1. A. W. Evans, quoted in Lucas, J., *War in the Desert* (London, 1982) p.74.
2. Quoted in Warner, P., *Alamein, Recollections of the Heroes* (London, 1979) p.39.
3. Quoted in Gilbert, A., (ed.) *The Imperial War Museum Book of the Desert War 1940–1942* (London, 1992) p.30.
4. Challoner, L., In the Desert Today quoted in Lewis-Stempel, J., *Autobiography of the British Soldier* (London 2007) pp.358–60.
5. Quoted in McGuirk, D., *Rommel's Army in Africa* (London, 1987) p.53.
6. Imperial War Museum, ('IWM') p.31.
7. Quoted in Bowen, R., *Many Histories Deep – the Personal Landscape; Poets in Egypt 1940–1945* (London, 1995) p.144.
8. *Ibid.* p.186.
9. H. A. Wilson, IWM p.41.
10. J. G. Harris 7th Rifle Brigade, IWM p.35.
11. *Ibid.* p.29.
12. Crawford R. J., *I was an Eighth Army Soldier* (London, 1944) p. 21.
13. *Ibid.* p.21.
14. McGuirk, p.55.
15. *Ibid.* p.55.
16. De Manny, E., 'Silver Fern Leaf up the Blue' in *Return to Oasis* (1980).
17. Lucas, p.9.
18. McGuirk, p.55.
19. Crawford, p.86.
20. Lucas, p.74.
21. DLI Sound Recording Project.
22. Crawford, p.20.
23. Manning, O., *Fortunes of War* vol. 2 (London, 1979) p.10.
24. Crawford, pp.19–21.
25. *Ibid.* pp.19–21.
26. *Ibid.* p.19.
27. *Ibid.* p.22.
28. McGuirk, p.58.
29. Quoted in Strawson, J., *The Battle for North Africa* (London, 1969) p.8.
30. McGuirk, p.58.
31. Crawford, p.27.
32. Strawson, p.10.
33. Warner, p.30.
34. Bowen, p.25.
35. IWM, p.37.
36. Bowen, p.41.
37. Ranfurly, Countess H., *To War with Whittaker* (London, 1995) p. 135.
38. *Crusader* issue no.57, 31 May 1943.
39. Lucas, p.31.
40. Bowen, p.122.
41. Challoner in *Autobiography* etc pp. 358–60.
42. McGuirk, p.59.
43. IWM, p.44.

1. Desert War
1. Ranfurly, p.134.
2. T. Powell, quoted in Warner, p.38.
3. Lt-Col-R. G. Green, quoted in Warner, p.53.
4. Warner, p.40.
5. *Ibid.* p.55.
6. *Ibid.* p.55.
7. Quoted in Kershaw, R., *Tank Men* (London, 2008) p.142.
8. *Ibid.* p.144.
9. *Ibid.* p.144.
10. *Ibid.* p.154.

11. Lucas, p.37.
12. Kershaw, p.166.
13. Lucas, p.70.
14. Kershaw, p.161.
15. Lt-Col-East, Lucas, p.91.
16. *Ibid.* p.91.
17. Lucas, p.89.
18. *Ibid.* p.89.
19. *Ibid.* p.157.
20. Strawson, p.97.
21. R. G. W. Mackilligan MC, Lucas, p.159.
22. Lucas, p.144.
23. *Ibid.* p.144.
24. Lt-Col-B. S. Jarvis, quoted in Lucas, p.144–145.
25. Warner, p.155.
26. Lt-Col-Jarvis, Lucas, p. 145.
27. *Ibid.* p.145.
28. *Ibid.* p.145.
29. *Ibid.* p.145.
30. *Ibid.* p.178.
31. *Ibid.* p.178.
32. *Ibid.* p.183.
33. Later Air Chief Marshal, IWM, p.142.
34. Later Lord Deramore, IWM, p.144.
35. IWM, p.46.
36. Jim Smith, (Bletchley Park), quoted in Smith, M., *Station X – Codebreakers of Bletchley Park* (London, 1998) p.99.
37. Smith, p.100.
38. Bill Williams, Smith, p.103.
39. Ralph Bennet, Smith, p.197.
40. Captain Sean Fielding, quoted in Parkinson, R., *The War in the Desert* (London, 1976) p.196.

2. 'Compass': June 1940 – March 1941
1. Quoted in Pitt, B., *The Crucible of War – Western Desert 1941* (London, 1980) pp.22–3.
2. Strawson, p.16.
3. *Ibid.* p.17.
4. *Ibid.* p.16.
5. Quoted in Barr, N., *Pendulum of War – the Three Battles of El Alamein* (London, 2005) p.4.
6. Pitt, pp.22–3.
7. *Ibid.* p.49.
8. IWM, p.2.
9. Bowman, p.111.
10. IWM, p.189

11. *Ibid.* p.191.
12. *Ibid.* p.193.
13. OH vol. 1 pp.259–60.
14. *Ibid.* p.260.
15. *Ibid.* p.260.
16. Bierman, J. S. & S. Smith, *Alamein – War without Hate* (London, 2002) p.46.
17. *Ibid.* p.47.
18. Strawson, p.39.
19. IWM, p.3.
20. Bierman & Smith pp.48–9.
21. *Ibid.* p.49.
22. IWM, p.5.
23. IWM, p.8.
24. Strawson, p.39.
25. IWM, p.8.
26. Challoner, *op. cit.*
27. Strawson, p.39.
28. OH vol. 1 p.272.
29. IWM, p.6.
30. Strawson, p.37.
31. *Ibid.* p.47.
32. OH vol. 1 p.315.
33. Bowman, p.138.

3. 'Brevity' & 'Battleaxe': May – July 1941
1. Prince, F. T., 'Soldiers Bathing' in *Poetry of the Forties*, ed. R. Skelton (London, 1968) p.104.
2. Garret, D., *The Campaign in Greece and Crete* (HMSO, 1942) pp. 5–6.
3. IWM, p.13.
4. *Ibid.* p.14
5. Clark, A., *The Fall of Crete* (London, 1962) p.9.
6. Simpson, A., *Operation Mercury – the Battle for Crete* (London, 1981) p.52.
7. ANZAC doggerel.
8. Clark, p.20.
9. Dickinson, P., 'War' in *Poetry of the Forties* p.123.
10. Parkinson, p.40; Pitt, p.241.
11. Pitt, p.243.
12. OH vol. 2 p.41.
13. Pitt, p.250.
14. *Ibid.* p.250.
15. Parkinson, p.41.
16. IWM, p.17.
17. OH vol. 2 pp.31–2.
18. Ranfurly, p.84.
19. IWM, p.16.
20. Parkinson, p.44.

21. OH vol. 2 pp.31–2.
22. *Ibid.* p.41.
23. Strawson, p.57.
24. IWM, p.18.
25. OH vol. 2 pp.31–2.
26. McGuirk, p.78
27. *Ibid.* p.78.
28. IWM, p.19.
29. OH vol. 2 pp.31–2.
30. McGuirk, p.80.
31. Pitt, p.288.
32. McGuirk, p.83.
33. Pitt, p.281.
34. Strawson, p.68.
35. IWM, p.22–3.
36. *Ibid.* p.23.
37. McGuirk, pp.84–5.
38. OH vol. 2 p.159.
39. *Ibid.* p.161.
40. McGuirk, p.86.
41. Strawson, p.63.
42. Parkinson, p.55.
43. McGuirk, p.65.
44. Parkinson, p.55
45. McGuirk, p.66.
46. Strawson, p.67.
47. McGuirk, p.89.
48. Challoner, *op. cit.*

4. 'Crusader': August 1941 – January 1942
1. McGuirk, p.83.
2. Pitt, p.354.
3. Parkinson, p.59.
4. *Ibid.* p.61.
5. *Ibid.* p.61.
6. *Ibid.* p.63.
7. Ranfurly, p.113.
8. McGuirk, p.94.
9. Pitt, p.355.
10. Ranfurly, pp.118–20; Pitt, pp. 349–52.
11. OH vol. 3 p.40.
12. Strawson, pp.79–80.
13. IWM, p.55.
14. OH vol. 3 p.44.
15. Pitt, p.387.
16. Parkinson, p.82.
17. OH vol. 3 p.44.
18. Strawson, p.80.
19. Lewis-Sempel, p.359.
20. *Ibid.* p.324.
21. *Ibid.* p.340.
22. *Ibid.* pp.340–1.

23. *Ibid.* p.341.
24. *Ibid.* p.342.
25. IWM, p.56.
26. Bowen, p.81.
27. OH vol. 3 p.59.
28. Parkinson, p.79.
29. Strawson, p.83.
30. OH vol. 3 p.53.
31. Parkinson, p.67.
32. Ranfurly, p.114.
33. OH vol. 3 p.70.
34. IWM, p.58.
35. OH vol. 3 p.96.
36. Crawford, p.34.
37. OH vol. 4 p.96.
38. *Ibid.* p.71.
39. *Ibid.* p.71.
40. Parkinson, p.85.

5. 'Msus Stakes' & 'Gazala Gallop': January – June 1942
1. OH vol. 3 p.136.
2. *Ibid.* p.139.
3. An expression put forward by the distinguished Great War historian C. R. M. F. Cruttwell.
4. Strawson, p.96.
5. Lt. D. F. Parry, IWM, p.60.
6. Parkinson, p.91.
7. Strawson, p.96.
8. OH vol. 3 p.145.
9. Strawson, p.97.
10. OH vol. 3 p.151.
11. *Ibid.* p.152.
12. *Ibid.* pp.153–4.
13. *Ibid.* p.154.
14. Parkinson, p.92.
15. *Ibid.* p.93.
16. OH vol. 3 p.153.
17. *Ibid.* p.153.
18. Strawson, p.100.
19. *Ibid.* p.101.
20. Parkinson, p. 95.
21. *Ibid.* p.94.
22. *Ibid.* p.95.
23. *Ibid.* p.95.
24. *Ibid.* p.96.
25. OH vol. 3 p.213.
26. IWM, p.96.
27. Parkinson, p.103.
28. *Ibid.* pp.103–4.
29. *Ibid.* p.104.
30. IWM, p.97.

31. *Ibid.* p.98.
32. Strawson, p. 104; Parkinson, p.105.
33. OH vol. 3 p.229.
34. *Ibid.* p.233.
35. IWM, p.102.
36. OH vol. 3 p.237.
37. Crawford, p.79.
38. OH vol. 3 p.243.
39. *Ibid.* p.243.
40. IWM, p.100.
41. Parkinson, p.110.
42. *Ibid.* p.110.
43. OH vol. 3 p.246.
44. IWM, p.110.
45. *Ibid.* p.110.
46. Barr, p.16.

6. Mersa Matruh & First Alamein: June – August 1942

1. IWM, p.113.
2. OH vol. 3 p.285.
3. *Ibid.* pp.281–3.
4. Barr, p.18.
5. *Ibid.* p.19.
6. *Ibid.* p.24.
7. *Ibid.* p.27.
8. IWM, p.12.
9. Crawford, p.79.
10. *Ibid.* p.41.
11. Bowman, p.108.
12. Warner, p.203.
13. Barr, p.31.
14. *Ibid.* p.32.
15. *Ibid.* p.33.
16. Crawford, p.48.
17. OH vol. 3 p.296.
18. Strawson, p.96.
19. Warner, p.64.
20. H. Metcalfe, Warner, p.64.
21. Ranfurly, p.39.
22. IWM, p.113.
23. *Ibid.* pp.113–4.
24. *Ibid.* p.114.
25. J. R. Oates, IWM, p.155.
26. Strawson, p.109.
27. Ranfurly, p.139.
28. Crawford, p.55.
30. Bowman, p.82.
31. Warner, p.219.
32. Crawford, p.52.
33. *Ibid.* p.56.
34. *Ibid.* p.46.
35. *Ibid.* p.46.

7. Alam Halfa: August – September 1942

1. Currey, R. N., 'Burial Flags, Sind' in *Poetry of the Forties*.
2. Barr, p.186.
3. *Ibid.* p.189.
4. *Ibid.* p.189.
5. OH vol. 3 p.367.
6. Barr, p.199.
7. *Ibid.* p.200.
8. *Ibid.* p.201.
9. *Ibid.* p.203 – Gott's demise was lamented by some but by no means by all.
10. OH vol. 3 p.370.
11. *Ibid.* p.370.
12. *Montgomery of Alamein, Memoirs* (London, 1958) p.90.
13. *Ibid.* p.93.
14. IWM, p.157.
15. *Ibid.* p.157.
16. OH vol. 3 p.370.
17. Montgomery, p.97.
18. OH vol. 3 p.384.
19. *Ibid.* p.383.
20. Warner, p.206.
21. *Ibid.* p.54.
22. OH vol. 3 p.386.
23. Montgomery, p.99.
24. OH vol. 3 p.387.
25. Warner, p.50.
26. OH vol. 3 p.388.
27. Montgomery, p.99.
28. OH vol. 3 p.389.
29. Montgomery, p.97.
30. OH vol. 3 p.391.
31. *Ibid.* p.391.
32. IWM, p.159.

8. Second El Alamein: Break-in

1. Montgomery, p.100
2. Sergeant J. Longstaff, 2nd Batt. Rifle Brigade, quoted in Arthur, M., *Forgotten Voices of the Second World War* (London, 2004) p.201.
3. Montgomery, p.100.
4. Sergeant J. Fraser, RTR quoted in Arthur, pp.201–202.
5. Montgomery, p.101.
6. Sergeant Longstaff, Arthur, p.210.
7. Montgomery, p.103.
8. *Ibid.* p.104.
9. Barr, p.295.
10. IWM, p.161.

11. Carver, M., *El Alamein* (London, 1962).
12. Strawson, p.127.
13. IWM, p.161.
14. Barr, p.305.
15. *Ibid*. p.305.
16. Montgomery, p.110.
17. Arthur, p.204.
18. Warner, p.213.
19. Montgomery, p.111.
20. Montgomery, p.107.
21. *Ibid*. p.108.
22. *Ibid*. p.108.
23. Arthur, p.204.
24. Montgomery, p.108.
25. *Ibid*. p.109.
26. *Ibid*. p.109.
27. *Ibid*, p.110.
28. *Ibid*. p.110.
29. Warner, p.204.
30. IWM, p.160.
31. *Ibid*. p.160.
32. Montgomery, p.110.

23. Lewis-Stempel, p.360.
24. Warner, p.205.
25. The Revd C. W. Potts (The Buffs), Warner p.93.
26. Warner, p.205.
27. Captain D. Smiley, Royal Armoured Car Regiment, Arthur, p. 206.
28. OH vol. 4 pp.34–5.
29. Warner, pp.40–1.
30. OH vol. 4 p.41.
31. IWM, pp.166–7.
32. *Ibid*. p.168.
33. Arthur, p.206.
34. *Ibid*. p.206.
35. J. W. Telford, Warner, p.74.
36. Major D. J. Watson, Warner, p.103.
37. Mackilligin, Warner, p.159.
38. Warner, p.205.
39. 1st Lt Brian (Barney) O'Kelly, Intelligence Corps, Warner p.205.
40. Lt-Col-Jarvis, Warner, pp.145–6.
41. Montgomery, p.117.
42. *Ibid*. p.118.
43. *Ibid*. p.118.
44. Brigadier C. E. F. Turner, Warner, p.215.
45. Mrs G. Trevern, Warner, p.217.

9. Second El Alamein: 'Lightfoot'

1. Jarmain, J., 'Ring Plover at El Alamein' in *Poetry of the Forties*.
2. Martin Ranft, 220th Artillery Regiment, Panzerarmee Afrika, Arthur, p.207.
3. OH vol. 4 p.34.
4. R. G. W. Mackilligin MC, Warner, pp.157–8.
5. Col. L. C. East, ibid. p.80.
6. Lewis-Stempel, p.360; this anonymous verse was blown into a slit trench at El Agheila.
7. Arthur, p.204.
8. Lewis-Stempel, p.360.
9. Warner, p.88.
10. OH vol. 4 p.33.
11. *Ibid*. p. 37.
12. Warner, p.89.
13. *Ibid*. pp.89–90.
14. Lewis-Stempel, p.360.
15. IWM, p.63.
16. Major H. P. Samwell, Argyll & Sutherland Highlanders, Strawson, p.139.
17. IWM, p.166.
18. Strawson, p.140.
19. Lewis-Stempel, p.352.
20. Strawson, p.139.
21. Corporal V. Scammel, Argyll & Sutherland Highlanders, Arthur, p.196.
22. Strawson, p.139.

10. Second El Alamein: 'Crumbling'

1. Trooper Jakes, Lucas, p.200.
2. *Ibid*. p.197.
3. F. A. Lewis, Warner, p.41.
4. McGuirk, p.60.
5. Warner, p.207.
6. *Ibid*. p.207.
7. Lewis-Stempel, pp.357–8.
8. Colonel R. F. Wright, Warner, p.175.
9. Arthur, p.205.
10. Warner, p.175.
11. Rifleman Suckling, Lucas, p.221.
12. Arthur, p.205.
13. Lucas, p.222.
14. Warner, p.175.
15. *Ibid*. p.42.
16. *Ibid*. pp.175.
17. Arthur, p.205.
18. *Ibid*. p.205.
19. Carver, p.153.
20. Warner, p.93.
21. OH vol. 4 p.59.
22. Warner, p.94.
23. *Ibid*. p.95.
24. McGuirk, p.125.
25. Warner, p.95.
26. *Ibid*. p.96.

27. Arthur, p.207.
28. *Ibid.* p.207.
29. *Ibid.* p.207.
30. OH vol. 4 p.63.
31. Montgomery, pp.120–121.
32. *Ibid.* p.121.
33. *Ibid.* p.121.

11. Second El Alamein: 'Supercharge'
1. Montgomery, pp.121–3.
2. *Ibid.* p.125.
3. *Ibid.* p.125.
4. S. J. C. Cross MBE, Warner, p.170.
5. Roy Cooke, Lucas, p.236.
6. *Ibid.* p.236.
7. L. R. Symonds, Warner, p.132.
8. IWM, p.72.
9. *Ibid.* p.72.
10. Lucas, p.242.
11. Carver, p.168.
12. IWM, p.74.
13. *Ibid.* p.174.
14. Lucas, p.243.
15. *Ibid.* p.242.
16. McGuirk, p.60.
17. Lucas, p.243.
18. Montgomery, p.125.
19. Lucas, p.246.
20. Lewis-Stempel, p.352.
21. *Ibid.* p.354.
22. *Ibid.* pp.354–5.
23. *Ibid.* p.355.
24. *Ibid.* p.356.
25. *Ibid.* p.357.
26. Col R. F. Wright, Warner, p.176.
27. Carver, p.173.
28. OH vol. 4 p.72.
29. Carver, p.177.
30. Montgomery p.125.
31. Carver, p.169.
32. Lucas, p.241.
33. F. Jackson, Lucas, p.253.
34. McGuirk, p.60.
35. Montgomery, p.125.
36. Warner, p.211.
37. *Ibid.* p.171.
38. Lewis-Stempel, p.344.
39. Montgomery, p.126.
40. *Ibid.* p.127.
41. *Ibid.* p.126.
42. Strawson, p.149.
43. IWM, p.175.
44. *Ibid.* pp.151–153.

12. The Long Pursuit
1. OH vol. 4 p.79.
2. Montgomery, pp.132–3.
3. McGuirk, p.96.
4. Arthur, pp.206–7.
5. Arthur, p.208.
6. *Ibid.* p.208.
7. Warner, p.201.
8. *Ibid.* p.200.
9. OH vol. 4. p.82.
10. *Ibid.* p.82.
11. *Ibid.* Appendix 3, pp.476–7.
12. Lucas, p.255.
13. *Ibid.* p.256.
14. IWM, p.82.
15. Warner, p.127.
16. OH vol. 4 p.90.
17. Arthur, p.208.
18. IWM, p.48.
19. *Ibid.* p.49.
20. *Ibid.* p.178.
21. Strawson, p.175.
22. Parkinson, p.163.
23. IWM, p.200.
24. Strawson, pp.205–206.
25 McGuirk, p.60.
26. Strawson, p.204.
27. McGuirk. p.60.
28. Strawson, p.207.
29. *Ibid.* p.206.
30. McGuirk, p.63.
31. Parkinson, p.196.
32. Ranfurly, p.189.

MAPS

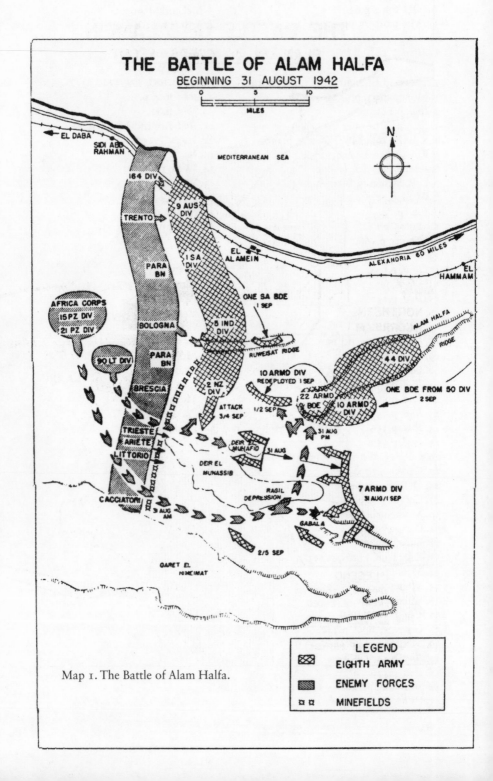

Map 1. The Battle of Alam Halfa.

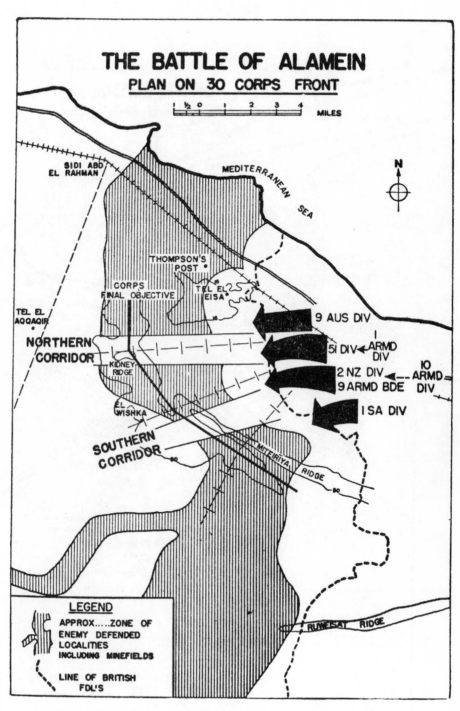

Map 2. The Break-in – Operation 'Lightfoot'.

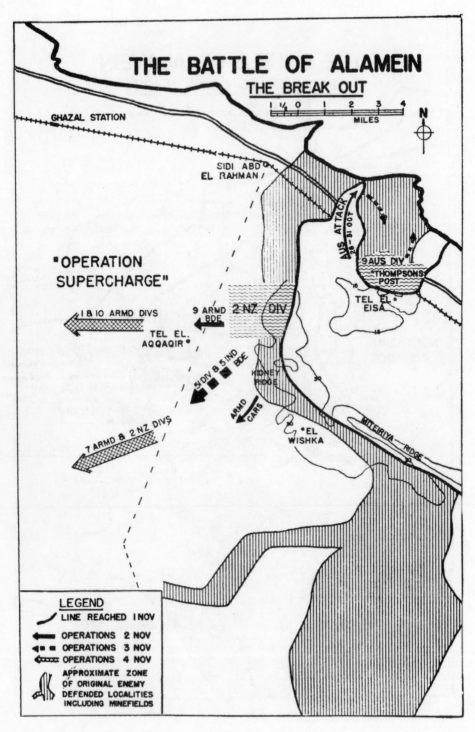

Map 3. The Break-out – Operation 'Supercharge'.

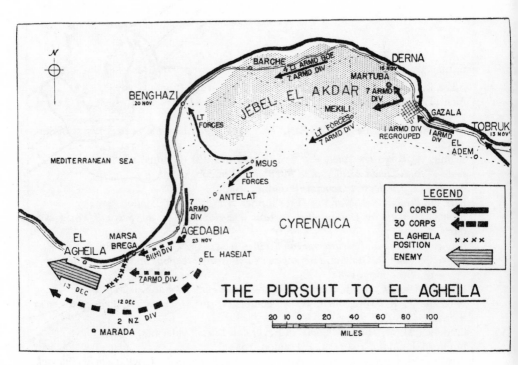

Map 4. The Pursuit to El Agheila.

Bibliography

Published Sources

Adair, R., *British Eight Army, North Africa 1940–1943* (London, 1974).

Agar-Hamilton, J. A. I. & L. C. F. Turner, *Crisis in the Desert May–July 1942* (Oxford, 1952).

Alexander, Field Marshal the Earl, *The Alexander Memoirs 1940–1945* (London, 1962).

Arthur, M., *Forgotten Voices of the Second World War* (London, 2004).

Bailey, J. B. A., *Field Artillery and Firepower* (London, 1989).

Barnett, C., *The Desert Generals* (London, 1960).

Barr, N., *Pendulum of War, the Three Battles of El Alamein* (London, 2004).

Beale, P., *Death by Design, British Tank Development in the Second World War* (Stroud, 1998).

Bennet, R., *Ultra and Mediterranean Strategy 1941–1945* (London, 1989).

Bidwell, S., and D. Graham, *Firepower, British Army Weapons and Theories of War 1904–1945* (London, 1982).

Bierman, J. and C. Smith, *Alamein, War Without Hate* (London, 2002).

Bingham, J., K. Wordsworth & W. Haupt, *North African Campaign 1940–1943* (London, 1969).

Braddock, D. W., *The Campaigns in Egypt and Libya* (Aldershot, 1964).

Bradford, E., *Malta 1940–1943* (London, 1985).

British Troops Egypt *Official Handbook for British Troops in Egypt, Cyprus, Palestine and the Sudan* (BTE, 1936).

Bryant, Sir Arthur, *The Turn of the Tide* Vols I and II (London, 1957–1959).

Carver, M., *El Alamein* (London, 1962).

Carver, M., *Tobruk* (London, 1964).

Carver, M., *Dilemmas of the Desert War* (London, 1986).

Chalfont, A. J., *Montgomery of Alamein* (London, 1976).

Clark, A., *The Fall of Crete* (London, 1962).

Connell, J., *Auchinleck: A Biography of Field Marshall Sir Claude Auchinleck* (London, 1959).

Crawford, R. J., *I was an Eighth Army Soldier* (London, 1944).

Crimp, R. L. *The Diary of a Desert Rat* (London, 1971).

Crisp, R., *Brazen Chariots: An Account of Tank Warfare in the Western Desert, November–December 1941* (London, 1959).

De Guingand, Major-General Sir F., *Operation Victory* (London, 1963).

Delaney, J., *Fighting the Desert Fox* (London, 1998).

Die Oase – Journal of the Afrika Korps Veterans Association

Eighth Army Weekly.

Douglas, K., *Alamein to Zem Zem* (Oxford, 1979).

Ellis, J., *Brute Force: Allied Strategy and Tactics in the Second World War* (London, 1980).

Fergusson, Sir Bernard, *Wavell, Portrait of a Soldier* (London, 1961).

Fletcher, D., *The Great Tank Scandal: British Armour in the Second World War* Part 1 (HMSO, 1989).

Ford, K., *El Alamein* (Oxford, 2001).

Fraser, D., *Alanbrooke* (London, 1982).

Garret, D., *The Campaign in Greece and Crete* (HMSO, 1942).

Gilbert, A., (ed) *The Imperial War Museum Book of the Desert War 1940–1942* (London, 1992).

Greacen, L., *Chink: A Biography* (London, 1989).

Greenwood, A., *Field Marshal Auckinleck* (London, 1990).

Griffiths, P., 'British Armoured Warfare in the Western Desert 1940–1945' in J.P. Harris and F. H. Toase (eds), *Armoured Warfare* (London, 1990).

Hamilton, N., *Monty: The Making of a General 1887–1942* (London, 1982).

Hamilton, N., *The Full Monty: Montgomery of Alamein 1887–1942* (London, 2001).

Harrison, F., *Tobruk: The Great Siege Reassessed* (London, 1996).

Harrison-Place, T., *Military Training in the British Army, 1940–1944: From Dunkirk to D-Day* (London, 2000).

Humble, R., *Crusader: Eighth Army's Forgotten Victory November 1941 to January 1942* (London, 1987).

Horrocks. Lieutenant-General, Sir B., *A Full Life* (London, 1960).

Irving, D., *The Trail of the Fox* (London, 1977).

Johnson, M. and P. Stanley, *Alamein: The Australian Story* (Oxford, 2002).

Joslen, Lieutenant-Colonel H. F., *Orders of Battle: Second World War* (HMSO 1960).

Kippenburger, Major-General Sir H., *Infantry Brigadier* (Oxford, 1949).

Latimer, J., *Alamein* (London, 2002).

Lewin, R., *Rommel as Military Commander* (London, 1968).

Lewin, R., *Montgomery as Military Commander* (London, 1971).

Lewin, R., *The Life and Death of the Afrika Korps* (London, 1977).

Lewis, P. J., & I. R. English, *Into Battle with the Durhams: 8 DLI in World War II* (London, 1990).

Lewis-Stempel, J., *The Autobiography of the British Soldier* (London, 2007).

Liddell Hart, Sir B. H., *The Tanks: The History of the Royal Tank Regiment and its Predecessors, Heavy Branch Machine Gun Corps, Tank Corps and Royal Tank Corps, 1914–1945*, 2 vols (London, 1959).

Lucas, J., *War in the Desert – the Eighth Army at El Alamein* (London, 1982).

Lucas, J., *Panzer Army Africa* (London, 1977).

MacDonald, C., *The Lost Battle: Crete 1941* (London, 1993).

Macksey, K., *Rommel: Battles and Campaigns* (London, 1979).

Majdalany, F., *The Battle of El Alamein* (London, 1965).

Montgomery, Field Marshall the Viscount B. L., *Memoirs* (London, 1958).

Moorehead, A., *Mediterranean Front* (London, 1942).

Moorehead, A., *Years of Battle* (London, 1943).

Moorehead, A., *The End in Africa* (London, 1943).

Neillands, R., *The Desert Rats: 7th Armoured Division, 1940–1945* (London, 1991).

Nicolson, N., *Alex: The Life of Field Marshal Earl Alexander of Tunis* (London, 1971).

Parkinson, R., *Blood, Toil, Sweat and Tears* (London, 1973).

Parkinson, R., *A Day's March Nearer Home* (London, 1974).

Parkinson, R., *The War in the Desert* (London, 1976).

Philips, C. E. L., *Alamein* (London, 1962).

Pitt, B., *The Crucible of War 1: Wavell's Command* (London, 1986).
Pitt, B., *The Crucible of War 2: Auchinleck's Command* (London, 1986).
Pitt, B., *The Crucible of War 3: Montgomery and Alamein* (London, 1986).
Playfair, Major-General I.S.O., Official History, UK Military Series, Campaigns: *Mediterranean and Middle East* Vols 1–4, (London, 1962–1966).
Osprey *Elite* 105 'World War II Infantry Tactics: Squad and Platoon'.
Osprey *Elite* 122 'World War Two Infantry tactics: Company and Battalion'.
Osprey *Elite* 124 'World War Two Infantry Anti-Tank Tactics'.
Osprey *Elite* 162 'World War II Desert Tactics'.
Osprey *Battle Orders* 20 'Rommel's Afrika Korps Tobruk to El Alamein'.
Osprey *Battle Orders* 28 'Desert Rats: British 8th Army in North Africa 1941–1943'.
Osprey *New Vanguard* 28 'Panzerkampfwagen IV Medium Tank 1936–1945'.
Osprey *New Vanguard* 33 'M3 and M5 Stuart Light Tank 1940–1945'.
Osprey *New Vanguard* 46 '88mm Flak 18/36/37/41 and Pak 43 1936–1945'.
Osprey *New Vanguard* 98 'British Anti-Tank Artillery 1939–1945'.
Osprey *New Vanguard* 113 'M3 Lee/Grant Medium Tank 1941–1945'.
Osprey *Campaign* 158 'El Alamein 1942'.
Quarrie, B., *Afrika Korps* (Cambridge, 1975).
Quarrie, B., *Panzers in the Desert* (Cambridge, 1978).
Rommel, E., *Infantry Attack* (London, 1990).
Samwell, H. P., *An Infantry Officer with the Eighth Army: The Personal Experiences of an Infantry Officer During the Eight Army's Campaign Through Africa and Sicily* (London, 1945).
Schmidt, H. W., *With Rommel in the Desert* (London, 1951).
Smith, M., *Station X – The Codebreakers of Bletchley Park* (London, 1998).
Stewart, A., *The Eighth Army's Greatest Victories: Alam Halfa to Tunis 1942–1943* (London, 1999).
Stewart, A., *The Early Battles of Eighth Army: 'Crusader' to the Alamein Line 1941–1942* (London, 2002).
Strawson, J., *The Battle for North Africa* (London, 1969).
Terraine, J., *The Right of the Line* (London, 1983).
Toase, F. H., & J. P. Harris, *Armoured Warfare* (London, 1990).
Van Creveld, M., *Supplying in War: Logistics from Wallenstein to Patton* (Cambridge, 1977).
Verney, G. L., *The Desert Rats: History of 7th Armoured Division 1938–1945* (London, 1954).
War Office, *Military Report on the North-Western Desert of Egypt* (London, 1937).
Warner, P., *Alamein – Recollections of the Heroes* (London, 1979).
Young, D., *Rommel* (London, 1950).

Unpublished Sources

Pinkney, M., *Maurice and Mary*.
Akam, E. A., *A Memoir*.

Illustration credits

All illustrations are courtesy of the author apart from 1. JR1732b91p15B 19391945; 2. JR1733b91p17 19391945; 3. JR1734b91p22 19391945; 4. JR1735b91p23 19391945; 5. JR1737b91p42M19391945; 6. JR1736b91p3919391945; 7. JR1738b91p42B19391945; 8. JR1739b91p45 19391945; 9. JR1740b91p50 19391945; 10. JR1741b91p57 19391945; 11. JR1742b91p59 19391945; 12. JR1743b91p60T 19391945; 13. JR1744b91p60B 19391945; 14. JR1745b91p64T 19391945; 15. JR1746b91p64BL 19391945; 16. JR1747b91p64BR 19391945; all courtesy of Jonathan Reeve.

Index